MW00910230

Dr. Kindbud's

WEED-O-PEDIA

Primo Nuggets of Marijuana Facts and Stoner Trivia

DR. SEYMOUR KINDBUD

CIDER MILL PRESS

BOOK PUBLISHERS

13-Digit ISBN: 978-1604332681
10-Digit ISBN: 1604332689

This book may be ordered by mail from the publisher. Please include $4.50 for postage and handling.
Please support your local bookseller first!

Books published by Cider Mill Press Book Publishers are available at special discounts for bulk purchases in the United States by corporations, institutions, and other organizations. For more information, please contact the publisher.

Cider Mill Press Book Publishers
"Where good books are ready for press"
12 Port Farm Road
Kennebunkport, Maine 04046

Visit us on the Web!
www.cidermillpress.com

Typography: AtSackersGothic Light, Adobe Garamond, Garamond 3, DIN, Goudy Trajan, Muleshoe WF, No. 10 Type Regular.
Illustrations courtesy of Shutterstock.com.
Printed in China
1 2 3 4 5 6 7 8 9 0
First Edition

DEDICATION

To Buz, who hooked us up

CONTENTS

INTRODUCTION: Dr. Kindbud's First Deep Hit.........6

CHAPTER 1: A Long Strange Trip Through History...14

CHAPTER 2: Cannabis in Popular Culture.................92

CHAPTER 3: 420: The Cannabis Subculture.............334

CHAPTER 4: Cooking with Cannabis.....................388

CHAPTER 5: Lighting Up and the Law....................416

CHAPTER 6: Far-Out Science.................................468

CHAPTER 7: How to Grow Your Own.....................530

INDEX...596

DR. KINDBUD'S FIRST DEEP HIT

Getting high on weed is fun. It makes music more entrancing, movies and television shows funnier or freakier, video games more challenging, food and drink more appealing, and sex more amazing. When you're high, you think a little deeper, you laugh a little more. You find nature and the supernatural more awe-inspiring. All of your senses feel more attuned to the subtle stimuli around you that at other times go unnoticed. You're relaxed yet ready to deftly swerve to avoid any hassles that come your way.

Sometimes, you've surely noticed, your mind wanders when you're high. You can get to ruminating and pondering. And in all that thinking, you eventually get around to questions like how weed gets you high, when did people figure out it was so enjoyable to smoke, who decided it should be illegal, what are the greatest weed-influenced songs, shows, movies and books, and why the number 420 became code for getting high. My friends and partying partners have their own theories about these questions and many others, which often provoke intense, if sometimes ill-informed, debates when we're kicking back and passing a joint.

After one very impassioned discussion that resolved nothing—blame short-term memory loss that I can't even remember what was the bone of contention—I decided to go find the answer. On the Internet, I came across quite a few answers to the question I was researching—the problem was, the answers contradicted each other and I knew our dispute about the subject would linger long after the joint had been roached.

That's when I realized we needed a definitive source, an encyclopedia we could turn to for answers. So I set out to research everything I could find out about the Cannabis plant, its habits and effects, its long association with people and its current status as both medicine and illicit substance around the world. I went to expert sources and sought out the facts on all the scientific or historical matters. I checked in with experienced cooks for recipes and dug up the plans for of the most inventive smoking devices. And I consulted with many friends and acquaintances,

and a critic here and there, to come up with the list of best movies, songs, TV shows, and more for stoners. You're now holding the product of all that research. And it's my hope that it answers your questions and leaves you feeling enlightened.

The book is organized by subject (rather than alphabetically) so you can browse through those areas that interest you now and find information you're searching for later. Each chapter covers a wide range of topics addressed in the order in which my mind took me—that is, not necessarily in an indisputably logical pattern. Entire books have been written about some of the topics, but all of the entries here are short—you should be able to finish each one between hits. I've also dropped in a lot of nuggets—information nuggets—just right for sharing with friends. And I hope you do. Like really fine bud, high-quality info should be passed around.

One more thought: In the sections on Cannabis as medicine and your health, I tried to let the science speak for itself and relied as much as possible on credible, peer-reviewed research. I avoided as best I could imposing my opinions or personal views in those areas and in the legal section, too. I'm a devout believer in sharing unbiased information so that all people can come to their own conclusions. But I also want to take the opportunity here to share my conclusions.

The novelist Merry Prankster and LSD pioneer Ken Kesey appeared on the *Tomorrow Show* with Tom Snyder in 1981. The host asked Kesey if he felt any residual effects from all the LSD he had taken in the 1960s. After a quick, fun answer, Kesey looked sincere for a moment and said, "You don't get anything for free... everything bruises something... so you trade off." This comment struck home for me—there are undeniable benefits of using non-addictive, mind-expanding drugs, including genuine conscious-raising as well as fun times. But those benefits don't come without some cost to the user, even when those costs are not easily discerned.

All my research and experience leads me to believe that use of Cannabis by mentally and physically healthy adults has significant benefits for their psyche and overall well-being. Its value as medicine has been and continues to be documented. And so far science has not yet identified any

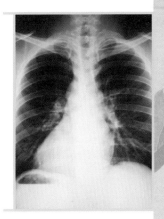

long-term physical or psychological harm that results from adults enjoying Cannabis.

That said, smoking anything can put a strain on your respiratory system. And frequent Cannabis use has been known to dampen ambition and productivity and often leads to an unhealthy sedentary lifestyle and excessive snacking.

Yet I am confident that if you otherwise take care of your health and make a conscious effort to prevent getting high from becoming a way to avoid responsibilities and life's experiences, it can be a lot of fun and in many ways adds richness to your days. In other words, getting high can make your life better if you manage it wisely. So, puff on!

CHAPTER 1

A LONG STRANGE TRIP THROUGH HISTORY

Humans' relationship with the cannabis plant dates back to before people could write. The earliest civilizations recognized all of its values: as fiber, food, and medicine for body and soul. Cannabis has been used ever since as an intoxicant—ritually and recreationally—in many regions of the world. Along the way, it has been associated with many strange tales and wild misbehavior. I've laid out its story in chronological order, but feel free to skip around and see where your mind leads you.

ORIGIN MYTH

The Dogon are a tribe of cliff-dwelling people living in the African country of Mali. Until the 1930s, they were almost completely isolated from the outside world and, therefore, retained their ancient culture and beliefs long after most other people adopted one of the major religions.

Anthropologists who studied the Dogon people in the 1970s learned that tribal legends connected them to Sirius, the very bright star often called "the dog star." Though they lacked the knowledge and the tools of modern astronomy, the Dogons knew Sirius has a larger twin that is invisible to the

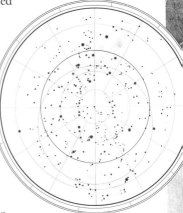

naked eye, and celebrated a ritual on the completion of the twins' 50-year orbit cycle. Their awareness of the invisible star and duration of its orbit is hard to explain. The Dogon believe that a race of mermaid-like beings, called Nommos, visited them eons ago and gave them knowledge of the solar system.

The Dogons, like some other African tribes, use Cannabis in their rituals and in their daily lives. The root of the word "cannabis" meant "dog" (as in *canine*) and "bi" means "two." Those facts have led some to the conclusion that Cannabis is the "two dog plant" that came from the two dog stars, brought to the Dogon people by the Nommos when they visited thousands of years back. This myth has been circulated by a variety sources, but it has not been documented as part of the Dogons' belief system.

Dr. Kindbud enjoys a good myth as much as the next guy, but I have to point out that the earliest fossil record of Cannabis is in Central Asia (think Afghanistan), not Africa. And I won't argue against the existence of other advanced civilizations in the universe. Yet I see no need of an alien race to explain the wonder that people found Cannabis. Like so much else in our world, Cannabis seems to be a small but perfectly natural miracle of whatever force of creation you believe in.

ANCIENT CHINESE SECRET

Fossils found in Afghanistan and other areas of Central Asia establish that the Cannabis plant and relatives lived in the region at least 15,000 years ago. But the earliest evidence of people using it comes from oldest known human culture, the Yang-shao, a prehistoric people living in

China's Yellow River Valley 6,500 years ago. Evidence suggests they wore clothes made of hemp and used hemp fiber rope and nets.

By 2700 BC, people in China were using Cannabis as medicine. The *Pên-ts'ao Ching*, an early text on medicine, noted the hallucinogenic properties of the flowers and prescribed it for treating symptoms of malaria, beriberi, constipation, joint pain, and female disorders. The book also described a paste ground from Cannabis root used to ease the pain of wounds and injuries. Cannabis seeds were an early staple grain for the ancient Chinese, though they were later replaced by rice. The Chinese also learned to extract the oil, which they used for cooking and a variety of other purposes. They fed the residue from the pressed seeds to their domesticated animals.

 The Chinese character for *hemp*

ONWARD AND OUTWARD

The Aryans were an early race of people who flourished in Central Asia about 4,000 years ago. They worshipped the spirits of plants and animals, and Cannabis was an integral part of their rituals. Their sacred texts, known as the four Vedas, were compiled between 1400 and 1000 BC. They identify the *bhangas* (Cannabis) spirit as a healer and soother.

The Assyrian Empire covered a large area of what is now Iran and Iraq in 700 BC. One of its last kings, Ashurbanipal, gathered thousands of clay tablets into a vast library stored in the ancient city of Nineveh, his capital. In the 1840s, British archeologists found many of the tablets preserved and  brought them to the British Museum, where they can still be viewed today. One set of tablets was a kind of medical text, listing 400 useful plants, including cannabis, which is prescribed for ailments familiar (nausea) and not so familiar (sorcerer's spells).

Archeologists have found evidence that Cannabis was cultivated in Europe as early as 400 BC, but it appears to have been grown only for its fiber and seeds, not the flowers.

The Thracians, a civilization that grew up in southern Europe around the same period as the Greek city-states, piled Cannabis flowers into fires and inhaled the smoke to get intoxicated. Romans relied on hemp imported from Gaul (today French-speaking Europe) for sails and rope, and understood its effects. Galen, an influential Roman physician around 200 AD, wrote that his neighbors and friends shared Cannabis "to produce hilarity and enjoyment." Scythians, a group of loosely related tribes from Siberia to the steppes of Central Asia that flourished in the BC era, included Cannabis seeds in their burial grounds—a sign that it was a necessity for the afterlife.

As a sacrament, medicine, and intoxicant, marijuana use spread along with trade from the areas now known as India and Afghanistan to Persia, Assyria, and Arabia. *The Koran*, the sacred book of Islam, expressly prohibits alcohol consumption but does not forbid use of Cannabis. As the faith spread rapidly from 700 to 1000 and beyond, the use of marijuana grew with it—increasingly in the form of hashish, potent balls of resin collected from the buds.

Cannabis use reached Africa, where to this day a variety of tribes still use it ritually and recreationally. The Mfengu people of south Africa, for instance, smoke marijuana to treat the pain caused by snakebites and childbirth—which, having never experienced either, I am surprised to know have anything in common. The Riamba tribe of the Congo revere the Cannabis plant as a god who protects from physical and spiritual harm.

HASHISH ASSASSINS

Marco Polo brought back to Europe spices, silks, and other treasures from his travels through Asia. He also had a load of information and stories of wonders the West had never seen. One story he related told of a powerful tribal chief named Hasan Ibn al-Sabbah, who was known as the Old Man of the Mountain. The chief lived in Persia in the thirteenth century and was said to have attracted the fiercest fighters to his band of rebels by giving them large doses of hashish that gave them visions of Paradise. The warriors were highly lethal and fueled, the story goes, by hashish. They became known as "assassins," which has long been rumored to be Arabic for "hashish killers."

But that translation may be a misinterpretation, according to modern scholars. The current understanding, based on contemporary documents that have survived to this day, is that al-Sabbah referred to his men as *Asasiyun*, a word for people who are faithful to the Asās, or "founda-

tion" of Islam. That translation is not as titillating as "hashish-crazed murderers," so either intentionally or not, Marco Polo's version has lasted.

THOSE DARK AGES

While appreciation for the flowers of the Cannabis plants (that would be your buds) grew throughout the Middle East, Africa, and Spain, Europe (caught in the Unenlightenment of the Medieval Period) valued Cannabis only for its fiber.

The great sea power, England, powered its navy on sails and rigging made from hemp. Its monarchs, including Henry VIII and Elizabeth I, mandated that landowners devote a specific percentage of their fields to growing hemp. Hemp is a strain of the Cannabis plant that's low on the psychoactive ingredients and high in strong fibers, so that may explain why very few Europeans knew about or appreciated its intoxicating power. Or maybe that laidback feeling of enjoying whatever you can in life ran up against the Protestant work ethic or the challenge of survival in tough times.

Pope Innocent VIII was one of the key architects of the Inquisition, the Catholic Church's brutal campaign against people it deemed heretics. In 1484, he issued a papal bull that ordered severe—often lethal—punishments for practitioners of magic and witchcraft. Specifically, it condemned Cannabis use as an "unholy sacrament of the Satanic Mass," which sounds like he saw the day coming when thousands of stoned fans would cheer for Ozzy Osbourne as he bit the head off a chicken on stage.

Not every ruler in the Muslim world in this time accepted Cannabis use. In 1378, Emir Soudon Sheikhouni, a powerful chieftain in Persia, tried to crack down on hashish use, demanding that all Cannabis plants be destroyed and users be imprisoned. He reportedly also had their teeth removed, for reasons that elude me.

As you might surmise, these early Wars on Drugs didn't do any more to curb Cannabis use than the more recent one.

Cannabis does show up in one of the widely circulated early medical books, *Culpepper's Complete Herbal*, published in 1652. It lists hemp, and declares that it is so familiar to even laypeople that it needs no description. And it prescribes different parts of the plant for use in treating colic, burns, inflammation, and worms.

NAME THAT PLANT

In the Age of Enlightenment of the seventeenth and eighteenth centuries, scientists began studying the world systematically and thousands of new species were discovered every year. European explorers brought home many species from Asia, Africa, and the Americas and were sharing information about them like never before. A standardized naming system became necessary, so researchers and collectors could be clear about which species they were studying and discussing.

In 1735, a plant-crazy Swede named Carolus Linnaeus published *Systema Naturae,* a book detailing his classification and naming scheme that organized species by their reproductive characteristics. In 1753, he published a two-volume *Species Plantarum* (*The Species of Plants*) that listed

the plants known to him and other botanists at the time.

Included in that book is the *Cannabis* genus. By the time Linnaeus came along, the plant had long been called "Cannabis," a word linked back to ancient Greek, possibly even to the Scythians or Thracians, the early Hellenic cultures that used it as a sacrament. Linnaeus named the species "sativa," Latin for "sown" or "cultivated."

In 1783, a French biologist identified a separate species, *Cannabis indica*. The third species now recognized,

Cannabis ruderalis, was named in the twentieth century by Soviet scientists who found it growing wild in their country. You can learn more about the botanical classification of Cannabis in the Far-Out Science chapter.

BRAVE NEW WORLD

While the Inquisition was rooting out and punishing Cannabis users in Europe, Spanish conquistadors began cultivating the hemp strains of the plant in South and Central America. In 1564, Spain's King Phillip ordered that Cannabis be grown throughout the Spanish empire to produce canvas and rope to outfit the Spanish Navy, which was locked in a battle with Great Britain for supremacy of the seas.

When the Jamestown colony was founded in Virginia

in 1819, hemp cultivation was made mandatory and hemp seeds were accepted as tax payment. The commitment to Cannabis cultivation continued in the American colonies through the time of the founding fathers. The two great gentlemen farmers of the group, George Washington and Thomas Jefferson, both had hemp growing on their plantations. Jefferson's farm diaries and letters include many references to the plant that, along with cotton and flaxseed, was the primary source of fiber for clothing and other textiles used on his farm. He noted, for instance, that his plantation used about 400 yards of hemp fabric—that is, canvas—every year and that each hemp plant yielded a quart of seed. "A bushel of good brown seed is enough for an acre," he wrote.

Jefferson designed an improved a "hemp brake," a machine that extracted the fibers from the stalks. He also used hemp paper when drafting the Declaration of Independence on 1776. That paper may well have come

from Benjamin Franklin's mill, which manufactured hemp fiber into sheets for documents, newspapers, and other uses.

In his diary entry for August 7, 1765, George Washington wrote, "Began to separate the Male from the Female hemp." Now you might conclude that our first president was doing what many growers do today: pulling up the males, which contain no THC, to leave behind only budding females. But it's more likely that he wanted to divide the plants because the female plants produced the seeds, which he would need for the next year's crop, but the males yielded the stronger fiber.

No one has suggested that any of the founding fathers used cannabis for medicine or pleasure, but it was neither illegal nor unknown at the time. Some historians claim that one of Napoleon's objectives for his invasions of Russia and Egypt was to cut off the supply of hemp to his mortal enemy, Great Britain. We can't say for sure if

NAPOLEON

that worked. But in 1798, during the French occupation of Egypt, Napoleon issued a ban on the purchase and use of cannabis among his troops. As always, the prohibition did not stop users from enjoying it or the troops from bringing it home with them and introducing it to their fellow citizens.

THE HASH CLUB

In the nineteenth century, European scholars, scientists, physicians, poets, and artists began to discover and explore the psychoactive effects of cannabis consumption.

French psychologist Jacques-Joseph Moreau de Tours encountered hashish users while traveling in Asia in the 1830s, and its effects reminded him of the delirium suffered by his mentally ill patients. In 1846, Dr Moreau published a 439-page book, *De Hachish et de l'Alienation Mentale–Études Psychologiques* (*Hashish and Mental–*

Psychological Studies). He was an early proponent of treating mentally ill people with medicine, making him the father of psychopharmacology. He tested hash and other cannabis preparations, such as oils and tinctures made from the resin, first on laboratory animals, then on healthy people, and ultimately as a treatment for patients suffering from what was then called melancholia and other mood disorders.

Dr. Moreau was one of the founders of Le Club des Hachichins in Paris, a gathering of artists, writers, and others who wanted to experience the mind-altering effects

of the hash high. Among the full- and part-time participants were some of the leading literary lights of the day, including novelists Victor Hugo (author of *Les Miserables*), Alexandre Dumas (*The Three Musketeers*), and Gustave Flaubert

VICTOR HUGO

(*Madame Bovary*), poet Charles Baudelaire, and journalist Théophile Gauthier. The latter published a detailed description of hashish intoxication in the Paris newspaper *La Presse* that was widely read and discussed. He called hash "an intellectual intoxication," unlike the "ignoble heavy drunkenness" caused by alcohol.

From 1844 to 1849, the club met at the Hotel Lauzun, and the members, dressed in Arab clothing, drank a strong brew of coffee laced with hash and spiced with cinnamon, cloves, and nutmeg. (Bet you'd like to order one of those at your local coffee shop.) They talked, wrote, painted, and contemplated. In an article published in 1860, titled "Les Paradis Artificiels" ("Artificial Paradises"), Baudelaire wrote of his experiences and observations. You might recognize these thoughts:

> *At first, a certain absurd, irresistible hilarity overcomes you. The most ordinary words, the simplest ideas assume a new and bizarre aspect... Next your*

senses become extraordinarily keen and acute. Your sight is infinite. Your ear can discern the slightest perceptible sound, even through the shrillest of noises. The slightest ambiguities, the most inexplicable transpositions of ideas take place. In sounds there is colour; in colours there is a music... You are sitting and smoking; you believe that you are sitting in your pipe, and that your pipe is smoking you; you are exhaling yourself in bluish clouds. This fantasy goes on for an eternity. A lucid interval, and a great expenditure of effort, permit you to look at the clock. The eternity turns out to have been only a minute.

FIRST MEDICINE

William Brooke O'Shaughnessy was a young Irishman who studied medicine, chemistry, and forensic toxicology at the University of Edinburgh and earned his degree in

1829. He moved to London to practice medicine. When he was unable to obtain a license, he established a laboratory that performed chemical analysis for doctors, hospitals and courts. During an outbreak of cholera in the 1830s, O'Shaughnessy's studies led him to a critical conclusion: cholera deaths were often caused by dehydration, the result of excessive diarrhea and vomiting. He reported his findings in the medical journal *Lancet* (still published today) and recommended treating cholera patients with intravenous fluid replacement, which is still part of cholera therapy.

This breakthrough earned O'Shaughnessy fame and the commission as assistant surgeon to the East India Company in Calcutta. There he traveled among the natives and learned about their medicinal plants. He learned all about cannabis and its healing properties from the healers he met and began to experiment with it in a variety of forms, first on laboratory animals and then on his patients. He found it useful treating rheumatism, rabies, cholera, tetanus, convulsions, and menstrual cramps. With hashish he had found a well-suited medicine to give his patients relief, and in the case of cramps, even total disappearance of symptoms. In a paper he presented in 1839 titled "On the Preparations of the Indian Hemp or Gunja," he wrote, "I believe that this medicine is an anticonvulsivum of great value."

O'Shaughnessy would be well-remembered enough for this contribution to science. But I can't finish telling

you about him without mentioning his other major accomplishment. While he was studying cannabis, he also conducted experiments in electromagnetism—in the 1840s! He went back to India and played the lead role in setting up a nationwide telegraph system for the country and devised an alternative to the copper wires that worked in the United States and Britain but were too fragile for India's less developed landscape. O'Shaughnessy was later knighted by Queen Victoria. He might today be thought of as the Patron Saint of Medical Marijuana.

LITTLE CANNABIS PILLS

Word about O'Shaughnessy's findings spread throughout Europe and scientists, particularly in Germany, began to systemically study cannabis as a treatment for many ailments. Franz von Kobylanski, George Martius, Carl

Damian Ritter von Schroff, Ernst Freiherr von Bibra, and Bernhard Fronmüller published the results of their testing of different forms of cannabis as treatment for everything from insomnia to insanity. The private physician of Queen Victoria, Sir John Russell Reynolds, prescribed it to her for menstrual cramps.

Until the 1880s, physicians concocted their own

cannabis cures, and many reported on the inconsistent strengths of their preparations. Patent medicines were the over-the-counter drugs of the day. A German company, E. Merck, began to manufacture cannabis medicines. In the United States, companies whose names you recognize, such as Squibb, Parke-Davis, and Eli Lilly produced and distributed cannabis medicines. They had names like Dr. Brown's Sedative Tablets, Casadein, and Bromida. The latter, produced by Battle & Co., was marketed as a sleep aid and became one of the most popular products of its day.

The Gunjah Wallah Co. in New York marketed Hasheesh Candy. It promoted the candy as "The Arabian "Gunjh" of Enchantment confectionized. A most pleasurable and harmless stimulant. Cures Nervousness, Weakness, Melancholy. Inspires all classes with new life and energy. A complete mental and physical invigorator."

Cannabis as medicine was never more mainstream than it was in the late nineteenth century. Scientists continued to study it and find new ways it could be used to heal. And then its day was over, as newer and more targeted treatments were introduced. Vaccines for diseases such as cholera and tetanus replaced cannabis because they protected against infections along with treating the symptoms. Aspirin, introduced in 1899, quickly became the primary treatment for headaches and other aches and pains for which cannabis had previously been the most popular cure. Cannabis medicine slowly faded into irrelevance until interest was revived in the 1970s.

THE HASHISH EATER

The son of a New York minister, Henry Ludlow, a fiery abolitionist who hosted a stop on the Underground Railroad and later became a leading voice in the temperance movement, Fitzhugh Ludlow was a bookish young man who studied medicine at Union College in Schenectady, New York. He developed a professional interest in anesthesia and maybe a taste for altered states after being treated with morphine as a boy. Ludlow began visiting a friend who ran an apothecary and, as he later wrote, to "trial of the effects of every strange drug and chemical which the laboratory could produce."

Among the substances Ludlow sampled was a tetanus remedy called Tilden's Extract, a concentration of *Cannabis indica* (advertised as "Indian hemp") sold in pill form. One expert has estimated that its THC content was equivalent to about seven joints of potent marijuana. Ludlow was entranced by the high he got from the pills, reporting fantastic visions and surges of creativity. He took them regularly, almost daily, for several years before he began to feel addicted to it in the same way that author Thomas DeQuincey described in his book *Confessions of an English Opium-Eater* (published in 1821).

Ludlow sought treatment for his addiction—which we know was psychological, not physical in the way that heroin, cocaine, and alcohol are addicting—and his physician urged him to write about his experiences as a form of therapy. In 1856, Ludlow published an article in the popular magazine *Putnam's Monthly*, called "The Apocalypse of Hasheesh." A year later, his book *The Hasheesh Eater* became available to readers. It was an almost immediate sensation, and it was reprinted more than four times over the next several years.

The book's impact was widespread. Private hash parlors opened in major cities across the United States. At the Centennial Exposition in Philadelphia, the exhibit from Turkey offered visitors the chance to toke on a hash pipe. Asked about the book, writer H.P. Lovecraft answered that he had "frequently reread those phantasmagoria of exotic colour, which proved more of a stimulant to my own fancy than any vegetable alkaloid ever grown and distilled."

Ludlow concludes his book with his harrowing (but maybe exaggerated) tale of breaking his addiction and a condemnation of cannabis use. This part of the book became part of the argument during the 1930s for outlawing cannabis use in the United States. But in the 1950s, the book was rediscovered by the Beat Generation and republished by the iconic City Lights Books.

The Fitzhugh Ludlow Memorial Library was established in the 1970s, when four researchers merged their private collections of books. It became and remains a leading resource for those studying psychoactive drugs.

THE HEARST STORY

William Randolph Hearst was one of America's first media moguls. He took over the *San Francisco Examiner*, a newspaper that had published renowned authors such as Mark Twain, Ambrose Bierce, and Stephen Crane, after his father accepted it as payment for a gambling debt in 1887. Hearst's holdings grew and he eventually came to be the owner and publisher of 28 newspapers and magazines. Hearst's papers became widely popular and influential, in large part because of the sensational, scandal-driven stories Hearst insisted upon. Historians credit Hearst's newspapers with rousing public opinion in support of the Spanish-American War and against immigrants of all kinds.

To support the paper needs of his many publications, Hearst invested in a substantial amount of timberland, in particular 800,000 acres in northern Mexico. Those lands were seized during the Mexican revolution, led by Pancho Villa in the 1910s. Hearst had long denigrated Mexicans, but after losing the land he began to focus his newspapers' coverage on a terrible scourge that came across the border with them. He published lurid stories linking "marihuana, the new Mexican drug," to murder, rape, and all manner of lawlessness.

Stay with me here, if you like a good conspiracy theory. Around the same time that Hearst was fanning fears of cannabis and crime, two inventions were on the verge of having a significant impact on hemp production. A new machine design had made breaking down hemp fibers and processing them much more effectively, so they could suddenly be made into paper as cheaply as tree pulp. Hemp paper would be a threat to Hearst's investment in timberlands.

Meanwhile, at the laboratories of Dupont, chemists had developed a strong new synthetic fiber: nylon. It would take the place of hemp in rope production. Dupont had many influential investors, including the billionaire businessman and Secretary of the Treasury Andrew Mellon. So here we have two of America's most powerful men with an interest in suppressing hemp production. And that's just what happened. The Hearst newspapers roused the public about the dangers of marijuana and when Congress banned its production, sale, and use, it also banned the production of harmless hemp.

GOT THAT SWING

The Prohibition years were one of the best parties America ever threw for itself. In the 1920s, speakeasies and jazz clubs served champagne and cocktails to the well-heeled, while roadhouses and moonshiners met the needs of the rest of the population. There was plenty of access to the weed increasingly known as *marijuana,* too. Drugstores sold patent cannabis medicines. Tea pads—apartments used as marijuana social clubs—sprouted up all over the major cities. Fun-seekers could always be sure they'd find it in dance halls and bordellos.

In New Orleans, public health officials sounded the alarm about the growing use of marijuana in the city. They stirred up fears of crime in local newspapers and wrote to the surgeon general of the United States about the threat. In a 1931 article published by *The American Journal of Police Science,* the district attorney of New Orleans stated:

> *It has been the experience of Police and Prosecuting Officials in the South, that immediately before the commission of many crimes the use of marihuana cigarettes has been indulged in by criminals, so as to relieve themselves from the natural restraint which might deter them from the commission of criminal acts, and to give them the fake courage necessary to commit the contemplated crimes.*

Marijuana use wasn't spurring a crime spree, but it did fuel the joy and wild abandon of the city's jazz musicians, who were inventing a liberated new music and playing it for hours on end. Songs such as Louis Armstrong's "Muggles," Cab Calloway's "That Funny Reefer Man," and Fats Waller's "Viper's Drag" celebrated the pleasures of the weed that was often spoken of as "Muggles."

As jazz caught on around the country, marijuana rode along with the musicians to Chicago, Kansas City, and New York. Milton Mezzrow, a clarinetist living in Harlem like many other jazz musicians, became so well known as a dealer that "mezz" was slang for marijuana there. He was only a fair musician, but he attracted a lot of attention by proclaiming himself a "voluntary Negro" marrying a black woman. He later published a fun and honest autobiography called *Really the Blues,* which included his arrest for attempting to bring sixty joints into the 1939 New York World's Fair. When he was imprisoned, he asked to be transferred to the black section of the segregated jail.

Mezzrow may not have been truly able to choose his race, but race became the choice of New York's politicians and newspapers when they wanted to enflame the public about the spread of marijuana use. They told tales of black men crazed on reefer and jazz, murdering, stealing, and most horrible of all, raping white women in their deranged lust. The same types of stories appeared in other cities, and the public began to clamor for law enforcement to take action. Jazz musicians, including Armstrong and Dizzy Gillespie, were followed by federal officers, hoping to catch them violating marijuana laws.

THE TOP COP

Harry Anslinger was a legendary police officer in 1930. At the age of twenty-three, he solved a fraud case while working as an investigator for the Pennsylvania Railroad. Over the next few years, he consulted with the military and police departments around the world, becoming an expert in drug trafficking. In 1929, he was appointed Assistant Commissioner of the Bureau of Prohibition, when it was gripped by scandal and corruption. After bringing reform to that federal department, Anslinger was named the first Commissioner of the Federal Bureau of Narcotics a year later. Both bureaus, Prohibition and Narcotics, were part of the Treasury Department—as illegal substances, they were evading payment of sales tax. The Secretary of the Treasury, you may recall, was Andrew Mellon. (Go back to "The Hearst Story" to find out why that's intriguing.)

Anslinger was America's top drug cop for the next thirty-two years. He published three books on the topic— *The Traffic in Narcotics, The Murders,* and *The Protectors.* His article "Marijuana: Assassin of Youth," was published in magazines, including *Reader's Digest* in 1937. He was the source of the most-repeated horror story about marijuana and crime:

An entire family was murdered by a youthful (marijuana) addict in Florida. When the officers arrived at the home they found the youth staggering about in a human slaughterhouse. With an axe he had killed his father, mother, two brothers and a sister. He seemed to be in a daze... he had no recollection of having committed the multiple crime. The officers knew him ordinarily as a sane, rather quiet young man; now he was pitifully crazed. They sought the reason. The boy said he had been in the habit of smoking something which youthful friends called "muggles," a childish name for marijuana.

The story was a complete fabrication concocted by Anslinger. When he took office in 1930, sixteen states had passed laws prohibiting marijuana use. By 1937, all states had passed it.

In 1948, Anslinger abandoned the claims that linked marijuana use to violence and declared that it would make

Americans too peaceful and weaken their will to fight Communism.

TAX HASSLE

The federal tax code had come in handy for law enforcement on more than a few occasions in American history. The notorious gangster Al Capone evaded jail for years until he was finally arrested and convicted on charges of income tax evasion. In 1937, the Treasury Department proposed a bill that was passed by Congress—the Marihuana Tax Act. It levied a tax of one dollar on every buyer, seller, producer, and user and required that all involved in the commercial trade of marijuana purchase a tax stamp from the Treasury Department. Physicians who wished to prescribe it to their patients were required to file extensive paperwork with the Treasury Department. All were subject to fines and imprisonment for failure to comply with the law.

The law defined marijuana as:

(A)ll parts of the plant Cannabis sativa L., whether growing or not; the seeds thereof; the resin extracted from any such plant; and every compound, manufacture, salt, derivative, mixture, or preparation of such plant, its seeds, or resin; but shall not include the mature stalks of such plant, fiber produced from such stalks, oil or cake made from the seeds of such plant, any other compound, manufacture salt, derivative, mixture, or

preparation of such mature stalks (except the resin ex-
tracted therefrom), fiber, oil, or cake, or the sterilized
seed of such plant which is incapable of germination.

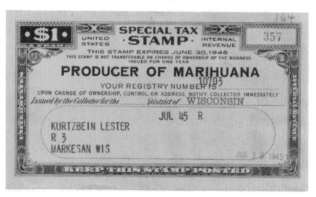

That description sounds like it also bans the production
and use of hemp for paper, rope, and other products.
Therefore, Harry Anslinger and other Treasury Department officials had to reassure Congressmen from those
states where hemp had become an important crop that its
production was not threatened by the law. Anslinger testified before the Senate committee that those in the domes-

tic hemp industry "are not only amply protected under this act, but they can go ahead and raise hemp just as they have always done it."

The Federal Bureau of Narcotics circulated a similar bill to state legislatures around the country, more than forty of which enacted it.

THE LAGUARDIA REPORT

Public outcry over marijuana use prompted New York Mayor Fiorello LaGuardia in 1939 to appoint a commission of public health experts, psychiatrists, law enforcement officials, and others to study the question of whether it should be a legal medical treatment. The commission's report, released in 1944, took a "Not Clearly Pro or Con" position on the question, and expressed these conclusions:

Under the influence of marihuana the basic personality structure of the individual does not change but some of the more superficial aspects of his behavior show alteration.

With the use of marihuana the individual experiences increased feelings of relaxation, disinhibition and self-confidence.

The new feeling of self-confidence induced by the drug expresses itself primarily through oral rather than through physical *activity. There is some indication of a diminution in physical activity.*

The disinhibition which results from the use of marihuana releases what is latent in the individual's thoughts and emotions but does not evoke responses which would be totally alien to him in his undrugged state.

Marihuana not only releases pleasant reactions but also feelings of anxiety.

Individuals with a limited capacity for effective experience and who have difficulty in making social contacts are more likely to resort to marihuana than those more capable of outgoing responses.

The report also stated these findings:

1. *Marijuana is used extensively in the Borough of Manhattan but the problem is not as acute as it is*

reported to be in other sections of the United States.

2. The introduction of marijuana into this area is recent as compared to other localities.

3. The cost of marijuana is low and therefore within the purchasing power of most persons.

4. The distribution and use of marijuana is centered in Harlem.

5. The majority of marijuana smokers are Blacks and Latin-Americans.

6. The consensus among marijuana smokers is that the use of the drug creates a definite feeling of adequacy.

7. The practice of smoking marijuana does not lead to addiction in the medical sense of the word.

8. The sale and distribution of marijuana is not un-

der the control of any single organized group.

9. *The use of marijuana does not lead to morphine or heroin or cocaine addiction and no effort is made to create a market for these narcotics by stimulating the practice of marijuana smoking.*

10. *Marijuana is not the determining factor in the commission of major crimes.*

11. *Marijuana smoking is not widespread among school children.*

12. *Juvenile delinquency is not associated with the practice of smoking marijuana.*

13. *The publicity concerning the catastrophic effects of marijuana smoking in New York City is unfounded.*

The Commission and the report were criticized by the

Federal Bureau of Narcotics and every effort was made to keep the document from reaching the media or the public.

HEMP FOR VICTORY

World War II's battle for the Pacific cut off the U.S. supply of Manila hemp, the raw ingredient for rope, canvas, and other sturdy fabrics, which was imported from the Philippines. Domestic hemp production was amped up to fill the need. The U.S. Department of Agriculture, with the support of the Army, produced a film about ten minutes long, extolling to farmers the virtues of hemp and

calling them to their patriotic duty to grow it.

The film's narrator says:

… with Philippine and East Indian sources of hemp in the hands of the Japanese, and shipment of jute from India curtailed, American hemp must meet the needs of our Army and Navy as well as of our Industry. In 1942, patriotic farmers at the government's request planted 36,000 acres of seed hemp, an increase of several thousand percent. The goal for 1943 is 50,000 acres of seed hemp.

The message got through. Between 1942 and 1945, more than 400,000 acres of hemp were cultivated in the United States. The Federal Government established the War Hemp Industries Corporation, which built 42 hemp mills in the Midwest. The Agriculture Department published at least 14 papers on growing and processing hemp, the last of them in 1956. Then the Controlled Substances

Act of 1970 banned hemp production throughout the United States.

The "Hemp for Victory" film disappeared from circulation after World War II ended and the USDA and the Library of Congress later denied its existence. But copies eventually found confirm that the U.S. government once advocated hemp growing. You can watch it today on YouTube.

THE FORD HEMPSTER

Henry Ford, automobile and manufacturing pioneer, had another bright idea in the 1940s. With steel and petroleum in short supply for domestic use during World War II, Ford engineers developed a car that was made primarily with plastic parts. The plastic was synthesized from soybeans, wheat, hemp, and other agricultural products, and it produced a car that was nearly 1,000 pounds lighter than an all-steel car. The so-called "Soybean Car" never went into mass production, but Ford continued to support research into ethanol and other petroleum alternatives.

"Why use up the forests which were centuries in the making and the mines which required ages to lay down," Ford said, "if we can get the equivalent of forest and mineral products in the annual growth of the hemp fields?"

TRUTH SERUM

The USDA wasn't the only federal agency interested in the cannabis plant. The spy division was exploring its possibilities, too. The Office of Strategic Services, the predecessor to the CIA, tested marijuana's effects and possible uses as a "weapon." A secret group of intelligence officers within the agency began trying out the value of cannabis as a truth serum on each other and unwitting subjects.

They reported that the subjects became "loquacious" and "freely imparted information."

In May 1943, George Hunter White, a former narcotics officer who became the head of O.S.S. counter-intelligence operations in the United States during the war, met with Augusto Del Gracio, an associate of gangster Lucky Luciano. Del Gracio was given THC-laced cigarettes, and he subsequently talked openly about Luciano's criminal operations.

After the war, White continued to be involved in testing drugs for use in military intelligence. He was part of the team that tested LSD as a weapon and interrogation tool in the 1950s, which ultimately led to the Acid Tests and all the liberation of the 1960s. (*Acid Dreams*, by Martin A. Lee and Bruce Shlain, is a fascinating and thoroughly documented history of this era.)

ON THE BEAT

The sounds of jazz became a siren call to those rebelling against the conformity of the 1950s, the so-called beatniks. And like the musicians they admired, the beatniks partook of marijuana and their leading literary lights celebrated it.

On the Road, written in 1949 and published in 1955, introduced several generations to the uninhibited, experience-seeking world of the Beats. When the narrator meets up with the main character, Dean Moriarity, in San Francisco, the latter tells his friend that he had bought "bad green" (fresh, uncured buds) and smoked too much of it.

"The first day," he said, "I lay rigid as a board in bed and couldn't move or say a word; I just looked straight up with my eyes open wide. I could hear buzzing in my head and saw all kinds of Technicolor visions and felt wonderful. The second day everything came to me, EVERYTHING I had ever done or known or read or heard of or conjectured came back to me and rearranged itself in my mind in a brand-new logical way and because I could think of nothing else in the interior concerns of holding and catering to the amazement and gratitude I felt, I kept saying 'Yes, yes, yes, yes.' Not loud. Just 'Yes' real quiet, and these green tea visions lasted until the third day. I had understood everything by then, my whole life was decided…"

William Burroughs is best known as the author of *Naked Lunch* (1959) and for his heroin addiction (and for shooting his wife while showing off his marksmanship a la William Tell). In an earlier book, *Junky* (1953), Burroughs noted differences between heroin and marijuana users:

> *Tea [marijuana] heads are not like junkies. A junky hands you the money, takes his junk and cuts. But tea heads don't do things that way. They expect the peddler to light them up and sit around talking for half an hour to sell two dollars' worth of weed… I soon*

found out I couldn't get along with these characters... I decided right then I would never push any more tea...

JFK AND JOINTS

The revelations and rumor-mongering about the wild times in the White House of John F. Kennedy never seem to be exhausted. It's hard to know what is true and what is made up to generate hype. A respected history professor, Michael O'Brien, wrote in his 2006 book *John F. Kennedy: A Biography* about an affair JFK had with Mary Pinchot Meyer, the former wife of a CIA agent and sister-in-law of *Washington Post* editor Ben Bradlee. O'Brien's book reports that Kennedy and Mary Meyer smoked marijuana together in July 1962.

"The White House was hosting a conference on narcotics in two months, and Kennedy joked about it to Mary," O'Brien writes. "The president smoked three of the six joints Mary brought to him. At first he felt no effects. Then he closed his eyes and refused a fourth joint. 'Suppose the Russians did something now,' he said."

Pinchot was murdered less than a year after JKF was assassinated, and her personal diary disappeared at the same time, so there is no corroboration of this first-person account. But given all the other substantiated revelations about JFK it's not hard to believe this story.

STONED IN THE SIXTIES

In the early 1960s, folk music festivals and jazz clubs were the most likely places to find people enjoying marijuana. But as the youth rebellion in the form of civil rights and antiwar protests spread across the country, "grass" became the social norm at every sit-in and march, rock concert, and party. Within a short time, marijuana went from being an underground habit of an elite, hip crowd to a part of the lifestyle of masses of teens and young adults. Whenever, wherever they got together, joints were passed.

"When a young person took his first puff of psychoactive smoke, he also drew in the psychoactive culture as a whole," stated Michael Rossman, one of the leaders in the Free Speech Movement that erupted on the campus at the University of California at Berkeley in 1964. "One inhaled a certain way of dressing, talking, acting, certain attitudes."

In the mid-1960s, however, marijuana was not the star attraction for the emerging counter-culture or the media. So-called psychedelic drugs, such as peyote, psilocybin mushrooms and, most notably, LSD, became the sacraments of a new faith and the admission ticket to uninhibited experiences of all varieties. Acid (street slang for LSD) first reached the public in the late 1950s and early 1960s through researchers working for the military and intelligence services, who tested its effects on students at Stanford University and elsewhere. (This was the same crowd that tested cannabis as a "truth serum"; see page 65.) Acid soon became the subject of study by psychologists looking for a new understanding of and treatment for mental illness.

Because of interest in the therapeutic value of LSD, it was not prohibited by law anywhere in the United States until 1966 and was still legal in some states until 1968. Before then, however, law enforcement began to take notice of the LSD movement and their followers, and when the authorities wanted to pressure them to stop their acid celebrations that were becoming increasingly popular, the laws against marijuana possession became the net to ensnare them.

Timothy Leary was a psychology professor at Harvard until his experiments with psychedelic drugs caught the attention of the school's administration. He moved his studies to a mansion in Millbrook, New York, that belonged to one of his devotees. By the mid-1960s, Leary had become an outspoken proponent of LSD and an icon of the new counter-culture. In late 1965, Leary had been in Mexico, working on a book, and when he re-entered the United States, he was arrested and charged with marijuana possession. He had about a half-joint's worth of the drug, but he was fined $30,000, sentenced to thirty years in jail and ordered to undergo psychiatric treatment. While

he was still appealing this conviction, Leary was arrested again, in 1968, in California and charged with possession of two roaches (partially smoked joints), which he claimed were planted by the arresting officer. He appealed this conviction all the way to the U.S. Supreme Court, his lawyers asserting that The Marihuana Tax Act of 1937 was unconstitutional. In the case of *Leary v. The United States,* the court sided with Leary and declared that the law was unconstitutional. Still, Leary was sentenced to ten years for the arrest and another ten were added for the prior conviction. Leary escaped from prison and spent the next few years as a fugitive outside the United States until he was recaptured in Afghanistan in 1973 and brought back to finish his prison sentence.

Meanwhile, Ken Kesey, a novelist best known for the book *One Flew Over The Cuckoo's Nest,* began hosting parties at his Northern California home that were referred to as "Acid Tests." He and his band of Merry Pranksters traveled across the country in a psychedelic school bus, challenging the "straight" populace with their outrageous appearance, loud music, street theater, and confrontational pranks. In late 1965, when law enforcement decided to stop Kesey and his band from continuing their parties and antics, they raided his home in La Honda, California, found a small amount of marijuana, and charged the writer with illegal possession. Before his sentencing, Kesey faked his suicide and drove with friends to Mexico, where he stayed for nine months. When he returned, he was arrested again on possession charges, convicted, and sentenced to five months in the San Mateo County Jail. Under pressure from the law to renounce LSD and other drugs, Kesey announced the "Acid Test Graduation," which was to be the final gathering of the psychedelic clan on Halloween 1966.

Neal Cassady was a critical link between the 1950s beatniks and the 1960s hippies. He was the inspiration for the central character of Jack Kerouac's book, *On The Road* (see "On The Beat" on page 67), and a participant in the Acid Tests hosted by Ken Kesey. Cassady's drug of choice seems to have been speed (methamphetamines), but in 1958, he was arrested in California for possession of one joint of marijuana and sentenced to two years in San Quentin prison. He met Ken Kesey shortly after his release.

HEAD FIRST

In 1966, an Army veteran named Ron Thelin and his brother Jay opened the Psychedelic Shop on Haight Street in San Francisco, and a few months later Jeff Glick opened the Head Shop on East Ninth Street in New York. They were the first stores that openly sold pipes, bongs, and other supplies for smoking grass. They also were the place heads could find underground newspapers and comics, tarot cards, and other heads to talk to.

Head shops like these opened up in many cities and even progressive small towns in the 1970s. They helped broaden the reach of the alternative press and were an outlet for glass art, rock posters, and other accessories of the counter-culture lifestyle. By the 1980s, most head shops had been hassled enough by their local authorities that they posted signs warning customers to refrain from directly mentioning marijuana or any slang about its use. The War on Drugs, pressed so aggressively by President Ronald Reagan, had forced many head shops out of business by the 1990s, though some persisted and remain open for business today. Count yourself lucky, though, if you live near a cool head shop that offers more than just pipes and rolling papers.

A NORM(A)L SITUATION

A $5,000 grant from the Playboy Foundation, the nonprofit founded by the magazine's publisher Hugh Hefner, was the seed money to establish The National Organization for the Reform of Marijuana Laws (NORML) in 1970. An attorney who had worked with Ralph Nader at the Consumer Product Safety Commission, Keith Stroup founded NORML, whose stated mission is "the removal of all criminal penalties for the private possession and responsible use of marijuana by adults, including the cultivation for personal use, and the casual nonprofit transfers of small amounts," and "the development of a legally controlled market for cannabis."

In addition to lobbying and supporting candidates who share its views, NORML today conducts research, publishes reports, hosts seminars for lawyers, and promotes its cause through advertisements. On April 20, 2009, NORML released the first national pro-marijuana television advertisement, which was covered by the *New York Times* and the *CBS Evening News.*

NIXON'S REPORT

In 1970, Congress and the Nixon Administration were eagerly enacting stricter laws to deal with the "growing drug problem" in America. The National Commission on Marijuana and Drug Abuse was formed to study the causes and possible responses, with a tough, law-and-order type of politician,

Pennsylvania Governor Raymond Shafer, as the chairman.

Two years later, the Shafer Commission delivered a report to Congress, which stated that "Neither the marijuana user nor the drug itself can be said to constitute a danger to public safety." The Commission recommended decriminalizing possession for personal use. The report was celebrated by users and those who supported their rights, but Richard Nixon—the tough, law-and-order president, who named the members of the Commission—refused to read it and rejected its conclusion. At a news conference, he said, "Even if the Commission does recommend that it be legalized, I will not follow that recommendation."

THE HASH BASH

Each year, on the first Saturday in April, the annual Hash Bash erupts on the campus of the University of Michigan in Ann Arbor. Launched in 1972, the event features speeches, live music, and a street fair all in support of legalization of marijuana. While the event is not condoned by the city, Ann Arbor has made possession of marijuana a civil infraction rather than a crime. It levies fines of just $25 for the first offense, $50 for a second, and $100 for all subsequent infractions.

The 2009 Hash Bash attracted an estimated 1,600 participants, the largest crowd since the 1973 event drew more than 3,000. That year, the participants included Perry Bullard, a Vietnam veteran who had been elected to the Michigan House of Representatives in 1972. Bullard was photographed while smoking marijuana at the event.

Two other cities now host large-scale legalization events. The Freedom Rally in Boston (established in 1989) and Hempfest in Seattle (established in 1991) now attract tens of thousands of attendees and feature noteworthy speakers along with prominent bands and lots of public cannabis consumption. Former Seattle Police Chief Norman Stamper appeared at the 2006 Hempfest. The city of Boston has tried several times to block the Freedom Rally by refusing it permits to assemble, but the courts have upheld the organizers' rights to gather.

Steven Hager, editor and chief of *High Times* magazine, established The High Times Freedom Fighters Award at the 1987 Hash Bash, presented annually to an individual with a positive impact in the world of cannabis. Recent recipients include:

- 2011, Debbie Goldsberry
- 2010, Dale Gieringer
- 2009, Rick Simpson
- 2007, Tommy Chong
- 2006, Richard Lee
- 2005, Alex Whiteplume
- 2004, Eddy Lepp
- 2003, Valerie and Mike Corral
- 2002, Shawn Heller

- 2001, Vivian McPeak
- 2000, Keith Stroup
- 1999, Gideon Israel
- 1994, Jack Herer
- 1993, Gatewood Galbraith
- 1992, Elvy Musikka
- 1991, Rodger Belknap
- 1990, Thom Harris

RASTA AND REEFER

On the Caribbean island of Jamaica, where high-grade cannabis has been grown for decades, a new faith grew up alongside it. Rastafari is a not exactly a religion, though its adherents worship a single deity, known as *Jah,* and share the Christian beliefs in the Holy Spirit and the divinity of Jesus. *Rastas* (a term they prefer to *Rastifarians*) also revere Africa as the mother country of all humanity and Haile Selassie, late Emperor of Ethiopia, as the direct descendent of Jesus.

Rastas treat the plant they know as *ganja* (from the Sanskrit word *Ganjika*) as a sacrament. Smoking cannabis, they believe, raises their consciousness, heals their oppressed souls, and brings them closer to Jah. They also believe that it links them to their African forebears. They cite a variety of Bible references from both the Old Testament and New Testament that they believe express the importance of ganja to proper worship.

Historians theorize that the cannabis plant and the enthusiasm for smoking it came to Jamaica along with the thousands of South Asian and Muslim workers imported to the island by British business interests after the abolition of slavery. Rastafari first attracted followers in the 1930s, but most Americans first became aware of it in the 1970s through the increasing popularity of reggae music and Bob Marley, its best-known performer.

In 1988, the Attorney General Janet Reno refused to grant Rastas an exception to U.S. drug laws to allow them to smoke ganja as a part of their religious practices. Courts in the United Kingdom came to the same conclusion. But in 2008 the Italian Supreme Court ruled that Rastas may possess and use Cannabis in that country.

NUGGET

"I NOW HAVE ABSOLUTE PROOF THAT SMOKING EVEN ONE MARIJUANA CIGARETTE IS EQUAL IN BRAIN DAMAGE TO BEING ON BIKINI ISLAND DURING AN H-BOMB BLAST."
—RONALD REAGAN, PRESIDENT OF THE UNITED STATES, 1981–1989

REMEMBER PARAQUAT?

If you were a weed smoker in the 1980s, you probably

remember paraquat. At that time, the U.S. government sponsored a program to spray the herbicide on marijuana fields in Mexico to kill the crop. It did not eliminate all the weed growing in Mexico and coming into the United States, but the government encouraged the belief that smoking pot treated with paraquat would be dangerous to people and urged everyone to stay away from the crop.

Subsequent research has not found any link between smoking paraquat-treated pot and ill health effects in people. The residue appears to be converted to harmless compounds when burned on leaves. No injury or illness has been linked to smoking pot contaminated by paraquat.

However, ingesting *pure* paraquat is highly toxic to people and other mammals and there are no specific antidotes. In some parts of the developing world, the availability of paraquat has made it an all-too-common choice for desperate people who wish to commit suicide. Paraquat is still available in the United States, but only to licensed applicators. The U.S. government no longer sponsors the spraying of marijuana fields with the herbicide.

PARTYING POTUS

Jimmy Carter, the 39th President, supported the decriminalization of marijuana in his 1976 campaign, but Bill Clinton, the 42nd President, was the first to acknowledge using it. In a TV interview during his first presidential campaign, Clinton was asked if he had ever violated international law. "When I was in England, I experimented with marijuana a time or two, and didn't like it," he said. "I didn't inhale and I didn't try it again." The statement "I didn't inhale" became a punchline for countless comedians and, for Clinton's critics, emblematic of his habit of blurring unpleasant facts.

Al Gore, Clinton's vice-president and Democratic candidate for President in 2000, admitted to smoking and inhaling marijuana as did his opponent, George W. Bush. The candidate who opposed Bush in the next election, Senator John Kerry, also acknowledged that he had smoked marijuana—like Gore, as a soldier in the Vietnam War. Barack Obama, the 44th president, also owned up to sampling marijuana in his youth.

CANDIDATE FOR CANNABIS

Gary Johnson was the Governor of New Mexico from 1993 to 2005, and a candidate for the Republican nomination in the 2012 presidential election. Johnson is also a proponent of legalizing, regulating, and taxing marijuana. He has stated that "90 percent of the drug problem is prohibition-related, not use-related." Johnson argues that legalization would have positive effects and "would lead to a lower price for the product and eliminate the criminal element from its distribution, much like the repeal of the prohibition of alcohol many decades back."

A NEW PRESCRIPTION

The settlement of a 1978 lawsuit brought by patients suffering from glaucoma compelled the U.S. Department of Health and Human Services to allow them to use cannabis to treat their symptoms. Under the Compassionate Investigational New Drug program, the National Institute of Drug Abuse was authorized to license the University of

Mississippi to grow cannabis for research purposes (the patients would be test subjects for the new drug) and to provide it to licensed physicians. With a flood of AIDS patients applying to the program in 1992, a new HHS Secretary canceled it, though patients already in the program continued receiving the cannabis grown in Mississippi. By 2010, only four patients remained in the program.

The federal government supported little research into the medicinal value of cannabis in the 1970s and 1980s, but several state health departments sponsored rigorous scientific studies on it. Some states had decriminalized possession of marijuana. But in 1996 California became the first state to authorize physicians to prescribe smoked cannabis to their patients and to license dispensaries and growers. More than a dozen other states, from Rhode Island to Washington, Michigan to New Mexico, have passed similar legislation.

Growing, distributing, possessing, and using marijuana

is still a violation of federal law, which has been enforced against only a few flagrant distributors. To clear up the gray area between federal and state laws, Governors Christine Gregoire (Washington) and Lincoln Chafee (Rhode Island) sent a request in 2011 for the Food and Drug Administration (FDA) and Drug Enforcement Agency (DEA) to reclassify marijuana from a Schedule I Controlled Substance (like heroin, no medicinal value, prone to abuse) to Schedule II Controlled Substance (like morphine, with medicinal value, prone to abuse). The change would allow licensed pharmacies to dispense it like other drugs.

NJ WEEDMAN

Edward Forchion is a native of New Jersey, a father of five, a candidate for state assemblyman, and the founder of the Legalize Marijuana Party. The party's platform? That current federal laws classifying marijuana as a Schedule I drug are unconstitutional and hypocritical. Schedule I drugs have "no medicinal value" and the highest potential for abuse.

Forchion, who goes by the handle "NJ Weedman," asserts that laws allowing use of marijuana for medicinal purposes—in many states, including New Jersey—contradict its Schedule I status.

To gain attention for his cause, Forchion mailed a gram of medical marijuana to New Jersey Governor Chris Christie and other state officials each month in 2010. Forchion has in the past run for Governor, U.S. Senator, and Congressman, always with the same mission.

CHAPTER 2

CANNABIS IN POPULAR CULTURE

What do you do when you've got a good buzz on? Listen to music? Watch movies or TV? Talk with your baked buddies about the best tunes and funniest scenes? Then you're like a lot of other stoners. And just for you I filled this chapter with information about all the best media appearances of our favorite herb. I'm not saying I've listed every reference to cannabis in every art form—just those that Dr. Kindbud rates as the best of the best, the funniest of the funny, the worst of the worst.

FILMS: FUNNY, FREAKY, AND FAR-OUT

Did you finally get up the nerve to ask that special stoner someone over to your place for some Mary Jane, munchies, and a movie? The following compendium of stoner films has a flick for every mood, from laughing until you're in tears comedic masterpieces, to scientific mind-expanding journeys, to the scary, dark, and twisted. Each film contained herein provides a brief synopsis, a quotable highlight, and a nugget of interesting information to guide you on your journey for the perfect movie. Dr. Kindbud's Rating System will help you discover some new classics, impress your friends, and set the right mood.

ALICE IN WONDERLAND (1951)

SYNOPSIS: The protagonist Alice, a young curious

girl, comes upon a mysterious and wondrous world. After impulsively chasing a tardy white rabbit down his burrow hole, Alice's adventure begins to unfold before her. As she attempts to get home, a wicked queen stands in her way. Adventurous, strange, and psychedelic Disney classic of the famous children's story by Lewis Carroll.

FAVORITE QUOTE: *The White Queen:* Sometimes I've believed as many as six impossible things before breakfast.

NUGGET: In the original book, the Caterpillar really likes to smoke his hookah (don't we all) and gives Alice a crucial lesson in magic mushrooms upon their meeting.

RATING: 🍁🍁🍁🍁

ANIMAL HOUSE (1978)

SYNOPSIS: National Lampoon's Animal House is an all-time classic set in 1962 starring Tim Matheson, John

Belushi, Peter Riegert, Karen Allen, Donald Sutherland, John Vernon, and Kevin Bacon, among others. Dean Vernon Wormer of Faber College is determined to expel the members of the Delta frat and enlists the help of the Omega house, whose members are all rich Anglo-Saxon white males. Dean Wormer enlists the help of the Omega house, whose members are all rich Anglo-Saxon white males. With all of Delta's misdoings and general disregard for authority, it shouldn't be difficult for him. This movie is filled with toga parties, food fights, horse heart attacks, and such.

FAVORITE QUOTE:

Pinto [after being handed his first joint]: I won't go schizo, will I?

Jennings: It's a distinct possibility.

NUGGET: Did you know that when John Belushi is teaching the "dirty lyrics" of The Kingsmen's song "Louie Louie" to everyone he is referencing an actual FBI investigation that took place from 1963 to 1965? Due to complaints from parents claiming their kids knew the profane "secret hidden lyrics," the agency dedicated more than two years in an effort to decode them. Alas, to no avail.

RATING: 🍁🍁🍁🍁🍁 *"Stoner Classic"*

BAD TEACHER (2011)

SYNOPSIS: In this flick Cameron Diaz plays Elizabeth Halsey, who, as it turns out, is a very *bad* teacher. After a breakup with her fiancé and a desire for breast implants, she returns to teach junior high. Upon her arrival, she meets Scott Delacorte, a new colleague, played by Justin Timberlake, who turns out to be rich. She quickly crafts a plan to woo him.

FAVORITE QUOTE: *Cameron Diaz [to friend]:* Let's get baked [sees a student overheard]… goods. We're going to go get some baked goods.

NUGGET: Star Cameron Diaz not only enjoys the cheeba in this film, she's been known to praise the "higher" things in life off-screen as well.

RATING: 🌿🌿🌿

THE BIG LEBOWSKI (1998)

SYNOPSIS: "The Dude" Lebowski, played by Jeff Bridges, just wants to relax, smoke a joint, and keep the peace. A series of events, all stemming from a ruined rug and a mixup concerning another Lebowski, who happens to be a millionaire, takes Dude and his bowling teammates on a wild misadventure. This movie is packed with so many classic lines and some of the most beautifully choreographed bowling sequences ever shot on film.

FAVORITE QUOTE: *The Dude:* Mind if I do a J?

NUGGET: Annual Lebowski Fests occur all over the country where faithful fans or, as they are known to each other, "Achievers" pay homage to the film. It's costumes, contests, live music, bowling, and more. 2011 was the festival's ten-year anniversary, and the subculture shows no sign of slowing down. Check out what's currently going on by visiting http://www.lebowskifest.com/.

RATING: 🌿🌿🌿🌿🌿 *"Stoner Classic"*

BONGWATER (1997)

SYNOPSIS: Artsy-fartsy David (Luke Wilson), whose dream is to become an artist, deals the green bud on the side. He meets Serena, a weed lovin' lady who has some issues that need tissues. Serena soon decides to head for the Big Apple leaving David yearning for her return. This movie has all the makings for an entertaining weed lover's flick *(weed not included)*.

FAVORITE QUOTE: *Devlin, played by Jack Black singing and playing guitar around a campfire:* It was a big day on Jesus Ranch, Jesus Ranch. I feel in love with a baked potato. That's when I started to dance, yeah, in France. I'm taking a walk in the woods, it's nice outside, smells of shit... I come across a silver stripped mushroom and I fly-la-la-la-ly-ly-ly.

NUGGET: *Bongwater* the film was adapted from a book of the same name penned by Michael Hornburg that has developed a large cult following.

RATING: 🌿🌿🌿

THE BREAKFAST CLUB (1985)

SYNOPSIS: A John Hughes small-town classic about a diverse group of five high school students attending a mandatory Saturday detention. They each have a different reason for being there, and each have a story. Throughout the day of detention they fight, laugh, commiserate, and get high. This film's all-star lineup includes Molly Ringwald, Emilio Estevez, Judd Nelson, Ally Sheedy, Anthony Michael Hall, and Paul Gleason.

FAVORITE QUOTE: Chicks cannot hold their smoke. Dat's what it is.

NUGGET: The character of Allison Reynolds (Ally Sheedy) does not utter a single word until 33 minutes into the film.

RATING: 🌿🌿🌿

CADDYSHACK (1980)

SYNOPSIS: This '80s classic has an all-star cast including Chevy Chase, Michael O'Keefe, Rodney Dangerfield, Bill Murray, Ted Knight, and, of course, the Gopher! Set at an exclusive snooty white-collar golf course, the story follows caddy Danny Noonan (O'Keefe) as he tries to figure out his future and what direction to head in. The story also follows groundskeeper Carl Spackler (Murray) in his stoned quest to catch a mischievous gopher ruining the course. The uptight regulars get shaken up with the arrival of a new member, Al Czervik (Dangerfield), whose eccentric behavior is not welcome by many.

FAVORITE QUOTE: This is a hybrid. This is a cross, ah, of Bluegrass, Kentucky Bluegrass, Featherbed Bent, and Northern California Sensemilia. The amazing stuff about this is, that you can play 36 holes on it in the afternoon, take it home and just get stoned to the bejeezus-belt that night on this stuff.

NUGGET: If director Harold Remis had his way, Pink Floyd would have composed the score. But once Kenny Loggins wrote the song "I'm Alright," the rest was history.

RATING: 🍁🍁🍁🍁🍁 *"Stoner Classic"*

CHEECH & CHONG... UP IN SMOKE (1978)

SYNOPSIS: The adventures of Cheech and Chong, smokin and tokin! Unbeknown to the dynamic duo, the vehicle they are driving over the border to L.A. from Mexico is made entirely of delicious herb. A weed lover's dream! Will the law catch them? Will they realize they are traveling in a weedmobile?

FAVORITE QUOTE:

Chong: You wanna get high, man?

Cheech: Does Howdy-Doody have wooden balls?

NUGGET: The film uses the word "man" 295 times—212 times before Cheech and Chong reach the border.

RATING: 🍁🍁🍁🍁🍁 *"Stoner Classic"*

CLERKS (1994)

SYNOPSIS: Have you ever thought you'd like to experience a day in the life of a convenience store clerk in a New Jersey town? Dante Hicks gets called into work on the Saturday that was supposed to be his day off. As he tries to just get through the day and get the hell out of work, he and Randal, who works at the video rental store next door, discuss the finer things in life, play hockey on the roof of the store, and annoy their customers to no end. This movie is dialogue-driven, and Kevin Smith's writing is uniquely hilarious. It is also the first film appearance of Jay and Silent Bob (aka Bluntman & Chronic), two staples of modern pop culture.

FAVORITE QUOTE: *Jay's rap:* Smokin weed, smokin weed. Doin' coke, drinkin beers. Drinkin beers, beers beers. Rollin' fatties, smokin blunts. Who smokes the blunts? We smoke the blunts. Rollin' blunts and smokin um.'

NUGGET: Filmed in black-and-white on a budget of only $27,000, *Clerks* began the career of writer-director Kevin Smith, who would go on to make such stoner classics as *Mallrats* (1995), *Dogma* (1999), and *Jay and Silent Bob Strike Back* (2001).

RATING: 🌿 🌿 🌿 🌿

CLUB PARADISE (1986)

SYNOPSIS: A tropical THC getaway! Firefighter Jack Moniker, played by Robin Williams, retires to a small Caribbean island named St. Nicholas after an injury on the job. He soon meets Ernest Reed, played by Jimmy Cliff, who owns a small beachfront resort. Jack learns that land developers are weaseling their way into stealing the land from Ernest and steps in to help.

FAVORITE QUOTE:

Jack Moniker: Tree, what's happenin'?

[offers Jack marijuana]

Jack Moniker: Oooooh, no thanks. Last time I smoked that stuff they found me on top of the Sears tower trying to build a nest.

NUGGET: Bill Murray was first considered to star in this film.

RATING: 🌿🌿🌿

DAZED AND CONFUSED (1993)

SYNOPSIS: This memorable flick is a classic must-have for all stoners. The name of the movie pretty much sums up how awesome this movie is. The movie has a killer soundtrack, memorable cast that takes the viewer on a journey through the glazed-over eyes of freshman and seniors on their final day of high school back in 1976. It's full of hook-ups, smoke-ups, and beat-downs as everyone tries to launch an awesome summer.

FAVORITE QUOTE:

Wooderson: Say, man, you got a joint?

Mitch: No, not on me, man.

Wooderson: It'd be a lot cooler if you did.

NUGGET:
Carl Burnett, played by Esteban Powell, appears wearing a T-shirt with the Kiss album cover for "Rock and Roll Over." That album was not released until November 1976. Classic stoner mistake!

RATING:
🌿🌿🌿🌿🌿 *"Stoner Classic"*

DOGMA (1999)

SYNOPSIS:
This Kevin Smith classic focusing on a fantastical story surrounding Catholicism and the Catho-

lic Church proves to be both funny and well written. The film follows two angels, played by Matt Damon and Ben Affleck, who have fallen from God's grace and are sentenced to live out the universe's existence on earth with wings and no genitals. After a long time spent wandering the planet, they believe they have found a loophole in Catholic dogma that will allow them to return to heaven. On God's side is Bethany Sloane, an abortion clinic worker played by Linda Fiorentino. She is aided by Jay and Silent Bob, who always bring the chronic with them wherever they go. Chris Rock plays the thirteenth apostle. Alannis Morissette plays the role of God in this movie. No joke!

FAVORITE QUOTE:

Jay: See, all these movies take place in a town called Shermer, in Illinois. And there's all this fine bush running around, and we could kick all the dude's asses because they're all whiney pussies. Except Judd Nelson—he was harsh. But best of all, there was no one selling weed. So

I says to Silent Bob, "Man, we could live phat if we were the blunt-connection in Shermer, Illinois!" So we collected some cash we were owed and caught a bus. But when we got here, you know what we found out? There is no Shermer in Illinois. What kind of shit is that?! Fucking movies are bullshit!

NUGGET: This satire definitely drew the attention of some Catholics. There were large protests and calls to boycott the film when it was released in theaters. Kevin Smith, who wrote and directed the film, is Catholic.

RATING: 🌿🌿🌿🌿

DUDE, WHERE'S MY CAR? (2000)

SYNOPSIS: The classic tale of two friends, Jesse and Chester, who love the mary jane and awake from a night of debauchery to find their vehicle is missing as well as their memory of the previous evening. A fantastical journey to recover their car with many strange encounters along the way, including hot female aliens who want some sort of mystical device and a transsexual stripper after a suitcase full of money.

FAVORITE QUOTE:

Mr. Pizzacoli: A trained dolphin could deliver pizzas better than you two!

Jesse: But then the pizzas would get all wet.

NUGGET:
Although the film was knocked by film critics, it became well regarded as a great stoner flick within cannabis subculture and developed a cult following. Michael Moore may have used this pop culture reference for his book *Dude, Where's My Country?*

RATING: 🌿🌿🌿

EASY RIDER (1969)

SYNOPSIS: Out in search of America's open road two counterculture bikers, Wyatt and Billy, make their way from Los Angeles to New Orleans for Mardis Gras. They fund their trip by buying weed in Mexico and selling it in LA before taking off. There are a lot of strange turns in this film including hitchhikers, a whorehouse, a drunken lawyer, and a jail cell.

FAVORITE QUOTE:

George Hanson [Jack Nicholson] (after seeing his first marijuana cigarette): Lord have mercy! Is that what that is?

NUGGET: It has been reported that Dennis Hopper, Peter Fonda, and Jack Nicholson were smoking real marijuana on camera during the scene.

RATING: 🍁🍁🍁🍁🍁 *"Stoner Classic"*

EMPEROR OF HEMP (1999)

SYNOPSIS: Cult folk hero Jack Herer, the emperor of hemp, dedicated his life (1939–2010) to bringing awareness and discussion to the topic of hemp cannabis. This video documents his effort to educate people on the many uses and benefits of hemp as a plant, the conspiracy against it, and the call for an end of cannabis prohibition.

FAVORITE QUOTE: *Michael R. Aldrich, Ph.D. (historian)*: The idea that it had other uses, that you could make paper out of it, that you could make cloth out of it, you could make cord out of it, you could make oil, you could make medicine, those had never occurred to Jack, and boy did he take that idea and run with it.

NUGGET: This movie has a great soundtrack with cuts from Kara's Flowers, who later changed their name to Maroon5 and won a Grammy, as well as Cheap Trick, The

Rascals, Bonnie Raitt, Joe Walsh, and Kris Kristofferson.

RATING: 🌿 🌿 🌿 🌿

EYES WIDE SHUT (1999)

SYNOPSIS: This twisted tale from director Stanley Kubrick follows Dr. William "Bill" Harford through the bizarrely void and empty streets of Manhattan on a mysterious night. After he and his wife, Alice, smoke up, she confesses she once almost cheated on him and has since fantasized about it. When he refuses to admit that he too fantasizes, she becomes angry and chastises him. He leaves his home and through a series of odd events ends up on a nightlong journey that includes sneaking into a masked ceremonial orgy ritual thrown by the New York elite. Kubrick thought that it was important to cast an authentic married couple to play the married couple in this film and cast Tom Cruise and Nicole Kidman to play the roles.

TRIPPY QUOTE:

Dr. Bill Harford: Now, where exactly are we going... exactly?

Gayle: Where the rainbow ends.

Dr. Bill Harford: Where the rainbow ends?

Nuala: Don't you want to go where the rainbow ends?

Dr. Bill Harford: Well, now that depends where that is.

Gayle: Well, let's find out.

NUGGET: One popular theory about this film is that once Bill and Alice smoke, the film goes into a strange THC dream sequence for the duration. It certainly does take a turn for the peculiar.

RATING: 🌿🌿🌿

FAST TIMES AT RIDGEMONT HIGH (1982)

SYNOPSIS: A classic '80s flick that follows the lives

of a group of southern California teenagers who love sex, drugs, music, and the mall. One of the greatest stoner characters in the history of film is Sean Penn's portrayal of Jeff Spicoli, a laid-back surfer who is always stoned out of his gourd. Many other soon-to-be stars acted in this movie as well, including Jennifer Jason Lee, Judge Reinhold, Phoebe Cates, and Forest Whitaker.

FAVORITE QUOTE:

Brad Hamilton: Why don't you get a job, Spicoli?

Jeff Spicoli: What for?

Brad Hamilton: You need money.

Jeff Spicoli: All I need are some tasty waves, a cool buzz, and I'm fine.

NUGGET:
This film was written by Cameron Crowe, who based it on real-life misadventures he chronicled in his book *Fast Times at Ridgemont High: A True Story.*

RATING:
🌿🌿🌿🌿🌿 *"Stoner Classic"*

FEAR & LOATHING IN LAS VEGAS

(1998)

SYNOPSIS: Hunter S. Thompson's drug-fueled story of a journey from LA to Las Vegas and back with his lawyer, Dr. Gonzo, in search of the good old American dream. Johnny Depp's depiction of Thompson's off-beat characteristics are extremely entertaining while Benicio Del Toro holds his own as Dr. Gonzo. Be prepared for a drug-infused and psychedelic trip of vast proportions!

FAVORITE QUOTE: *Raoul Duke (reacting to the song "One Toke Over the Line" playing on the radio):* One toke? You poor fool! Wait till you see those goddamn bats.

NUGGET: What was originally Hunter S. Thompson's 250-word photo-caption job for *Sports Illustrated* grew to a novel-length feature story for *Rolling Stone*. Thompson said publisher Jann Wenner had "liked the first 20 or so jangled pages enough to take it seriously on its own terms and tentatively scheduled it for publication—which gave me the push I needed to keep working on it." He had first submitted a 2,500-word manuscript to *Sports Illustrated* that was "aggressively rejected."

RATING: ⬤⬤⬤⬤⬤ *"Stoner Classic"*

THE 40 YEAR OLD VIRGIN (2005)

SYNOPSIS: Steve Carell plays Andy, a man who loves his job at Smart-tech, his action figures, and his video-games. The only problem is that he's never loved a woman. Once word gets out that he's a virgin, his coworkers will stop at nothing to get him laid. Andy just wants a nice girl and has his eyes set on a cutey named Trish, played by Catherine Keener.

FAVORITE QUOTE:

Cal: Listen, when I was growing pot, I realized that the more seeds I planted, the more pot I could ultimately smoke.

Andy: I think I've got all the advice I can handle right now.

NUGGET: One of the best scenes in the movie is when Andy has his chest hair waxed off. Steve Carell is quoted as saying, "It has to be real. It won't be as funny if it's mocked up or if it's special effect. You have to see that this is really happening." So the crew set up five cameras to capture the gloriously funny moment in one take.

RATING: 🌿🌿🌿🌿

FRIDAY (1995)

SYNOPSIS: Two guys, Smokey (Chris Tucker) and Craig (rapper Ice Cube), are just chilling on the front porch on a Los Angeles afternoon trying to enjoy a high

Friday and find something fun to do. After smoking weed from a pot dealer dubbed Big Worm, they must scramble to get the dealer his money or face the consequences.

FAVORITE QUOTE:

Smokey: I know you don't smoke weed. I know this, but I'm gonna get you high today, cause it's Friday. You ain't got no job... and you ain't got shit to do.

NUGGET: This film was shot in just 20 days in director F. Gary Gray's childhood neighborhood. Most of the houses used for the film belonged to his friends, and he even used the home he grew up in.

RATING: 🌿🌿🌿🌿🌿 *"Stoner Classic"*

GET HIM TO THE GREEK (2010)

SYNOPSIS: Young, hard-working music exec Aaron Green (Jonah Hill) is given the task of escorting (supervising)

a washed-up rock star named Aldous Snow (Russell Brand) from his mother's house in London to Los Angeles for his comeback performance at the famous Greek Theatre. The only thing standing in his way is the hard-partying antics of this crazy superstar. Sean "P. Diddy" Combs plays Green's boss who has some very unusual antics of his own and even demonstrates to Green how to "mind fuck" someone. Be prepared for a raunchy drug-induced ride of a comedy!

FAVORITE QUOTE:

Jonathan Snow: That's the best part about the Jeffrey… it goes away and then it comes back.

Aldous Snow: When the world slips you a Jeffrey, stroke the furry wall.

NUGGET: Aldous Snow is a spinoff character from the movie *Forgetting Sarah Marshall*, which was also directed by Nicholas Stoller.

RATING: 🌿🌿🌿🌿

Grandma's Boy (2006)

Synopsis: Alex, a talented, 35-year-old video game tester must move in with his grandma who lives with two other older women all because his roommate spent the rent money on hookers. As far as Alex's coworkers at the video game company know, he's living with "three hot babes." Alex is no exception to the preconceived notion that video games and pot go hand in hand. In one scene, his grandma mistakenly uses his pot she found, and the three women get more than they bargained for.

Favorite quote:

Dante: Wow... where do you get your weed?

Mr. Cheezle: From you, Dante.

Dante: Oh... That's right! What's up, Mr. Cheezle!

Nugget: The film did not do so well in its theatrical release, grossing only $6 million, but it soon gained cult stature among potheads and sold over $50 million in DVD sales.

RATING: 🌿🌿🌿

GOOD MORNING, VIETNAM
(1987)

SYNOPSIS: Robin Williams plays Adrian Cronauer, a disc jockey who is assigned to the U.S. Armed Services Radio station's base in Vietnam in 1965 during the war. Adrian shakes up the scene with his humor and becomes extremely popular among the troops, but his superiors don't always see eye to eye with him. The movie executes an excellent blend of comedy and drama.

FAVORITE QUOTE: Speaking of things controversial, is it true that there is a marijuana problem here in Vietnam? No it's not a problem, everybody has it.

NUGGET: The first draft of the script was written by the real Adrian Cronauer and was much different than what ended up making it on to the big screen. After several failed attempts to get it produced as a TV show or Movie-of-the-Week, Robin Williams came upon the script. Realizing it was a great platform from which he could promote his unique comedic style, he had it reworked into the film we know today.

RATING: ⚜ ⚜ ⚜ ⚜

HALF BAKED (1998)

SYNOPSIS: Three roommates need to raise money to bail out their friend, Kenny, who gets sent to jail for feeding popcorn to a diabetic police horse and killing it. Why not sell some sticky-icky? Thurgood Jenkins (Dave Chappelle) just found a sweet weed supply, and it may be the only way for he and his buds to raise the money and save Kenny from Nasty Nate in prison. Trouble and hilarity ensue, including a cameo from Bob Saget who proclaims his history of exchanging fellatio for coke. Dave Chappelle broke onto the mainstream scene with this stoner masterpiece. Filled with a ton of one-liners, this movie has provided countless hours of fried fun.

FAVORITE QUOTE: *Enhancement Smoker (played by John Stewart):* You ever see the back of a twenty-dollar bill... on weed? Oh, there's some crazy shit, man. There's a dude in the bushes. Has he got a gun? I don't know! Red team go! Red team go!

NUGGET: Even though this movie is revered as a stoner classic, Dave Chappelle said that the script that he co-wrote with his partner Neal Brennan was funnier than the finished movie, which he called "a weed movie for kids."

RATING: 🌿🌿🌿🌿🌿 *"Stoner Classic"*

HAROLD & KUMAR GO TO WHITE CASTLE (& SEQUELS)

(2004)

SYNOPSIS: We're going to take the liberty of squeezing all three movies from this series into one entry. They are all great stoner flicks. In the beginning (*Harold & Kumar Go To White Castle*), Harold and Kumar are just two stoned college students who have a serious case of the munchies that can only be satisfied by a visit to White Castle. Should be a simple trip, but of course it is not, including getting their car stolen by Neil Patrick Harris (you know… Doogie Howser, M.D.). In the sequel, *Harold & Kumar Escape From Guantanamo Bay* (2008), the two get sent away after being mistaken as terrorists while trying to smoke-up on a plane to Amsterdam. They escape and set out to prove their innocence. In the third movie, *A Very Harold & Kumar 3D Christmas* (2011), the pair reunites six years after their last adventure. After Kumar inadvertently sets Harold's prized Christmas tree ablaze, the two take to the streets of Manhattan in search of a replacement. 3D trouble ensues.

FAVORITE QUOTE:

Harold: I want 30 sliders, five French fries, and four large cherry Cokes.

Kumar: I want the same, except make mine diet Cokes.

NUGGET: This movie was released in Europe, where there are no White Castles, with the title *Harold & Kumar Get the Munchies.*

RATING: 🌿🌿🌿🌿🌿 *"Stoner Classic"*

HOMEGROWN (1998)

SYNOPSIS: After Malcom Stockman (John Lithgow) is killed by an unknown perpetrator, his three helpers take over his business, a marijuana plantation. Unfortunately, the business side of things isn't as easy as they had hoped and they run into all sorts of trouble. Billy Bob Thornton gives a stellar performance as Jack Marsden.

FAVORITE QUOTE:
Jack Marsden: You guys are the biggest fuck-ups in the history of dope dealing. That's a huge fuckin' statement.

NUGGET:
This movie is set somewhere in northern California where in reality some of the finest bud is grown in places such as Humboldt County.

RATING: 🌿🌿

HOT TUB TIME MACHINE (2010)

Synopsis: A magical hot tub transports four men reliving a great night at a ski resort back to the year 1986. Adam (John Cusack) must ensure that he, his two buddies, and his nephew Jacob (Clark Duke) do not do anything to stop the conception of Jacob—a kind of *Back to the Future* paradox situation.

FAVORITE QUOTE:

Lou: Fuckin' Russian energy drink, Chernobly. It's got this shit in it, not even legal here.

Adam: Whats in it?

Lou: How the fuck am I supposed to know dude, but it's illegal!

NUGGET:
When the guys first arrive back in the '80s they unpack their suitcases and find Adam's is stocked with drugs. Jacob asks "Who are you, Hunter S. Thompson?" Adam responds, "I thought I was." This comment is said to be an inside joke because Cusack is close friends with Thompson in real life and had been considered for the role of Raoul Duke in Thompson's movie *Fear & Loathing in Las Vegas*.

RATING: 🌿🌿🌿

HOW HIGH? (2001)

SYNOPSIS: Silas and Jamal played by Method Man and Redman have some magical ganja in their possession. They grew it from a seed planted in the ashes of their departed friend who suffered death by dread-lock fire while smoking. The good news is that this new weed gives them all the knowledge they need to get accepted to Harvard. But what will happen when their stash runs out?

FAVORITE QUOTE:

Silas: So, you trying to get something to bring your nerves down too, huh?

Jamal: Yeah. I figure if I study high, take the test high, get high scores! Right?

Silas: Right.

NUGGET: In one scene Silas and Jamal have just finished smoking in their car. If you pay attention you'll notice it's really smoky in the first shot then totally clear in the next. Oops.

RATING: 🌿🌿🌿

HUMBOLDT COUNTY (2008)

SYNOPSIS: This dramatic comedy follows proper straight-laced Peter Hadley (Jeremy Strong), who ponders his future after he flunks a class taught by his father at medical school and becomes stranded with a bunch of off-the-radar hippies who grow pot to support themselves. As he spends time witnessing the operation, he contemplates the type of life he would like to have and can see the pros and cons of both.

FAVORITE QUOTE:

Peter: Hey, why do they call your mom Bogart?
Charity: Uh, she's not my mom.

Peter: Oh.

Charity: Because she bogarts the pot, a verb which means to hold instead of pass.

NUGGET: Humboldt County took its name from Humboldt Bay. Humboldt Bay was named after Alexander von Humboldt, a renowned naturalist and explorer from Germany.

RATING: 🌿🌿🌿

IT'S COMPLICATED (2009)

SYNOPSIS: A divorced couple, Jake (Alec Baldwin) and Jane (Meryl Streep), reunite and reignite their old flame at their son's college graduation. Jake happens to be remarried, and Jane is also drawn to an architect named Adam played by Steve Martin. It's complicated.

FAVORITE QUOTE: I don't know what they've done

to pot in the last 30 years, but it rocks!

NUGGET: Writer and director Nancy Meyers has written, produced and directed several big Hollywood hits including *What Women Want* (2000), *Something's Gotta Give* (2003), and *The Parent Trap* (1998).

RATING: 🌿🌿

JAY & SILENT BOB STRIKE BACK (2001)

SYNOPSIS: The dynamic stoner duo Jay and Silent Bob, played by Jason Mewes and writer/director Kevin Smith, get a feature film of their own. They are pissed after Dante gets a restraining order prohibiting them from selling weed in front of the Quick Stop, and the find themselves with nothing to do. When they are informed that their comic book alter egos, Bluntman and Chronic, are being adapted into a film and that people are trashing it on the Internet, they set out to get paid and put an end to the rumors.

FAVORITE QUOTE:

Jay: Yo! You guys need to turn those frowns upside down, and I got just the thing for that [produces a bag of pre-rolled joints]. We call them... Doobie Snacks.

NUGGET:
Did you know Kevin Smith has a comic book store of his own dubbed Jay & Silent Bob's Secret Stash? It is located in Red Bank, New Jersey, where parts of *Chasing Amy* (1997) were filmed.

RATING: 🌿 🌿 🌿

KNOCKED UP (2007)

SYNOPSIS:
After a fun one-night stand, stoner party dude Ben Stone (Seth Rogan) has to face the reality that

his fling, Alison Scott (Katherine Heigl), is pregnant with his baby. Can Ben pull his shit together enough to raise a baby and prove his worth? A coming-of-age story of life, love, and stoner struggles. A great date-night flick!

FAVORITE QUOTE:

Ben Stone: You know, the best thing for a hangover is weed. Do you smoke weed?

Alison Scott: Not really.

Ben Stone: You don't?

Alison Scott: No.

Ben Stone: At all?

Alison Scott: Uh-uh.

Ben Stone: Like... in the morning?

Alison Scott: No... I just... don't.

Ben Stone: It is, like, the best medicine. Cause it fixes everything. Jonah broke his elbow once. We just... got high and... it still clicks but, I mean, he's ok.

NUGGET: This film contains one of the funniest psychedelic mushroom scenes of all time. Characters Ben and Pete travel to Las Vegas and indulge in shrooms at a Cirque du Soleil. Will it work out for them?

RATING: 🍁🍁🍁🍁

LEAVES OF GRASS (2009)

SYNOPSIS: Edward Norton plays two roles in this film as identical twin brothers. One is a Ivy League professor and thinker, and the other is still back in their Oklahoma hometown starting an impressive high-tech cannabis growing operation. After the stoner lures the professor back home by faking his death, he enlists his help to overthrow the local drug kingpin, played by Richard Dreyfuss.

FAVORITE QUOTE: You can't synthesize that. That is nature's delivery system for goodness. Distilled into a pure form. It glides down into your belly, and blooms into a feeling of peace, in this world beset by evil.

NUGGET: Writer Tim Blake Nelson already had Norton in mind when writing the screenplay. He stated that if Norton had declined "there would have been no second choice." Lucky for Nelson, Norton wanted to star in the film so badly he took a pay cut saying he "actually got paid half" what he usually made.

RATING: 🌿 🌿 🌿 🌿

MAGIC TRIP (2011)

SYNOPSIS: This documentary was put together from long-stored video of Ken Kesey and the Merry Pranksters making their way across the county in the trippy bus named "Further" in the 1960s. After the trip had ended they realized there was problems with the audio they had recorded with the film and the footage got shelved. It was resurrected by Writer/Directors Alison Ellwood and Alex Gibbony and voiceover was added over the footage to re-tell the magical journey.

FAVORITE QUOTE: It looked like a traveling pleasure palace, it was big and roomy and spacious… until we got all the people in it… People didn't think that we were hippies or that we were drug freaks because it wasn't in the news yet.

NUGGET: Neal Cassady, a member of the Merry Pranksters, was Jack Kerouac's model for his character Dean Moriarty in his novel *On The Road*.

RATING: 🌿🌿🌿🌿

MALLRATS (1995)

SYNOPSIS: Two New Jersey guys, TS Quint and Brodie, are dumped by their girlfriends and decide to head to the mall and try to feel better. TS wants to win his girl, Brandi, back, but Brodie is convinced he wants nothing to do with his ex, Rene. It's amazing how much trouble two guys can get into at a Jersey mall. It wouldn't be a Kevin Smith film without Jay and Silent Bob debauchery strewn throughout the film.

FAVORITE QUOTE: *Jay says to Willam (Ethan Suplee) [who has not been able to see a Sailboat in a Magic-Eye picture]:* What you need is a fatty-boom-batty blunt! And I guarantee you'll be seeing a sailboat, an ocean, and maybe even some of those big-tittied mermaids doing some of that lesbian shit! Look at me, look at me, you sloppy bitch!

NUGGET: According to an imdb.com post, "Brodie's shirt is the merged faces of three actors that tried out for the part of Brodie and didn't get it."

RATING: 🌿🌿🌿🌿🌿 *"Stoner Classic"*

NAKED LUNCH (1991)

SYNOPSIS: This movie is crazy, twisted, dark, and psychedelic. The subtext can be read in many different ways. The story follows Bill Lee (Peter Weller), who becomes addicted to the propellant he spays to kill bugs as an exterminator. Then he must flee the country after accidentally killing his wife. The film has a number of odd hallucinations including his typewriter that transforms into a cockroach with a need for text.

FAVORITE QUOTE:
Bill Lee: What do you mean, "it's a literary high"?
Joan Lee: It's a Kafka high. You feel like a bug.

NUGGET: Although it shares the same name, the film is not based on William S. Burrough's novel. It is a culmination of part of Burrough's biography, part drug-fueled writings, and paranoia about a writer by the name of Bill

Lee, who accidentally shot his wife while attempting to shoot an apple off her head.

RATING: 🌿🌿🌿

NATIONAL LAMPOON'S VACATION (1983)

SYNOPSIS: Clark Griswold (Chevy Chase) wants his wife Ellen (Beverly D'Angelo) and two kids, Audrey and Rusty, to have an amazing vacation, unlike all those with his parents when he was a kid. That's why he's taking them on a road trip to Walley World family theme park. Unfortunately, little goes right, and the family finds themselves dealing with one self-inflicted calamity after another.

FAVORITE QUOTE:
Audrey Griswold (after seeing Vicki's trophy for hog raising): Uh, don't take this personally, Vicki, but being a farmer

isn't too cool you know.

Cousin Vicki: Oh, yeah? Well, how cool is this? *[She then reaches under her bed and produces a shoebox full of home-grown weed.]*

NUGGET: This film was based on a short story written by John Hughes titled "Vacation 58" that he wrote for the September 1979 issue of *National Lampoon* magazine.

RATING: 🌿🌿🌿🌿🌿 *"Stoner Classic"*

OLD SCHOOL (2003)

SYNOPSIS: Mitch Martin (Luke Wilson) has fallen on tough times. Upon finding his girlfriend cheating on him, Mitch must find a new place to live. After two of his friends, Frank and Bernard, coerce him into starting a fraternity in his newly rented college-located house, mayhem breaks loose. Now the boys can relive their crazy college haze.

FAVORITE QUOTE:

Jerry: That was great.

Frank: What happened? I blacked out.

NUGGET: These guys must love White Snake. Their song "Here I Go Again" is played four times throughout the film. It is played twice with the vocal, once without, and hummed once. Mitch also references White Snake while talking about Nicole's old jean jacket. Frank also wears a White Snake t-shirt at the end of the movie.

RATING: 🌿 🌿 🌿 🌿

OUTSIDE PROVIDENCE (1999)

SYNOPSIS: It's the mid-70s and Tim Dunphy (Shawn Hatosy) and his friends enjoy their beer and weed! After getting in trouble with the law a few too many times, Tim's father, played by Alec Baldwin, sends him away to a prep school in Cornwall, Connecticut, to get his life straightened out. There, Tim proves you can grow as a person while still partying hard.

FAVORITE QUOTE:

Jane: Put that away! It's time to study.

Tim: No, really, I study better when I'm stoned. It's like my brain becomes more focused or something.

Jane: Yeah, right. You haven't gotten higher than a D since you've been here.

Tim: That's cause there's no good weed around here.

NUGGET: Peter Farrelly, who wrote the book the film was based on, drew from his experiences at Kent State where he graduated from in 1975.

RATING: 🌿🌿🌿🌿🌿 *"Stoner Classic"*

PINEAPPLE EXPRESS (2008)

SYNOPSIS: Dale Denton (Seth Rogan) has an interesting job as a process server, constantly dressing in uniforms and costumes to gain access to the people he must serve. What could make his job better? Being high, of course! But after his dealer Saul Silver (James Franco) gives him some seriously potent and unique weed named Pineapple Express, Dale accidentally leaves a roach behind after witnessing a murder while trying to serve papers. Now the duo must go on the run.

FAVORITE QUOTE:

Saul: This is like if that Blue Oyster shit met that Afghan Kush I had—and they had a baby. And then, meanwhile, that crazy Northern Light stuff I had and the Super Red Espresso Snowflake met and had a baby. And by some miracle, those two babies met and fucked—this would the shit that they birthed.

Dale (takes a whiff of the weed): Wow. This is the product of baby fucking.

NUGGET: Seth Rogan told a *Rolling Stone* interviewer that they had hoped for a film budget of $50 million but could only get $25 million because of the intense drug content.

RATING: 🌿🌿🌿🌿🌿 *"Stoner Classic"*

THE PINK WIZARD OR THE DARKSIDE OF THE RAINBOW — *Dark Side of the Moon* (1973) *and The Wizard of Oz* (1939)

SYNOPSIS: This is the perfect Saturday night activity for you and a few choice friends. Get the popcorn ready, roll up a joint, and get your music and DVD ready. You are about to experience a sensory overload as you embark on the journey of "The Darkside of the Rainbow." You will need one copy of Pink Floyd's "Darkside of the Moon" and the classic fantasy film *The Wizard of Oz*. Cue up the music and then hit play on the third roar of the MGM lion at the beginning of the flick. Turn off the movie's sound, and sit back and get ready to be astounded!

HILARIOUS MASH-UP QUOTE: There is no place like home... to watch this amazing phenomenon.

NUGGET: One of the highlights of this amazing adventure is when the scarecrow dances away to the amazing tune "Brain Damage." It will blow your mind!

RATING: 🍁🍁🍁🍁🍁 *"Stoner Classic"*

PRIVATE PARTS (1997)

SYNOPSIS: Howard Stern stars in this autobiographical film that tells the story of a shy kid who loved music and weed and finds himself drawn to the disc-jockey profession. The film chronicles Stern's rise to the top, the mainstream resistance he faced, and his quest to bring his voice to the airwaves.

FAVORITE QUOTE: Now, because I had such a minuscule schlonger, I turned to drugs. Unfortunately, the drugs really made me paranoid.

NUGGET: The final scene of the movie in which Howard Stern speaks directly into the camera was improvised and they only filmed one take.

RATING: 🌿🌿🌿🌿

PULP FICTION (1994)

SYNOPSIS: A classic from writer/director Quentin Tarantino that intertwines the lives of two mob hitmen, a gangster's wife, a boxer, and a pair of diner-robbing bandits. The two hitmen, Vincent Vega (John Travolta) and

Jules Winnfield (Samuel L. Jackson), set out to reclaim a briefcase that was stolen from their boss, Marsellus Wallace (Ving Rhames).

FAVORITE QUOTE:

Lance: You're going to give her an injection of adrenaline directly to her heart.

Vincent: But she's got, uh, breastplate...

Lance: So you gotta pierce through that. So what you have to do is, you have to bring the needle down in a stabbing motion.

Vincent: I gotta stab her three times?

Lance: No, you don't gotta fucking stab her three times! You gotta stab her once, but it's gotta be hard enough to break through her breastplate into her heart, and then once you do that, you press down on the plunger.

Vincent: What happens after that?

Lance: I'm kinda curious about that myself...

NUGGET: Most of the clocks in the movie are set to 4:20 an international signal for cannabis.

RATING: 🌿🌿🌿🌿🌿 *"Stoner Classic"*

REEFER MADNESS *or* TELL YOUR CHILDREN (1936)

SYNOPSIS: This movie known throughout modern pop culture was originally released under the title *Tell Your Children.* It is a classic view into the 1930s American negative cannabis propaganda agenda. Today the film is mostly used as entertainment for stoners (how ironic is that?!) because its claims are outlandish and unfounded. Mae (Thelma White) and Jack (Carleton Young) are part of an underground marijuana distribution ring. They succeed in getting the local high school students high and hooked—with over-the-top effects.

FAVORITE QUOTE:

Bureau Official: Here is an example: A fifteen-year-old lad apprehended in the act of staging a holdup—fifteen years old and a marijuana addict. Here is a most tragic case.

Dr. Carroll: Yes. I remember. Just a young boy... under the influence of drugs... who killed his entire family with an axe.

NUGGET: In 2004 a special edition DVD of *Reefer Madness* was released as a colorized parody. In this revised version, all the characters exhale bright pastel pot smoke. Michael J. Nelson, of *Mystery Science Theater 3000,* recorded a commentary track to lighten the mood of this propaganda.

RATING: 🌿 Booooo.

REVENGE OF THE NERDS (1984)

SYNOPSIS: Lewis (Robert Carradine) and Gilbert

(Anthony Edwards) are dorky high school graduates on their way to the first year at Adams College. Many obstacles stand in their way, including a huge jock named Ogre. But luckily they find I tight-knit group of nerds to stand behind them. A classic feel-good film from the '80s.

FAVORITE QUOTE:

Judy: Maybe we should eat?

Harold Wormser: Maybe we should watch TV?

Booger: Hey guys... [*he opens his jack to reveal a bunch of joints*] wonder joints.

NUGGET:
Actors Robert Carradine and Anthony Edwards wanted to test out their nerd costumes before shooting began. They suited up and went to a college rush where, after one look, the fraternity leader told them, "No way!" And they knew their wardrobes were perfect.

RATING: 🍁🍁🍁🍁

ROAD TRIP (2000)

SYNOPSIS: When Josh Parker (Breckin Meyer) accidentally slips up and cheats on his long-time long-distance girlfriend while at college, it might not have been that big of a deal. That would be if he hadn't videotaped it and accidentally sent the tape to his girlfriend! Now he and four friends hit the road to get to the tape before she does. Great ready for a great stoner night adventure.

FAVORITE QUOTE:

Rubin: This is sort of an unusual question, but do you have any marijuana I might be able to buy from you? Our car exploded last night and I'm practically all out of my own.

Motel Clerk: Am I a drug dealer? No, I am not. Thank you for asking, though.

Rubin: No? OK. That's OK. Thanks.

Motel Clerk: Is there anything else I can help you with? Perhaps you'd like an 11-year-old prostitute sent to your room.

NUGGET: Andy Dick makes a cameo as the clerk at the motel. When the camera first reveals him he is reading a copy of *Celebrity Skin* magazine with Drew Barrymore on the cover. This is rumored to be an inside joke played by writer/director Todd Phillips on Tom Green, who also stars in the movie, who was engaged to Drew at the time.

RATING: 🌿🌿🌿🌿

ROLLING KANSAS (2002)

SYNOPSIS: The three Murphy brothers, Dave, Dink and Dick, have just run into a treasure map of sorts. Just when hard times are looming in Texas they are presented a map left to them from their stoned parents leading to a magical weed field in Kansas. The three brothers hit the road to get their hands on the green.

FAVORITE QUOTE: Tomorrow we will be getting

in a car and harvesting hundreds of pounds of marijuana.

NUGGET: While approaching a highway patrol police checkpoint, the boys ditch their weed in a cornfield. When they come back to grab it, the field has been mowed with only hay bails remaining. Only problem… corn isn't used to make hay. Oops.

RATING: 🌿🌿🌿

SCARY MOVIE 2 (2001)

SYNOPSIS: Here's a silly, silly stoner flick from the Wayans brothers that's fun to watch with baked friends. Professor Oldman (Tim Curry) decides to perform some research in Hell House, a house where an exorcism was performed a year earlier. He disguises it as a sleep disorder study and recruits college students to participate. The students must face the horrors of the house including a carnivorous marijuana bud that smokes humans. Luckily it can be easily distracted with some munchies. This gets our vote as one of the best weed scenes ever.

FAVORITE QUOTE:

Shorty Meeks (as he's being rolled up like a joint from a giant weed bud): I'll never smoke you again!

NUGGET: The film originally had an NC-17 rating due to the scene where Tori Spelling's character performed fellatio on the Invisible Man. The scene was pulled from the U.S. release of the movie and it received an R rating. But the scene can be found in the British version.

RATING: 🌿🌿

SEX POT (2009)

SYNOPSIS: Sex Pot is almost so bad it's good. It is the story of two potheads who find a stash of marijuana and realize its magical powers. It's an aphrodisiac for women, and soon they are swimming in ganja and girls. If you're looking for a chill, relaxed night, this comedy filled with buds and boobs might be just the trick.

FAVORITE QUOTE:

Mert: Take these pills.

Spanky: What are they?

Mert: They're vitamins for your dick. Take three.

Spanky: I need something to wash 'em down.

Mert: Drink the fuckin' bongwater!

NUGGET: Director Eric Forsberg makes a cameo in his film as the man who says, "Back off man!" at the liquor store and turns the boys down in their attempt to get booze.

RATING:

SMILEY FACE (2007)

SYNOPSIS: Anna Faris stars as stoner aspiring actress, Jane, who is trying to get stuff done, but her stoner ways always leave her a little short of the finish line. After a wake-and-bake session, she wanders into the kitchen to stumble upon her roommates cupcakes—his pot cupcakes. Jane eats them all before she realizes they contain pot. Her day just got a lot more difficult. Can she replenish her roommate's pot cupcakes, pay bills, get to an audition, and stay out of trouble?

FAVORITE QUOTE: They say a true pothead stops getting the munchies after a certain point. I mean, the true pothead wouldn't even say the word munchies. I mean, the true pothead wouldn't even say the word *munchies*. I don't know what the true pothead would say: "munchos" or "hungries" or something? At any rate, I still love to eat when I'm high. So fuck you if you're too cool to get hungry when you're stoned.

NUGGET: In Matt Zoller Seitz's review of *Smiley Face* for the *New York Times*, he commended Faris' "freakishly committed performance as Jane F. [that] suggests Amy Adams's princess from *Enchanted* dropped into a Cheech and Chong movie."

RATING: 🌿🌿🌿

THE STONED AGE (1994)

SYNOPSIS: Joe (Michael Kopelow) and Hubbs (Bradford Tatum) like blasting their rock 'n roll, driving around in the Blue Torpedo, and "chicks." Tonight they're trying to break the mold and find some fine girls they can party with.

FAVORITE QUOTE:
Hubbs: Hey Tack, we'll trade you this half-joint of burlsense bud for the chicks.
Tack: Fucking skank weed, man.

Hubbs: Ok. How about we give you this entire bottle of the Schnappster, you tell us where the chicks are?

Tack: That shit makes me hork.

NUGGET: Eric Bloom and Donald "Buck Dharma" Roeser, members of the band Blue Oyster Cult, can be seen selling bootleg t-shirts after the final credits of the movie.

RATING: 🌿🌿

SUPER HIGH ME (2007)

SYNOPSIS: Stand-up comedian Doug Benson takes the ultimate test for humanity and puts his body through a month-long journey of marijuana use to see the scientific effects of the drug on his internal system and mind. He is a funny man, but he also takes a serious look at the state of medicinal marijuana use in the United States. The film is divided into two sections (sort of). The first part documents Doug's life for a month with no pot. As a regular smoker, this was probably the most difficult part for him, but he had to clear all THC out of his system. The second part, aka the fun part, is his month of straight smoking. During both sections Doug takes a variety of tests and examinations and in the end they compare sober Doug to stoned Doug.

FAVORITE QUOTE: I know that I like it, I know that lots of people like it, so let's see what happens if you overdo it!

NUGGET: Benson endured a series of medical tests and a period of abstinence from any booze or weed before his 30-day use of the drug. Interestingly, his sperm count went up with his use of marijuana, contrary to the popular belief that cannabis lowers one's sperm count.

RATING: ⬤⬤⬤⬤⬤ *"Stoner Classic"*

Super Troopers (2001)

Synopsis: Mac, Thorny, Rabbit, Farva, and Foster are state troopers stationed in a remote area of Vermont close to the Canadian border. They say "an idle mind is the devil's playground," and without much to do up there these troopers like to have their fun and get into their share of trouble messing with the locals. When news of possible budget cuts that would put them out of business surface they must figure out a way to outdo the local police force. Could good old marijuana come to the rescue?

Favorite quote: You must have eaten, like, a hundred bucks worth of pot, and, like, 30 bucks worth of shrooms, man!

Nugget: In the weed-smoking scene where the troopers are watching the Johnny Chimpo cartoon, the makeup artist made the actors' eyes red and bloodshot by blowing menthol into them before filming. It was disappointing to find out they weren't really baked.

RATING: ⬤⬤⬤⬤

TENACIOUS D IN THE PICK OF DESTINY (2006)

SYNOPSIS: In *The Pick of Destiny* Jack Black and Kyle Gass meet in Venice Beach, California, and sparks fly. They immediately form a musical bond of brotherhood and set out to be the greatest band in the world. The band's name? Tenacious D, which is what the two birthmarks on their behinds spell out when joined. Their first goal is to kill at the open mic. The only thing they need is a magical pick that is housed at a rock history museum.

FAVORITE QUOTE:

Kyle: Go score me a dime-bag.

JB: A what?

KG: Ten dollars worth of weed. Now listen: Go down to Wake & Bake Pizza, ask for Jojo. Tell him you want the Bob Marley Extra Crispy. He'll know what you're talkin' about.

NUGGET: In addition to playing Satan in this film, Dave Grohl (of Foo Fighters fame) also played Lucifer in Tenacious D's music video for their song "Tribute" and played drums on the record.

RATING: 🌿 🌿 🌿

WAKING LIFE (2001)

SYNOPSIS: Take a strange journey through a dream-like state, as the nameless protagonist (played by Wiley Wiggins) is drawn into many philosophical conversations and debates with characters he meets along the way. As he tries to wake himself up from what he's convinced is a dream, he wanders and questions the difference between dreaming and waking life and other existential topics. This movie doesn't have any marijuana in it, but anyone who likes to think while baked will certainly enjoy it.

FAVORITE QUOTE: They say that dreams are only real as long as they last. Couldn't you say the same thing about life?

NUGGET: This movie used an interesting technique called rotoscoping, shooting every scene on digital video with the actors and then having a group of animators basically "paint" overtop the video on computers. The result is a very cool stylized film. Since its release many people have borrowed this technique.

RATING: 🌿 🌿 🌿 🌿

WALK HARD: THE DEWEY COX STORY (2007)

SYNOPSIS: Dewey Cox, played by John C. Reilly, is a rock 'n roll star who transcends the ages. Tim Meadows plays Sam, a bandmate of Cox, who always has a sweet stash around. In his career he sleeps with 411 woman, is married to three of them, become friends with The Beatles and Elvis, and gets hooked and kicks just about every drug you can imagine. Luckily he has the love of a good woman, Darlene (Jenna Fischer). Other great cameos include Jack White playing Elvis and Jack Black as Paul McCartney as well as so many more.

FAVORITE QUOTE:

Sam (after Dewey walks in of them smoking a joint): No, Dewey, you don't want this. Get outta here!

Dewey Cox: You know what, I don't want no hangover. I can't get no hangover.

Sam: It doesn't give you a hangover!

Dewey Cox: Wha—I get addicted to it or something?

Sam: It's not habit-forming!

Dewey Cox: Oh, okay... well, I don't know... I don't want to overdose on it.

Sam: You can't OD on it!

Dewey Cox: It's not gonna make me wanna have sex, is it?

Sam: It makes sex even better!

Dewey Cox: Sounds kind of expensive.

Sam: It's the cheapest drug there is.

Dewey Cox (with no excuses left): Hmm.

Sam: You don't want it!

Dewey Cox: I think I kinda want it.

Sam: Okay, but just this once. Come on in.

NUGGET: When young Dewey is riding the tractor, the year is supposed to be 1946. But it's a 1950s Ford.

RATING: 🌿 🌿 🌿 🌿

YOUR HIGHNESS (2011)

SYNOPSIS: This recent classic from director David Gordon Green follows brothers Thadeous and Fabious (played by Danny McBride and James Franco) on a quest to rescue Fabious' soon-to-be bride. Fabious is a hero in the kingdom and has accomplished many successful quests while Thadeous has been hiding in his shadow not doing much of anything (well, except smoking weed). Will they be able to slay dragons and other fantastical obstacles to save their land?

FAVORITE QUOTE:

Fabious [after the two brothers smoke weed]: Thadeous, are you seeing what I'm seeing?

Thadeous: You making a fool of yourself. Handle your shit, Fabious, please.

NUGGET: James Franco took nine months of sword

training before filming this movie.

RATING: 🌿🌿🌿🌿🌿 *"Stoner Classic"*

STONERVISION

When you're sitting in front of the television, mellowing out with your buzz, every comedy good and bad (especially bad) is a little funnier. Plus, all the other shows seem a bit, you know, freakier. Tune in to Stonervision and you're sure to see weird and wacky shows like these.

ARRESTED DEVELOPMENT
(Fox, 2003–2006)

SYNOPSIS: This hilarious indie-style sitcom follows the Bluth family on their escapades. Michael Bluth (Jason Bateman) is a widowed father of a 13-year-old son (played by Michael Cera) constantly attempting to pick up the slack and save his family from their own devices. An alcoholic mother, white-collar criminal father, self-destructive/self-determined brother, and narcissistic sister keep his hands full.

FAVORITE QUOTE:

Michael Bluth: Look, you can't risk leaving the attic anymore.

George Sr.: When have you seen me outside?

Michael Bluth: Yesterday at the Ford Dealer.

George Sr.: Yeah, well, have you seen those new Mustangs? I'm telling you—you could hump the hood.

NUGGET: Ron Howard narrates this show.

RATING: ♦ ♦ ♦ ♦ ♦ *"Stoner Classic"*

Aqua Teen Hunger Force

(Adult Swim, since 2001)

Synopsis: This animated series starring Master Shake, Frylock, and Meatwad follows the absurd adventures of fast food characters. The only human character on the show, neighbor Carl Brutananadilewski, is often involved in some way, but it's the stoner alien Mooninites who like the green stuff.

Favorite quote:

Err: Ya all have any eggs?

Shake: I don't know guys. Lemme check.

Err: 'Cause I'm totally gonna mess someone's house up!

Ignignokt: Yes, eggs or pot... either one.

Meatwad: Hey, ah, Frylock, do we have any pot?

Frylock: No, we don't! Marijuana is illegal.

Err: What about nitrous, man?

Ignignokt: Shut up, Err.

NUGGET: Aqua Teen Hunger Force is the longest-running original series on Adult Swim.

RATING: 🍁🍁🍁🍁

BEAVIS & BUTTHEAD
(MTV, since 1993)

SYNOPSIS: Two socially inept, teenage, music-video-watching dumb-asses from Highland, Texas, try to impress chicks and do things that are "cool" in this animated series created by Mike Judge. Whether they actually smoked marijuana is never shown, but their behavior certainly indicates it at times.

FAVORITE QUOTE:

Teacher David Van Driessen: Today we're going to explore the world of haiku.

Beavis: We're going to explore the world of getting high? Cool!

Van Driessen: No, Beavis, not *high cool.* Haiku—the haunting Japanese form of three-line poetry.

NUGGET: Mike Judge voices Beavis, Butt-head, neighbor Tom Anderson, teacher David Van Driessen, coach Bradley Buzzcut, and principal McVicker. Most of the video commentary is improvised.

RATING: 🌿🌿🌿🌿🌿 *"Stoner Classic"*

THE BOONDOCKS

(Adult Swim, 2005–2010)

SYNOPSIS: In this cartoon culture clash, Brothers Huey and Riley were born in the big city but moved away to Granddad's house in a mostly white suburban middle-class neighborhood. Ten-year-old Huey, the main character and voice of reason, is motivated by social justice while his 8-year-old younger brother, Riley, is a bit of a troublemaker and very enthusiastic about hip-hop culture. The influence of anime in this cartoon series makes for some great stoner imagery.

FAVORITE QUOTE:

Delivery man [pulls out a joint]: Now this shit right here, nigga, this all the medicine I need.

Granddad: What is that? Is that reefer?

Delivery man: Nah, nigga it's weed!

Granddad: Reefer's the same thing as weed.

Delivery man: What?

Granddad: Keep it down, I have kids in the house.

Delivery man: What, I can't say weed?

NUGGET: The series was created and based on Aaron McGruder's comic strip of the same name that first debuted in newspapers in April 1999.

RATING: 🌿🌿🌿

BORED TO DEATH (HBO, 2009–2011)

SYNOPSIS: Created by Jonathan Ames, this quirky series follows a lead character of the same name (played by Jason Schwartzman), a struggling novelist/private investigator with an hilarious cast of stoner buddies, Ray and George, who establish a friendship for the first time on the show by sharing their love of marijuana. Together, they help each other solve detective cases, deal with women problems, and end up in some comical situations, often while high as a kite.

FAVORITE QUOTE:

I am so sorry Steven. Because of the marijuana my whole life is like the film Memento… and I'm nervous.

NUGGET:
Jonathan Ames is also an author of many novels, essays, and comics.

RATING: 🍁🍁🍁🍁🍁 *"Stoner Classic"*

CANNABIS PLANET (KJLA-TV, since 2009)

SYNOPSIS: This show covers the "merits of the cannabis plant (medicinally, industrially, agriculturally), and the benefits this plant brings to planet earth, mankind and the United States," according to the producers. It keeps its audience up to date on the latest marijuana news, horticulture, and cooking techniques.

FAVORITE QUOTE:

Chef Mike: You know—on those hot days—I really love a good fruit salad, and today I'm going to show you a simple way to make it medicated.

NUGGET: Though originally only aired in Los Angeles, it can now also be seen in Denver, Sacramento, San Diego, and the San Francisco Bay Area. The show hopes to air the program in every state that allows medical marijuana.

RATING: 🌿 🌿 🌿 🌿

THE COLBERT REPORT

(Comedy Central, since 2005)

SYNOPSIS: This spinoff/counterpart of *The Daily Show* features political humorist Stephen Colbert, whose news-anchorman persona is a "well-intentioned, poorly informed, high-status idiot." The show includes satirical news reports and pokes fun at recent headlines.

FAVORITE QUOTE:

Colbert: But look who's toking now!.. Our elderly are getting baked. No wonder they're eating dinner at 4 o'clock in the afternoon.

NUGGET: Colbert was one of the earliest correspondents for *The Daily Show*. He also worked on the show *Strangers with Candy* for Comedy Central in 1999.

RATING: 🍁🍁🍁🍁

COPS (Fox, since 1989)

SYNOPSIS: This reality show follows police officers in different cities as they pursue "bad boys" and make busts. Most of these cops frown on the use of marijuana, but it would appear that weed busts are the least of their worries in most of these cities.

FAVORITE QUOTE:

Officer: Can you run faster than 1,200 feet per second? In case you didn't know, that is the average speed of a 9mm bullet fired from my gun.

NUGGET: With the announcement that *America's Most Wanted* was being cancelled, COPS became Fox's longest-running program.

RATING: 🌿🌿

CHAPPELLE'S SHOW

(Comedy Central, 2003–2006)

SYNOPSIS: This sketch comedy series starring comedian Dave Chappelle features insanely funny clips with topics including race, drugs, and sexuality. The comedy sketches are introduced by Chappelle in front of a live audience and the show often ends with a musical performance.

FAVORITE QUOTE:

Tyrone Biggums [speaking to elementary school class]: Drugs is all around you, kids. Look at that magic marker cap. What the hell you think that is, some kind of crayon? Take it off and sniff it and get high.

NUGGET: Among the shows many notable guest stars, Wayne Brady was the only guest to appear on the stage.

RATING: 🍁🍁🍁🍁🍁 *"Stoner Classic"*

DA ALI G SHOW

(Channel 4 UK and HBO, 2000–2004)

SYNOPSIS: Whether playing Borat, Bruno, or Ali G, series creator and actor Sacha Baron Cohen brings on hilarious situations and funny interviews to unsuspecting people.

FAVORITE QUOTE:

Ali G.: What is the different types of hash out there? We all know that it's called the bionic, the bomb, the puff, the blow, the black, the herb, the sensie, the cronic, the sweet Mary Jane, the shit, Ganja, split, reefa, the bad, the buddha, the home grown, the ill, the maui-maui, the method, pot, lethal turbo, tie, shake, skunk, stress, whacky, weed, glaze, the boot, dimebag, Scooby Doo, bob, bogey, back yard boogie. But what is the other terms for it?

NUGGET: The 2006 spinoff mockumentary film *Borat: Cultural Learnings of America for Make Benefit Glori-*

ous Nation of Kazakhstan, received awards and both critical and commercial success.

RATING: 🌿🌿🌿🌿

THE DAILY SHOW WITH JON STEWART (Comedy Central, 1996–present)

SYNOPSIS: Fake news at its finest and Jon Stewart delivers it like no one can. He and his correspondents cover everything from politics to pop culture to current events and everything in between, including segments about marijuana. Conservative political pundit, Bill O'Reilly, refers to *The Daily Show* viewers as "stoned slackers."

FAVORITE QUOTE:

Jon Stewart: Children should not smoke pot, no matter how many times their Grandmother with glaucoma tells them its "cool"… or "in"… or "far-out"… or "the only way she can see."

NUGGET: Craig Kilborn was the original host of *The Daily Show* from 1996 to 1998.

RATING: 🌿🌿🌿🌿

DRAGNET (NBC, 1951–1970)

SYNOPSIS: This classic crime drama series solves all types cases including busting pesky reefer smokers. In one 1967 episode, a character being investigated by LAPD's Joe Friday and Bill Gannon predicts that "marijuana's going to be just like liquor—packaged and taxed and sold right off the shelf."

FAVORITE QUOTE:

Clyde Barton: I don't know much about it, Sergeant, but I got a hunch. I don't think I've made a mistake.
Sgt. Joe Friday: Yeah.
Clyde Barton: What do you think?

Sgt. Joe Friday: No sir, there's no mistake—marijuana.

NUGGET: Dragnet started as a radio program in 1949 and ran until 1957.

RATING: 🌿🌿

ENTOURAGE (HBO, 2004–2011)

SYNOPSIS: A group of friends follow movie actor Vincent Chase to Los Angeles and try to live the Hollywood lifestyle. This means fancy cars, beautiful women, and the finest marijuana—rolled, packed, delivered, and smoked by Turtle.

FAVORITE QUOTE:
Ari Gold: Smoke more weed, Turtle. Seriously, smoke more weed.

NUGGET: The show is loosely based on executive

producer Mark Wahlberg's life.

RATING: 🌿🌿🌿🌿

FAMILY GUY (Fox, since 1998)

SYNOPSIS: This animated comedy series about a dysfunctional family from Quahog, Rhode Island, is centered around parents Peter and Lois; their kids Meg, Chris, and Stewie; and of course the talking dog, Brian. In their "420" episode, Brian campaigns to legalize marijuana in Quahog and succeeds, allowing everyone to get high around town and decreasing the crime rate.

FAVORITE QUOTE: *The chorus lyrics from a song in episode 122, set to the tune of "Me Ole Bam-boo" from* Chitty Chitty Bang Bang:
A bag of weed, a bag of weed
Oh, everything is better with a bag of weed

It's the only hope that you'll ever need
Because everything is better with a bag of weed.

NUGGET: The show was cancelled after three seasons in 2001 but picked up again in 2004 after tremendous DVD sales and high ratings for syndicated reruns.

RANKING: 🌿🌿🌿🌿🌿 *"Stoner Classic"*

HOW TO MAKE IT IN AMERICA (HBO, since 2010)

SYNOPSIS: Characters Ben Epstein and his friend Cam Calderon try to make it in the competitive fashion scene of New York City in this comedy-drama. With their youth, energy, and entrepreneurial thinking, they use their street smarts and connections to give them a leg up. Cam's cousin Rene also has ambitious plans with his energy drink company called Rasta-Monsta. Friend Domingo Brown makes cash on the side selling weed to rich housewives.

FAVORITE QUOTE:

Domingo: Shake and bake, baby! What's up?

Cam: Looks like you are the man for the Real Housewives of the Upper East Side.

Domingo: That's right, nigga', the Stoner Edition!

NUGGET:

Actor Scott "Kid Cudi" Mescudi is a rapper whose first album, *Man on the Moon: The End of Day,* went gold.

RATING: 🍁🍁🌙

IT'S ALWAYS SUNNY IN PHILADELPHIA (FX, since 2005)

SYNOPSIS: The gang at Paddy's Pub is always up to something zany, manipulative, competitive, or just plain disgusting. The show's twisted humor gets any stoner laughing. Sunny's creators, Rob McElhenney, Glenn Howerton, and Charlie Day, are also the stars of the sitcom, with help from great performances by Danny DeVito and Kaitlin Olson.

FAVORITE QUOTE:

Frank: Roxy... God bless you. You were a good whore. You serviced me like no other whore ever did. Not only my crank but my heart.

NUGGET: The first pilot for the show was shot for under $200 and was called *It's Always Sunny On TV.*

RATING: 🌿🌿🌿🌿🌿

KENNY VS. SPENNY

(Comedy Central, 2005–2010)

SYNOPSIS: Two Canadian personalities face off in many competitions where the loser gets assigned a "humiliation" or embarrassing act. In one episode of this comedy series, the guys try to decide who can smoke more weed. They fail in their attempt to establish a legitimate competition, but it's all about trying!

FAVORITE QUOTE:

Spenny: It's amazing. I don't find him annoying when I'm high. It's weird.

NUGGET: Kenneth Joel "Kenny" Hotz started his career as a writer for the movie *Teenage Mutant Ninja Turtles,* in 1987.

RATING: 🌿🌿🌿

LOONEY TUNES

(Warner Bros., since the 1930s)

SYNOPSIS: This animated cartoon mainstay stars some of our favorite and most iconic cartoon characters the likes of Bugs Bunny, Daffy Duck, Porky Pig, and Sylvester.

The funny, colorful, wacky story-lines have provided stoners with endless hours of entertainment for decades.

HILARIOUS QUOTATION:

Daffy Duck: You'd never catch that rabbit doing something this heroic.

Bugs Bunny [appearing in the seat next to Daffy]: Eh, what's up, duck?

Daffy Duck: You're dethpicable.

NUGGET: The Cartoon Network started *The Looney Tunes Show* in 2011 and has also started showing reruns from the classics library.

RATING: 🌿🌿🌿🌿

MAD MEN (AMC, since 2007)

SYNOPSIS: This drama follows protagonist Donald Draper who works at an elite Madison Avenue New York advertising agency in the 1960s. These cigarette-wielding, whiskey-drinking ad men portray a moment in American history. Recreational marijuana use may not have been as common as it is today, but *Madmen* does pay homage to those in the early 60s on the hip cutting edge.

FAVORITE QUOTE:
Jeff: You're going to have to tell me your name, sweetheart.
Peggy: I'm Peggy Olson and I want to smoke some marijuana.

NUGGET: The show's creator, Matthew Weiner, also wrote and produced episodes for HBO's *The Sopranos*.

RATING: 🌿 🌿 🌿 🌿

THE MAN SHOW
(COMEDY CENTRAL, 1999–2003)

SYNOPSIS: Comedians Jimmy Kimmel and Adam Carolla originally co-hosted this show from the male per-

spective. The show has comedy sketches, girls on trampolines, and plenty of beer-guzzling. In one episode, the hosts visit Snoop Dogg's house to shoot a sketch but just end up getting really high.

FAVORITE QUOTE:
Jimmy Kimmel to Corolla and Snoop Dogg: This is the biggest pot tree I ever saw. You'd have to roll this thing in a bench press.

NUGGET: Jimmy and Adam left the show in 2003 and the job was passed down to Joe Rogen and Doug Stanhope.

RATING: 🌿🌿🌿

MR. SHOW WITH BOB AND DAVID (HBO, 1995–1998)

SYNOPSIS: Comedians Bob Odenkirk and David Cross host this hilarious sketch comedy series in which skits and pre-taped segments flow together in a very strange and often twisted way.

FAVORITE QUOTE:

Pharmacy "customer" old lady: I just need marijuana for my glaucoma.

Pharmacy "customer" (Brian Posehn): Yeah, I know what you mean... my doctor says I need marijuana to get high.

NUGGET:
Cross and Odenkirk used their clout at HBO to help produce the musical comedy series *Tenacious D,* which started the comedy duo and the career of Jack Black.

RATING: ⬤ ⬤ ⬤ ⬤

THE MUPPET SHOW
(Disney 1976–1981)

SYNOPSIS:
Featuring a new guest star each week, this variety show hosted by Kermit the Frog and his group of

plushy friends is sure to entertain both kids and adults. Nicely done, Jim Henson.

FAVORITE QUOTE:

Kermit: I just want to know more about this wedding sketch. I mean, I've got to learn my lines, Piggy.

Miss Piggy: Well… you only have one line.

Kermit: I do?

Miss Piggy: Exactly.

NUGGET: Jason Segal directed the most recent update, *The Muppets* movie released in 2011.

RATING:

PARTY DOWN (Starz, 2009–2010)

SYNOPSIS: This comedy follows a group of half-motivated semi-slackers from catering gig to catering gig in half-hour length episodes. Although only two seasons

long, the producers crammed in a lot of laughs and many members of the cast have continued to have successful careers in Hollywood.

FAVORITE QUOTE:

Hippie, pointing to a basket of weed brownies: Uh, looks like he ate three. That's a tenth of an ounce of high-grade marijuana.

Roman: Ohh, Ohh! So either I'm gonna die, any instant, or I've been dead a while...

Paramedic: You can't OD on marijuana.

Hippie: You're gonna be great, son.

NUGGETS: Paul Rudd, known from his acting in hilarious stoner movies such as *Knocked Up* and *The 40-Year-Old Virgin*, was an executive producer and writer on *Party Down*.

RATING: 🍁🍁🍁🍁

POT TV (Web-based, since 1999)

SYNOPSIS: This Web-based video channel features programs such as "The Big Toke" (comedy), "The Grow Show" (horticulture), "Cannabis Common Sense," "Shake 'n Bake" (cooking), "Healing Herb Hour" (medicinal), and "Yours in Defense" (legal). There's a lot of pot information to find on this station.

FAVORITE QUOTE:

Marijuana Man: Thrilled that you could be here. It's a cloudy, rainy day in "fun"couver, but we are high and dry inside.

NUGGET: Channel owner Marc Emery funded the station with his marijuana seed business until his arrest in 2005. User-created content and modern video tools have helped reduce the station's budget substantially, allowing it to exist as a Web-based channel.

RATING: 🌿🌿🌿

REN & STIMPY

(Nickelodeon, 1991–1995)

SYNOPSIS: Ren Höek, a scrawny chihuahua, and Stimpson J. Cat, a dumb-ass cat, star in this wild animated series doing all kinds of grotesque, funny, and weird activities. You might not even need to smoke anything to feel weirdly high after watching this one.

FAVORITE QUOTE:

Stimpy: Hey, Ren, this horse reminds me of your Uncle Eddie.

Ren: Why is that?

Stimpy: Because he's big and stinky.

Ren: Hey, you shouldn't say mean things like that! Didn't you ever consider that this horse might have feelings?

NUGGET: Many scenes, closeups, and even episodes were removed or censored during the show's run.

RATING: 🌿🌿🌿🌿

REAL TIME WITH BILL MAHER

(HBO, since 2003)

SYNOPSIS: A current events and political talk show hosted by comedian Bill Maher, a known marijuana advocate and opinionated funnyman. New Rule: Get high before watching this show.

FAVORITE QUOTE:

Bill Maher: New Rule: You can't make me dress like Peewee Herman. According to the *New York Times*, this is the hottest look in men's fashion. From the waist up, it says Wall Street; from the waist down, it says, "Hurricane Katrina." Let me tell you something. This "exposed sock" look is never going to fly in Hollywood, because that's where we keep our weed.

NUGGET: In support of the upcoming vote for California's Proposition 19, the Regulate, Control &

Tax Cannabis Act, actor/comedian Zach Galifianakis supposedly lit up a joint during a taping.

RATING: 🌿🌿🌿🌿

SCOOBY-DOO (CBS, NBC, 1969–1986)

SYNOPSIS: Shaggy is the quintessential stoner. He and Scooby prioritize munchies over monsters as they set off on a series of mystery adventures with the rest of the gang in this classic cartoon.

FAVORITE QUOTE:

Villain: I would have gotten away with it, too, if it wasn't for you meddling kids.

NUGGET: Shaggy's voice was performed by Casey Kasem.

RATING: 🌿🌿🌿🌿

THE SIMPSONS (FOX, since 1987)

SYNOPSIS: This animated family from Springfield brings on the laughs. When Homer gets prescribed medical marijuana in season 13, things get trippy as Homer and Smithers finally find Mr. Burns' jokes funny. The band Phish makes an appearance at a rally to support the local vote on the use of medical marijuana (too bad the vote already happened a day earlier). Homer also finds himself smoking a joint with bus driver and stoner Otto Mann.

FAVORITE QUOTE:

Homer: Whether you suffer from glaucoma or you just rented *The Matrix*, medical marijuana makes everything fabulous, medically.

NUGGET:
The Simpsons is recognized by the Guinness World Records as the world's longest-running sitcom.

RATING: 🍁🍁🍁🍁🍁 *"Stoner Classic"*

SKINS (Company Pictures–UK, since 2007)

SYNOPSIS: This UK TV series, now up to its third generation of cast members, follows a group of teenagers from Bristol, England, who are up to all types of controversial activities and tend to puff on a spliff every now and then.

FAVORITE QUOTE:

Sid [under Anka's covers]: Every time. Every fucking time. "Buy three ounces of weed, Sidney." "Oh yes, sir." "Shove a bag of pills up your ass, Sidney." "Oh right away." "Come help me save some random chick." "Oh could I?" What have we learned, Sidney? Your friends are shitheads.

NUGGET: MTV attempted to launch a U.S. version of the show, but it was cancelled after ten episodes because of its racy content and censorship issues.

RATING: 🌿🌿🌿�︎

SOUTH PARK (Comedy Central, since 1997)

SYNOPSIS: A lot has happened in South Park over the years, including a good amount of pot smoking. In Season 14, Colorado legalizes medical marijuana, causing Randy Marsh to take some ballsy actions to get a physician's reference. Recurring character Towelie is a pot smoking towel. These animated kids are always creating big laughs.

FAVORITE QUOTE:

Nurse: Why are there hamburgers in your underwear?

Cartman: Are you serious? You're saying I have Aspergers?

NUGGET: Creators Trey Parker and Matt Stone won nine Tony Awards for their musical *The Book of Mormon*.

RATING: 🌿🌿🌿🌿🌿 *"Stoner Classic"*

TELETUBBIES (BBC, 1997–2001)

SYNOPSIS: And you thought this show was just for kids! The bright colors and complete lack of plot or reason will soon have any stoner gazing in a trance at the TV.

FAVORITE QUOTE:
Opening Narrator: Over the hills and far away, Teletubbies come to play.

NUGGETS: To make the characters appear smaller than they actually were, they use rabbits called Flemish Giants in the program, which can grow to over 20 pounds.

RATING: 🌿🌿

TENACIOUS D (HBO, 1997–2000)

SYNOPSIS: This comedy rock duo will rock your fucking socks off with their absurd lyrics, their insane melodies and harmonies, and their confidence about being the greatest band in the world.

FAVORITE QUOTE: Sometimes you have to leave your zone of safety, you have to manufacture inspirado. You gotta get out of the apartment. You've got to run with the wolves. You have to dive into the ocean bite with the sharks, or sometimes just treat yourself to an ice cream sundae with nuts.

NUGGET: The movie version, *The Pick of Destiny* was released in 2006 along with their album, which features appearances by Ronnie James Dio, Meat Loaf, and Dave Grohl.

RATING: ⊛ ⊛ ⊛ ⊛ ⊛ *"Stoner Classic"*

THAT '70S SHOW (Fox, 1998–2006)

SYNOPSIS: This sitcom follows a group of Wisconsin teenagers and their families as they deal with the issues of the 1970s: women's rights, sexual freedom, and teenage drug use. Although it's never really shown, everyone knows what's going on around that strangely smokey table as the camera pans from goofy face to goofy face. Let's face it, this show is for stoners by stoners.

FAVORITE QUOTE:

Eric: Gentlemen, we have finally done it. A pot leaf on the water tower.

Fez: This is the proudest moment of my life.

Steven Hyde: It doesn't look like a pot leaf. It looks like it's giving me the finger.

Michael Kelso: Well, it doesn't have to look perfect, Hyde. It's art.

NUGGET: At the conclusion of every episode's opening credits, the year in which the current show is taking place is displayed on the right corner of the Wisconsin license place.

RATING:

TRAILER PARK BOYS (Showcase-Canada, 2001–2008)

SYNOPSIS: A group of dope growing, heavy drinking, ex-convicts living in Sunnyvale Trailer Park are constantly coming up with get rich schemes and avoiding trailer park supervisors Jim Lahey and Randy. Julian, Ricky, and Bubbles are always smoking dope and getting in trouble in this mockumentary-style series.

FAVORITE QUOTE:

[As they find the mountain lion that's been eating their weed]
Julian: Holy shit, boys, don't move! So that's who's been eating our weed...
Ricky: You little fucker... OK, you guys stay here. I'm gonna throw the net on him, put him in a headlock, and choke him out.
Bubbles: Ricky, put the net down! You're not fuckin' choking him out!

Ricky: Why?

Bubbles: He's just a big kitty, boys! I can deal with this, I know kitties!

Ricky: What if he has radies?

Bubbles: Ricky, it's rabies, with a *B*, not "radies." And he doesn't have rabies. He's been eating weed for a fuckin' month! He's baked out of his goddamn mind, I can tell just the way he's standing there. He only did that to Trevor because he had that leopard-print jacket on. See, he's just a big, stoned, horny kitty with the munchies! Trevor was eating chips, too! *[pets the mountain lion]* Who's a good boy?

NUGGET: Director Mike Clattenburg made a short film titled *One Last Shot*, which followed criminals Ricky and Julian and became the basis for the TV show.

RATING: 🌿 🌿 🌿 🌿

YO GABBA GABBA!

(Nick Jr., since 2008)

SYNOPSIS: Stoners can't avoid staring at the pleasing visual sequences and strange actions of costumed characters Muno, Foofa, Brobee, Toodee, and Plex in this made-for-kids show. With the frequent appearance of guest celebrities and musicians doing silly things, you don't feel as bad about trying DJ Lance's new dance.

FAVORITE QUOTE:

Plex: Toodee, do you really have magic beans and can fly?

NUGGET: The show performed live as special guests at Coachella in 2010.

RATING: 🍁🍁🍁🍁

THE WHITEST KIDS U' KNOW (IFC, 2007–2011)

SYNOPSIS: This sketch comedy troupe gets high during the Civil War and also with dinosaurs. Awesome.

FAVORITE QUOTE:

Bob the plantation worker: The white man will try anything to keep you down. This is not illegal. This is holy, this is from God!

Samuel: When is God gonna tell white people to suck it!

NUGGET: The show was first aired on the Fuse network but was too racy and moved to IFC. But it still only aired at certain times of the day because of its language and content.

RATING: 🌿🌿🌿🌿

WEEDS (Showtime, since 2005)

SYNOPSIS: The title of this TV comedy series says it all. A single mother chooses to sell pot to support her family and in the process makes a series of horrible decisions. With the help of stoner friends and family, she becomes a feared drug dealer in small-town Agrestic, California. They soon find themselves leaving of Agrestic and onto bigger and wilder things.

FAVORITE QUOTE:

Nancy Botwin: You listen, you stay away from my customer base. You don't deal to kids.

Josh Wilson: They're too young to bleed, they're too young for weed, no grass on the field no grass will they yield.

Nancy Botwin: You're a poet.

Josh Wilson: You know it.

NUGGET: The theme song used for the first three

seasons is called "Little Boxes." Written and recorded by folk singer Malvina Reynolds, the song was written after a drive through Daly City, California. That recording is used during the opening credits throughout the first season. During seasons two and three, the song is performed by a new artist every week, including Elvis Costello, Billy Bob Thornton, and The Shins.

RATING: 🌿🌿🌿

WILFRED (FX, since 2011)

SYNOPSIS: This strange sitcom starts its first episode with a young man named Ryan (Elijah Wood), a suicidal, washed-up lawyer who befriends the neighbor's dog, Wilfred. The weird thing is that only Ryan sees Wilfred as a talking man/dog. They spend a lot of time together smoking bongs in the basement and getting in trouble with owners and friends.

FAVORITE QUOTE:

Jenna: Wilfred pooped on your lawn.

Wilfred: There is symbolism in that poop Ryan... and some grass... and half a slipper.

NUGGET: This sitcom was adapted for American TV from an Australian series of the same name.

RATING: 🌿🌿🌿🌿

LATE-NIGHT MOMENTS

Late night talk show hosts know full well that pot smokers have their bloodshot eyeballs glued to the television after hours. From glaucoma gags to munchies punch lines, they have lots of material to joke about. And there are plenty of guests who want to talk about the green stuff, too.

TONIGHT SHOW WITH JOHNNY CARSON

The King of Late Night wasn't afraid to get a few laughs with pot humor. One classic line came in 1977 after President Carter recommended that possession under an ounce should not be illegal. "The trouble is that nobody in our band knows what an ounce or less means," joked Carson. To which Doc Severinsen replied, "It means you're about out."

Louis Armstrong supposedly said on the show: "I've been smoking weed every day for 50 years and I ain't addicted."

And from an episode from August 1981:

Tarzan: Tarzan get that from witch doctor! It called... "Say this some plant."
Jane: Say this some plant?
[Tarzan plucks plant and sniffs it]

Jane: Say! This some bad weed! Tarzan smoke no vine before its time!

LIGHT NIGHT WITH CONAN O'BRIEN

Conan O'Brien often talks about weed during his opening monologues and with guests. He went a little far on *Late Night* in skits like Tokey the Anti-Drug Bong:

"Tokey's my name and hating drugs is my game. Kids, don't smoke marijuana it causes memory loss, impotence, delayed reaction time, and marijuana can lead to harder drugs. ..."

[Conan asks what the smoke is]

"That's my sweet, sweet marijuana smoke. I mean I'm a bong, it happens, it's natural... I might be giving the kids a mixed message... Man, it does smell good."

[Kids run on stage and start hugging him.]

"No! No! DO NOT SMOKE ME! DO NOT SMOKE ME!"

JIMMY KIMMEL LIVE

Mr. Kimmel is not shy about weed jokes, featuring appearances by weed "humoredians" from *The Marijuana-logues*. Also, in his *Do You Use Marijuana?* segment, Jimmy asks people on the street if they use marijuana and gives the audience a chance to guess before revealing the answer.

JAY LENO, THE TONIGHT SHOW

Like Carson, Jay Leno is constantly giving the band a hard time for smoking pot. Tommy Chong appeared on *The Tonight Show* after being released from being arrested for selling paraphernalia in 2004.

LATE SHOW WITH DAVID LETTERMAN

In 1994, David Letterman had an infamous interview with Madonna where she refused to leave and when she asked Dave if he's ever smoked Endo, he tried to play it off like he "doesn't know what she's talking about" then does a classic Johnny Carson impersonation.

HIGH-LIGHTS OF TV HISTORY

For most television shows, weed may not be a recurring character but will often make a cameo. Whether it be an anti-drug life lesson on a family drama, or a flashback to a character's younger days, most classic television shows have had one "very special" weed episode.

7th Heaven, "Who Knew?"

One of Matt Camden's classmates slips him a joint that his parents find at home. Annie also confesses to experimenting with pot. Everyone learns a lesson about something. Awww.

21 Jump Street, "Raising Marijuana"

Ioki and Penhall act as undercover drug smugglers and befriend teenage boys working for them.

The Andy Griffith Show, "Quiet Sam"

The only mention of narcotics ever on the show occurred in this episode. Barney becomes suspicious that the new farmer, Sam, is growing marijuana.

Barney Miller, "Hash"

Pot brownies accidentally get eaten at the police station.

Blossom, "The Joint"

When a joint is found in the house, a father has to confront his kids, Blossom and Joey. It turns out that Blossom found the joint on a bus… where Joey left it.

Curb Your Enthusiasm, "Carpool Lane"

A helpful hooker assists an overwhelmed Larry score some medical marijuana for his dad's glaucoma.

The Cosby Show, "Theo and the Joint"

Theo confronts a friend who had hidden a joint in his textbook after Cliff and Claire discover it. Even though his parents believed Theo when he said the joint was not his, he still insisted on proving his innocence.

The Dukes of Hazzard, "Mason Dixon's Girls"

When Bo and Luke are mistakenly caught with a crate of marijuana, detective Mason Dixon and his attractive female associates help bring down the real culprits.

The Facts of Life, "Dope"

The girls are faced with a tough decision—smoke marijuana or be ostracized by the popular girls in "the group."

Fraiser, "High Holidays"

Fraiser's dad accidentally eats a special brownie.

Freaks & Geeks, "Chokin' and Tokin'"

Lindsay is giving Nick a hard time for smoking too much pot, but her curiosity prevails when she tries it for the first time. Too bad she forgot about a babysitting assignment that evening.

Glee, "Wheels"

To make money to take Artie and his chair to sectionals, the kids decide to have a bake sale. Sales don't go well until Puck's "special cupcakes" go on sale.

Home Improvement, "What a Drag"

Jill and Tim find a baggie of weed in their backyard.

Hooked: Illegal Drugs and How they Got that Way, "Marijuana and Methamphetamine"

This TV documentary follows the history of marijuana from the Indian hemp plant to medicinal attributes documented some 4,000 years ago.

How I Met Your Mother, "How I Met Everyone"

Ted and Marshall refer to weed as "sandwiches" in front of the kids.

The Kids in the Hall

A skit about a guy who trades in his jean jacket for hair made out of pot.

King of the Hill, "High Anxiety"

Hank smokes a joint by accident and is paranoid that he is a murderer.

Maude, "The Grass Story"

Maude and the local housewives arrange a protest over a grocery store employees' marijuana conviction. This political episode was in response to the Rockefeller Drug Laws.

Murphy Brown, "Waiting to Inhale"

Jim purchases some weed to help ease Murphy's pain from chemotherapy treatments.

Parks and Recreation, "Summer Catalog"

Former Pawnee Park Department director (played by Michael Gross) is on probation for a pot bust and preaches the case to legalize it.

Penn & Teller: Bullshit!, "War on Drugs"

Penn and Teller dissemble drug prohibition, show clips from *Reefer Madness,* and discuss the theory of medical marijuana.

Rosanne, "A Stash From the Past"

Roseanne finds a stash of pot in her house and accuses Darlene's boyfriend David. Dan later reminds her that the weed was in fact her own. Rosanne and her sister Jackie end up spending the night in the bathroom getting high and reminiscing about their stoner days in the late '70s.

The Sarah Silverman Program, "High, It's Sarah"

Sarah smokes weed for the first time, encouraged by Brian.

Saved By The Bell, "No Hope with Dope"

The usually squeaky-clean kids of Bayside High faced pressure from fictional "movie star" Johnny Dakota in this classic episode. Johnny helped the gang film an anti-drug public service announcement, when he himself was a stoner and tried to pressure Zach to get high.

Zach: You smoke pot?

Johnny: Yeah, sure! Who doesn't?

Sex and the City, "The Post-It Always Sticks Twice"

Carrie is caught puffing a joint on the street by the police. She was attempting to smoke away the trauma of being dumped via Post-It note that morning.

Step by Step, "Just Say Maybe"

The teenagers are eager to attend Rockfestival '97, but mother Carole is not so thrilled. Al is tempted to take a hit, but in the end declines.

Strangers With Candy, "Trails of Tears"

Will Ferrell lights up the "peace pipe" around the fire as Jerri and others try to explore their cultural heritage.

Three's Company, "Days Of Beer and Weeds"

Chrissy (Suzanne Somers) doesn't realize her new plant is a pot plant.

Two and A Half Men, "Gumby with a Pokey"

Charlie gets his hands on some medical marijuana and somehow starts hallucinating.

The Wonder Years, "Christmas Party"

At the Arnold's annual Christmas party, Jack's friend Mr. Ermin smokes weed in the basement.

POTHEADS ON TV

DARNELL "CRABMAN" TURNER (Eddie Steeples), *My Name Is Earl*. The "Crabman" is a former assassin placed in the witness protection program and working at The Crab Shack. He is known for smoking weed and hiding cell phones in his afro that self destruct after use.

QUOTE: Remember that time we got stoned?... It was Biblical.

DOUG WILSON (Kevin Nealon), *Weeds*. This accountant/city councilman for Agrestic loves—really loves—to smoke the marijuana.

QUOTE:
Andy Botwin: How can you be so blindly pro-Bush?

Doug Wilson: I like his wife, Laura... I used to buy weed from her at SMU.

DR. JOHNNY FEVER (Howard Hesseman), *WKRP In Cincinnati*. An eccentric deejay for WKRP, the "doctor" is assumed to be a frequent marijuana user.

QUOTE: Statistics, right? I don't trust 'em. Statistically speaking, anybody who's led the kind of life that I have should look completely wasted.

SALVATORE "TURTLE" ASSANTE (Jerry Ferrara) *Entourage.* Driver, personal assistant, and friend who you can count on to get you high.

QUOTE:

Drama (at the racetrack): Come on, King Maker—He came home for me at 10-to-1 at Belmont. That's how I bought the Lincoln. Any of this ringing a bell?

Vince: Not really.

Eric: No.

Turtle: I thought you bought your Lincoln from selling weed at the high school.

Eric: That rings a bell.

RICKY (Robb Wells) *Trailer Park Boys.* Dim-witted, pot growing, ex-convict who lives in his car.

QUOTE:

Ricky (playing "Spacemen"): Breaker breaker, come in Earth, this is Rocket Ship 27, aliens fucked over the carbonator on engine four, I'm gonna try to refuckulate it on Juniper. Uhh, and hopefully they've got some, space weed there, over. How... how was that buddy? I don't fuckin' know.

Bubbles: Ricky... that's not very good. Use space words, real ones, not talking about space weed.

Ricky: NAYSA, power rockets are firin' all over the place... they got lasers that are shootin' and uh... Bubbles, I can't fuckin' do this.

NATE FISHER (Peter Krause), *Six Feet Under.* Often seen taking a "walk" to get out of the funeral home and "clear" his head.

QUOTE: What would you rather have, some overly educated gas bag like Trevor, or a semi-literate fuck-machine like me? Come on.

NICK ANDOPOLIS (Jason Segel), *Freaks and Geeks.* Marijuana use may have gotten him kicked off the basketball squad, but at least he's got music to go back on...

QUOTE:
Lindsay: I don't smoke pot.
Nick: Come on, what's the big deal? It's from the earth, it's natural. Why would it be there if we weren't supposed to smoke it?
Lindsay: Dog crap is here and we don't smoke that.

OSCAR GEORGE BLUTH (Jeffrey Tambor), *Arrested Development*. George Sr.'s pothead twin brother.

QUOTE:

Michael: My mom is very stressed out, and uh, she needs something that I can't give her, um... maybe a little afternoon delight?

Narrator: Oscar thought that Michael was referring to a particular brand of cannabis named afternoon delight, a strand famous for slowing behavior.

Oscar: Well, sure, the question is: Which way do I try to get it in her?

Michael: I don't need any details.

Oscar: Maybe, I'll put it in her brownie.

Michael: Hey!

KENNY POWERS (Danny McBride), *Eastbound and Down*. Former professional baseball player and pot-smoking wild man known for "smoking weed on the reg."

QUOTE: Me sittin' round smokin' weed is awesome but it's not what a team manager is lookin' for.

MICHELANGELO (Robbie Rist) *Teenage Mutant Ninja Turtles*. This pizza-loving dude sure sounds like a stoner.

QUOTE:
April: So, what do you guys like on your pizza?
Michaelangelo: Oh, just the regular stuff: flies, stink bugs... It was a joke.

OTTO MANN (Harry Shearer), *The Simpsons*. Bus driver, metal music-loving pot smoker.

QUOTE:

Bart Simpson: I know you can do it, Otto. You're the coolest adult I know.

Otto Mann: Wow. I've never been referred to as an adult before. I've been tried as one.

FORSYTH PENDLETON "JUGHEAD" JONES III (Howard Morris), *Archie Comics*. Archie Andrews' best friend with a love of hamburgers, Jughead can get his friends out of any tough situation.

QUOTE: Why do houses burn down but paper burns up? If "he" is a "him," why isn't "she" a "shim"?

TOWELLIE (Vernon Chatman), *South Park*. This cartoon towel is always high and reminding us of the importance of bringing a towel.

QUOTE:

Towelie: You wanna get high!

Towelie: Well, I'm gonna get a little high.

SHAGGY (Casey Kasem), *Scooby Doo*. Classic stoner '70s dude, cartoon-style.

QUOTE:

Shaggy: Like chill out, Scooby-Doo, stop shaking.

Scooby Doo: Me? That's you.

Shaggy: Oh, right it's me, sorry.

TRON CARTER (Dave Chappelle), *Chappelle's Show*. Cocaine dealer by trade, this dice-rolling character blended a blunt into a smoothie drink in the *Mad Real World* sketch.

QUOTE: Hot hand in a dice game, baby. Talkin' 'bout clickity-clickity-clack!

STEVEN HYDE (Danny Masterson), *That '70s Show.* One of many tokers in this show, Steven just exudes *stoner*.

QUOTE: I can't believe they are wasting all their money on this stupid disco when they could buy a really big bag of... caramels.

REVEREND JIM "IGGY" IGNATOWSKI (Christopher Lloyd) *Taxi*. This smart but spacey character was part of the counterculture in the 1970s. He has been known to eat a "funny brownie" on occasion.

QUOTE:
Question asked while filling out the driver's exam form: Mental illness or narcotic addiction?
Reverend Jim: That's a tough choice!

GEORGE CHRISTOPHER (Ted Danson), *Bored to Death*. A partying, womanizing, magazine editor with a love of marijuana.

QUOTE: I'm going to drink as much booze and smoke as much pot as I want, thank you very much.

TARA LINDMAN (Mary-Kate Olsen), *Weeds*. Evangelical stoner girl who helps the crew in Majestic with their pot business.

QUOTE:
Silas: How can you be all into Jesus and still smoke weed?
Tara: Because pot is natural, it's not processed, it's made by God himself, so it's spiritual. It elevates you, opens your mind. And that's what God's love is all about.

JESSE PINKMAN (Aaron Paul) *Breaking Bad*. Meth

chef and all-around drug dealer Jesse is known to puff regularly.

QUOTE:

Jesse: Your freaking wife told me when she was here all up on my shit! Yeah, that's right. She almost caught me moving Emilio! Good job wearing the pants in the family! And why did you go telling her I was selling you weed?
Walter: Because somehow it seemed preferable to admitting that I cook crystal meth and killed a man.

SAMANTHA JONES (Kim Cattral) *Sex and the City.* A powerful and sexy New York publicist, Samantha likes to relax with a puff of weed once in a while.

QUOTE:

Charlotte: Where are we going to get any?
Samantha: Well, I'd call my dealer, but he's at the Cape.

SPACEY SOUNDS

In Dr. Kindbud's considered opinion, listening to and playing music are the best use of the power of THC to heighten your awareness. So crank up those jams and read all about the artists and songs that pay tribute to the ganja god, with songs written and created while under THC's inspiration, nuggets of facts and folklore about the songs' meanings and origins and songs that are just plain great to listen to while high. For your next weed-themed party, peruse these pages to make an ultimate pot-tastic playlist.

311

These guys produce a unique style of rock and have been known to support and smoke the cause.

SONG TITLE: "Hydroponic"

LYRIC: Mother Nature supreme, step back and dream the hydroponic scene. Found around, knocked out of bounds, wound into the mind of my stone cloud.

NUGGET: 311 bassist P-Nut has often been seen in a mock Adidas t-shirt where the logo has been modified into a cannabis leaf and the word *Indica* is in place of *Adidas*.

ADRIAN ROLLINI & HIS TAP ROOM GANG

Jazz musician best known as a multi-instrumentalist ripping it up on baritone saxophone, xylophone, and piano.

Song title: "Got a Need for You"

LYRIC:
Female vocal: Your kisses keep on haunting me. Their memory won't let me be.
Male vocal: Yeah.

Female vocal: I've gotta need for you.
Male vocal: I wish you had a weed for me.

AFROMAN

Joseph Edgar Foreman, the American rapper known as Afroman, received acclaim when his song "Because I Got High" was nominated for a Grammy in 2002, bringing attention to the cause (perhaps not positive attention, but hilarious nonetheless).

SONG TITLE: "Because I Got High"

LYRIC: I was gonna clean my room, until I got high; I was gonna get up and find the broom, but then I got high.

ANDY KIRK & HIS TWELVE CLOUDS OF JOY

Andrew Dewey Kirk is best known as a jazz saxophonist and

tubist who performed with his band during the swing era.

SONG TITLE: "All the Jive Is Gone"

LYRIC: The latest crave, the countries rave is jive, jive, jive. This modern treat, makes life complete, jive, jive, jive.

ARLO GUTHRIE

An American folk legend and son of famed Woody Guthrie, Arlo is known for his protest songs including the Thanksgiving favorite "Alice's Restaurant Massacree."

SONG TITLE: "Coming Into Los Angeles"

LYRIC: Coming into Los Angeles, Bringing in a couple of keys, Don't touch my bags if you please, Mister Customs Man.

BARNEY BIGARD SEXTET

Best known as an American jazz clarinetist and saxophonist, Albany Leon Bigard also played with Duke Ellington and Joe "King" Oliver.

SONG TITLE: Sweet Marijuana Brown

LYRIC: She don't know where she's going, She don't care where she's been. But every time you take her out, she's bound to take you in.

BEA FOOTE

While not as well known as some of her blues contemporaries, Foote's voice, which was strong with killer vibrato, landed her on recordings with artists such as Sammy Price.

SONG TITLE: "Weed"

LYRIC: I'm the queen of all vipers. I mean I smoke my weed. You know it makes me feel kind of happy, when I'm in need.

THE BEATLES

The Beatles' transition from young pop musicians with songs that are catchy as hell to mind-altering and expanding artists is laid out for you to take in as you stroll through their discography. There is no doubt that marijuana and LSD played an important role in the evolution of The Beatles' music.

SONG TITLE: "Got To Get You Into My Life"

LYRIC: I was alone, I took a ride; Another road where maybe I could see another kind of mind there.

NUGGET: According to Paul McCartney's 1998 book *Many Years From Now,* the song "Got To Get You Into My

Life" is not about a particular person but about his desire to smoke pot.

BEN HARPER

This Grammy Award–winning American guitar player and singer is known to put on a great show and also show up to support "good" causes.

SONG TITLE: "Burn One Down"

LYRIC: Herb the gift from the earth, and what's from the earth is of the greatest worth. So before you knock it try it first. You'll see it's a blessing and it's not a curse.

BENNY GOODMAN & HIS ORCHESTRA

Known as the "King of Swing," Goodman is an American jazz and swing musician clarinetist and bandleader.

SONG TITLE: "Texas Tea Party"

LYRIC: Now, momma, momma, momma, momma, mom oh, where did you hide my tea?

NUGGET: The term *Tea Party,* referring to a pot party, was used by musicians and artists of Goodman's era.

BLACK SABBATH

Hailing from England, original vocalist Ozzy Osbourne sure knew how to party. In fact his cocaine and alcohol (ab)use led to his dismissal from the band in 1979. He did return in 1997 to record a live record, *Reunion,* with the original lineup.

SONG TITLE: "Sweet Leaf"

LYRIC: My life was empty, forever on a down
Until you took me, showed me around

My life is free now, my life is clear
I love you sweet leaf, though you can't hear

NUGGET: A total of 22 musicians can claim to have been in Black Sabbath at one time or another.

BLUE STEELE & HIS ORCHESTRA

Blue Steele was known as an extremely talented yet eccentric and sometimes violent bandleader. Musicians in his band have recounted him chasing them half naked and sometimes assaulting them with their own instruments.

SONG TITLE: "All Muggled Up"

LYRICS: This song has some scatting but no lyrics. *Muggled* was a popular slang term meaning marijuana, and this classic track captures the mood perfectly.

BOB DYLAN

Robert Allen Zimmerman is an American folk hero who was never afraid to stick his voice out and say something controversial. He challenged both the powers that be and his generation to do something great and fight injustice.

SONG TITLE: "Everyone Must Get Stoned"

LYRICS: Yes, but I would not feel so all alone, Everyone must get stoned.

NUGGET: The year was 1964; the scene, the Delmonico Hotel in New York City. Bob Dylan changes the history of rock 'n roll when he introduces The Beatles to cannabis and smokes them out for the first time.

BOB MARLEY

The beloved reggae musician who stood up against

injustice and put his Rastafarian beliefs above all else. His convictions were strong, so strong in fact that he refused to have his toe amputated when he was diagnosed with melanoma, which unfortunately spread resulting in his death. Marley once said, "When you smoke the herb, it reveals you to yourself."

Song title: "Kaya"

Lyrics: Got to have kaya now
For the rain is falling
I'm so high, I even touch the sky
Above the falling rain

Nugget: Kaya has many different meanings throughout the world. Referencing *The Urban Dictionary* confirms what many of us may have thought. It's weed.

BONE THUGS-N-HARMONY

This American R&B/hip-hop group from Cleveland, Ohio, owes thanks to the late Eazy-E (of the group N.W.A) who signed them to Ruthless Records. In 1997 they won a Grammy for "Tha Crossroads," which was a tribute to Eazy-E.

SONG TITLE: "Weed Song"

LYRICS: I remember being a little thug
Weed, really didn't know what it was
Then I took a puff and I realized
I should always stay high

BOSTON

This American rock band from—you guessed it—Boston, Massachusetts, has rocked the world with hits such as "More Than a Feeling," "Peace of Mind," and "Smokin".

SONG TITLE: "Smokin'"

LYRICS: Smokin', Smokin'
We're cookin' tonight, just keep on tokin'
Smokin', Smokin'
I feel alright, mamma I'm not jokin', yeah.

BREWER & SHIPLEY

Mike Brewer and Tom Shipley comprised this American folk rock singer-songwriter duo. Their greatest success was the classic "One Toke Over the Line."

SONG TITLE: "One Toke Over the Line"

LYRICS: One toke over the line sweet Jesus, One toke over the line, Sittin' downtown in a railway station, One toke over the line.

QUOTE:

Tom Shipley: When we wrote "One Toke Over the Line," I think we were one toke over the line. I considered marijuana a sort of a sacrament... If you listen to the lyrics of that song, "one toke" was just a metaphor. It's a song about excess. Too much of anything will probably kill you.

BRIAN ROBBINS

After taking notice of a sign that read "WE DRUG TEST ALL OUR EMPLOYEES." in a window of a movie theater he was passing in Boston, Robbins wrote the hook for his song "Marijuana" in protest. He recorded a demo of it (circa 1997) that became widely popular online.

SONG TITLE: "Marijuana"

LYRICS: Oh marijuana. A gift of God to my brothers and me. Oh marijuana. Now the government wants to test me when I pee.

NUGGET: For some reason many people think this song is by the jam band Phish. It is not.

BUCK WASHINGTON

Half of the famous performing team Buck and Bubbles, Washington was a pianist who also played with the likes of Louis Armstrong and Bessie Smith.

SONG TITLE: "Save the Roach for Me"

LYRICS: Folks say that I'm lonesome, say I'm blue as I can be. Well, if you're smoking that jive when I pass by, Please save the roach for me.

THE BUSTER BAILEY RHYTHM BUSTERS

Originally from Memphis, Tennessee, Bailey was a jazz clarinetist and saxophonist and a well-respected session musician (1925–1940).

SONG TITLE: "Light Up"

LYRICS: Light up! Let's all get mellow. Light Up! There's smoke in your eyes. Light Up!

CAB CALLOWAY

Cabell "Cab" Calloway III (1907–1994) was known as a staple of American Jazz. His vocal stylings and band leading capabilities earn him a spot in American history.

SONG TITLE: "Reefer Man"

LYRICS: Man, what's the matter with that cat there? Must be full of reefer. Full of reefer!?
Yea man. You mean that cat's high?

NUGGET: Reefer Man was also performed by Baron

Lee & The Blue Rhythm Band.

THE CATS & THE FIDDLE

Formed in 1937 by singer/guitarist Austin Powell in Chicago, this band was known for their stellar vocal harmonies and full sound. You can see the band make appearances in the films "Too Hot to Handle"(1938) and "Going Places"(1939).

SONG TITLE: "Killin' Jive"

LYRICS: You will think you'll blow your top, oh baby you start laughing and you can't stop. Until you don't give him a smile, 'cause he's a sad man, not a bad man.

CEE PEE JOHNSON AND BAND

Johnson began playing in his brother Bert's band (The Sharps and Flats) in Dallas, and eventually became a bandleader himself known for playing a set of tom-tom drums while singing.

SONG TITLE: "The G Man Got The T Man"

LYRICS: They've arrested my connection, and I can't find any more, cause the G man got the T man and gone.

COUNTRY JOE & THE FISH

Co-founded by "Country Joe" McDonald and Barry "The Fish" Melton, this band is regarded as a serious influence to the psychedelic rock movement and a powerful voice in the protest against the Vietnam War.

SONG TITLE: "Don't Bogart That Joint"

LYRICS: Don't bogart that joint, my friend. Pass it over to me.

CORRADO

Philadelphia-based band Corrado sure knows how to get the party started with their classic catchy American folk-rock tunes. Be sure to check out their debut album *American Junkboat* (2008).

SONG TITLE: "Partying"

LYRICS: It's the hour of the day, to make my worries go away. Partying Woe-oh!

CYPRUS HILL

A Latino hip-hop group from Los Angeles probably most famous for their endorsement of marijuana, which is reflected in many of their songs such as "Hits From the Bong" and "Insane in the Membrane." They also did great work campaigning for cannabis's legalization.

LYRICS: Pick it, pack it
Fire it up, come along
And take a hit from the bong.

DAVE MATTHEWS BAND

Commonly referred to as DMB, this folk rock band was formed in 1991 in Charlottesville, North Carolina. Their unique blend of folk, rock, funk, and jazz has given them the reputation of putting on a great live show and packing venues around the world.

SONG TITLE: "Jimi Thing"

LYRICS: Lately I've been feeling low
A remedy is what I'm seeking
I take a taste of what's mellow
Come away to something better.

DAVID PEEL & THE LOWER EAST SIDE

David Michael Rosario formed his New York-based band in the late 1960s performing their unique version of aggressive "acoustic street rock." Much of their songs' contents were about weed and bad cops and had a large appeal in the stoner subculture.

SONG TITLE: "The Pope Smokes Dope" (1972)

LYRICS: The pope smokes dope,
God gave him the grass
The pope smokes dope
He likes to smoke in Mass.

DOA

This anarchist hardcore punk band hailing from Vancouver, Canada, has a hit song with a title worthy of some bleeping.

SONG TITLE: "Marijuana Motherfucker"

LYRICS: MaraMarijuana
MaraMarijuana
I like Marijuana
You Like Marijuana
We Like Marijuana too.

THE DOORS

This psychedelic blues-rock band led by singer Jim Morrison sprang up from Los Angeles in 1965 to expand listeners' minds and take them on a wild trip.

SONG TITLE: "Light My Fire"

LYRICS: Girl, we couldn't get much higher
Come on baby, light my fire.

Dr. Dre

Andre Romelle Young knows two things: hip-hop and weed. He is an American rapper, producer, and CEO of Aftermath Entertainment.

Song title: "Kush"

Lyrics: Now that puff puff pass shit!

Ella Fitzgerald & Chick Webb

Fitzgerald, also known as "Lady Ella," is one of the most stunning examples of an American jazz vocalist. Webb gave Fitzgerald's career an early kick start when he began featuring her as a vocalist in his sets when she was a teenager.

Song title: "When I Get Low, I Get High"

LYRICS: My man walked out, now you know that ain't right, well he better watch out if I meet him tonight. I said when I get low I get high.

EMINEM

Marshall Bruce Mathers III, also known as Slim Shady, brought a lot of attention to the world of hip-hop with his unique flow and outrageously offensive lyrics. His mass appeal to suburban teenagers got the uptight parents into a media frenzy. But that just sold more records.

SONG TITLE: "Drug Ballad"

LYRICS: Marijuana is everywhere
Where was you brought up?
It don't matter as long as you get where you're going
'Cause none of the shit is going to mean shit where we're going.

FLAMING LIPS

This band knows how to satisfy a baked audience—from their surreal album soundscapes, to their amazing music videos, to their one-of-a-kind live shows. Frontman Wayne Coyne knows how to throw a party on stage complete with costumes and a confetti gun and has been known to get into a blow-up transparent ball and roam into the audience.

QUOTE:

Wayne Coyne: I see young people all the time coming from the suburbs into my neighborhood, which is a horrible neighborhood… but they come into this area of town where there's a lot of hazards just to get something that's so wonderful to some people and so harmless to society. But you have to go into the belly of the beast just to get a joint.

GEORGIA WHITE

Georgia White was a popular African-American blues singer in Chicago in the 1930s and '40s.

SONG TITLE: "The Stuff Is Here"

LYRICS: Close the windows, and lock the door. Take the rug up off the floor. Hey, hey, let's all get gay. The stuff is here.

NUGGET: A version of this song was also performed and recorded by Cleo Brown under the title "The Stuff Is Here and It's Mellow."

THE GRATEFUL DEAD

The band and its fans were long associated in the media with the enjoyment (and maybe even the odor) of marijuana, yet none of their songs speak directly about it. This is not to say the Dead had nothing to do with pot! Several members of the band were arrested in New Orleans in 1970 for possession, an event commemorated in one of their most recognizable songs, "Truckin'." And in the original Woodstock film, the Dead's lead guitarist, Jerry Garcia, appears holding up a plastic bag, which he points to and says, while looking directly at the camera, "Marijuana, Exhibit A." He also appeared in 1973 on a recording of "Panama Red," an ode to grass by the New Riders of the Purple Sage.

GREEN DAY

Frontman Billie Joe Armstrong formed Green Day in 1987 in Berkeley, California. Although it took them several albums to break into the mainstream—not that they were trying to—their ability to craft West Coast punk rock pop hits is undeniable. The band's name is purportedly a reference to weed.

SONG TITLE: "Basket Case"

LYRICS: It all keeps adding up
I think I'm cracking up
Am I just paranoid?
Am I just stoned?

HAZEL MEYERS

This American blues and country-blues singer released more than forty cuts between September 1923 and August 1924.

SONG TITLE: "Pipe Dream Blues"

LYRICS: Someone woke me up just to amuse. Now I'm cryin' with the mean old pipe dream blues.

ICE CUBE

O'Shea Jackson is both an American rapper and actor. He

began his career in the group C.I.A. and then moved on to the more widely known N.W.A.. He then went on to have a successful solo career as a rapper, actor, and screenplay writer. Some of his more notable works include his role as Doughboy in *Boyz N The Hood* (1991) and his screenplay that would become the movie *Friday* (1995).

SONG TITLE: "Smoke Some Weed"

LYRICS: Snoop Dogg, all the way to Cheech and Chong, Cyprus Hill, Robert Downey hit the bong, Ricky Williams, how Miami feelin'? Smoke some weed!

THE HARLEM HAMFATS

Formed in Chicago in 1936, this jazz band got signed to Decca Records after their song "Oh Red" became a hit.

SONG TITLE: "Weed Smoker's Dream"

LYRICS: May's a good lookin' frail. She lives down by the jail. On her back though she's got hot stuff for sale.

JAZZ GILLUM & HIS JAZZ BOYS

William McKinley Gillum (1904–1966) from Indianola, Mississippi, released his first recording containing "Early in the Morning" and "Harmonica Stomp" in 1934.

SONG TITLE: Reefer Head Woman

LYRICS: I can't see why my baby sleeps so sound. Well, I can't see why my baby sleeps so sound. She must have smoked the reefer and it's bound to carry her down.

JEFFERSON AIRPLANE

Formed in 1965, this psychedelic rock band contributed to the soundtrack of the "Summer of Love" in San Francisco. Their release "Surrealistic Pillow" (1967) was and continues to be a staple of rock. The origin of the name is rumored to be slang for a matchstick split in half used to hold a joint that has become too short to hold (think: DIY roach clip). The band denies it.

SONG TITLE: "White Rabbit"

LYRICS: And if you go chasing rabbits, and you know you're going to fall. Tell 'em a hookah-smoking caterpillar, has given you the call.

JIMI HENDRIX

Praised as a guitar god, Hendrix's unique style of intense guitar skills and mesmerizing stage presence will live on throughout history. Although his life was cut short, his work and essence will not be forgotten. Wherever there is weed, Hendrix fans will exist.

SONG TITLE: "Purple Haze"

LYRICS: Purple haze all in my brain. Lately things just don't seem the same. Actin' funny, but I don't know why. 'Scuse me while I kiss the sky

JULIA LEE & HER BOY FRIENDS

Julia Lee, born in Boonville, Missouri, in 1902, began her musical career around the age of 18 singing and playing piano in her brother George's band. In 1944 she landed a contract with Capitol Records and released a string of R&B hits.

SONG TITLE: "The Spinach Song" ("I Didn't Like It the First Time")

LYRICS: I used to run away from the stuff, but now somehow I can't get enough. I didn't like it the first time. Oh, how it grew on me.

KID CUDI

Born Scott Ramon Seguro Mescudi in 1984, Kid Cudi is a rapper, songwriter, and actor. After moving to Brooklyn, New York, he released his first mix tape, "A Kid Named Cudi," which caught the ear of Kayne West and resulted in a record deal. He can also be seen acting in the HBO series "How to Make It in America."

SONG TITLE: "Marijuana"

LYRICS: Pretty green bud all in my blunt. Oh, I need it. We can take off, yeah. Oh, marijuana, yeah.

LARRY ADLER

Larry Adler (1914–2001), known as one of the best harmonica players in the world, had many famous composers writing pieces for him. In his later career he collaborated with artists such as Sting, Elton John, and Kate Bush.

SONG TITLE: "Smoking Reefers"

LYRICS: Oh, can't change this world you were born in, but I declare, you can be walking on air by smoking reefer.

LIL GREEN

Lillian Green (1919–1954) began performing as a blues singer in her teens and was highly regarded for her timing and sinuous vocal style. She passed away from pneumonia at just 34.

SONG TITLE: "Knockin' Myself Out"

LYRICS: Little girls and boys I've got one stick, give me a match and let me take a whip quick. I'm gonna knock myself out. Yes, I'm gonna kill myself.

NUGGET: A version of this song was also recorded and performed by Yack Taylor.

Louis Armstrong

An American trumpeter born in 1901 in New Orleans, Louisiana, Armstrong played a major role in the evolution of jazz music. He shifted the focus from collective improv to solo performance. He was also a highly skilled vocalist.

Song title: "Muggles"

Nugget: The slang term *muggles* was used by jazz musicians to remain covert in their dealings.

Musical Youth

Musical Youth was a British reggae band formed in 1979 comprised of two sets of brothers. They are most well known for their single "Pass The Dutchie" that received a Grammy Award nomination in 1984.

Song title: "Pass The Dutchie"

LYRICS: I say, pass the Dutchie on the left hand side, Pass the Dutchie on the left hand side.

NUGGET: According to legend, this song's title was changed from "Pass The Kutchie," which means a marijuana pipe, to "Pass The Dutchie" because the members of Musical Youth were ages 11–16. The name change also helped it get airplay on radio and MTV.

NEIL YOUNG

One of the most influential musicians in history, Neil Young has touched the hearts of many with his classic/folk rock tunes. The Canadian native was a co-founder of Buffalo Springfield, a member of Crosby, Stills, Nash & Young, and an award-winning solo artist.

SONG TITLE: "Roll Another Number"

LYRICS: Think I'll roll another number for the road, I

feel able to get under any load.

Noble Sissle's Swingsters featuring Sidney Bechet

Noble Sissle (1889–1975) was an American jazz composer, singer, and bandleader as well as a playwright. Sidney Bechet (1897–1959) was a phenomenal clarinet and saxophone player sought after to play on other musicians' records.

Song title: "Viper Mad"

Lyrics: Wrap your chops, round this stick of tea. Love this gage, and get high with me.

NOFX

California punk rock band NOFX loves to offend, push the limits of what's acceptable, and stick up for the little guy while giving a middle finger to hypocrisy and injustice.

SONG TITLE: "Drugs Are Good"

LYRICS: Drugs are good, they let you do things that you know you not should. And when you do 'em people think that you're cool.

THE NUGGETS COMPILATION

The Nuggets compilation series hold some of the finest psychedelic rock 'n roll that has ever been produced. From garage tracks to studio productions, these compilations of tunes from rock music's first psychedelic era hold some true gems—or "nuggets," if you will. The discs can be bought in box set form or individually.

OUTKAST

Dynamic duo Andre 3000 and Big Boi have produced some of the most slamming musical hip-hop tracks to come out of the American South. With six Grammy Awards, these members of the Dungeon Family were more experimental and unique back in the early 1990s than most of their peers are even today.

SONG TITLE: "Crumblin' Herb"

LYRICS: There's only so much time left in this crazy world. I'm just crumblin' erb, I'm just crumblin' erb.

PINK FLOYD

Whether or not the members of Pink Floyd smoked up is unknown, but one thing is for sure… their fans do! Anyone who has sat down with a doobie, closed their eyes, and listened in awe to the sonic masterpiece that is "Dark Side of the Moon" will agree.

PETER, PAUL AND MARY

The American folk-rock trio comprised of Peter Yarrow, Paul Stookey, and Mary Travers have had almost a fifty-year career. They got started in the early 1960s after being hand-selected by manager Albert Grossman and found great success, broke up for most of the 1970s, and then reunited from 1978 to 2009.

SONG TITLE: Although they adamantly denied it, there has been much speculation that "Puff the Magic Dragon" was a reference to smoking pot.

LYRICS: Puff, the magic dragon lived by the sea, and frolicked in the autumn mist in a land called Honah Lee.

PETER TOSH

Jamaican reggae musician Peter Tosh began his career playing as a member of The Wailers. After The Wailers breakup in 1974, he began a successful solo career by releasing the album "Legalize It" (1976) under CBS Records.

SONG TITLE: "Legalize It"

LYRIC: Legalize it, don't criticize it,
Legalize it and I will advertise it.

PHISH

This American jam band, featuring the lead guitar and vocal stylings of Trey Anastasio, is revered for its live extended improvisations. Phish is a band that drew stoners from across the globe to follow them on their magical tours much like The Grateful Dead did.

SONG TITLE: "Dear Mrs. Reagan"

LYRICS: Dear Mrs. Reagan, I hope you're feeling well. Fighting drugs and abortion will keep you out of hell.

QUEENS OF THE STONE AGE

Josh Homme founded this riff-based rock band in 1997 in Palms Desert, California. After the breakup of Homme's first band, Kyuss, he briefly toured as a guitarist with rock band The Screaming Trees in 1995.

SONG TITLE: "Feel Good Hit of the Summer"

LYRICS: Nicotine, Valium, Vicodin, Marijuana, Ecstasy and Alcohol. Nicotine, Valium, Vicodin, Marijuana, Ecstasy and Alcohol.

REEFER BLUES: VINTAGE SONGS ABOUT MARIJUANA
(Compilation Volumes 1–3)

This series of classic compilations is a must-have for any stoner. Show your friends you've got some class and culture and bring back the stoner voices of the Blues at your next party. Highlights include "I'm Gonna Get High" by Tampa Red & The Chicago Five and "Here Comes the Man With the Jive" by Stuff Smith & His Onyx Club Boys.

RADIOHEAD

Radiohead's modern rock masterpiece "OK Computer" (1997) is guaranteed to take a stoned listener on an amazing futuristic yet organic voyage. Be sure to check out "Paranoid Android" and "Exit Music (For a Film)."

RICK JAMES

Rick James, an American songwriter, singer, and producer, had a reputation as a wild party man onstage and off. He rose to fame in the late 1970s with hits such as "You and I" (1978) and "Super Freak" (1981).

SONG TITLE: "Mary Jane"

LYRICS: I'm in love with Mary Jane. I'm not the only one. If Mary wanna play around. I let her have her fun.

THE ROOTS

The Philadelphia-based hip-hop group The Roots create a unique brand of music using acoustic instruments to make a blend of rap, jazz, rock, and other eclectic styles. The Roots may now be seen as the house band on "Late Night with Jimmy Fallon" on NBC.

SONG TITLE: "Stay Cool"

LYRICS: The stress got me ignitin' the potent marijuana leaf, tryin' to play it cooler than a polar bear colony. You feel the music know I'm over there probably, pimpin' on the same system that forever shorted me.

ROSETTA HOWARD & THE HARLEM HAMFATS

Chicago-born Rosetta Howard (1914–1974) is known for her blues singing in the 1930s and '40s.

SONG TITLE: "If You're a Viper"

LYRICS: I'm the queen of everything. I've got to be high before I can swing. Light a T and let it be, if you're a viper.

NUGGET: This song was written by Stuff Smith and was also performed by Fats Waller.

SNOOP DOGG

Snoop Dogg, the West Coast Doggfather of rap, started as a protégé of rapper Dr. Dre. His first record *Doggystyle* (1993) was released by Death Row Records and debuted at Number 1 on Billboard's Hot 100 and R&B charts.

SONG TITLE: "Gin and Juice"

LYRICS: Rollin' down the street, smokin' indo, sippin' on gin and juice.

STEVE MILLER BAND

This American rock band formed in San Francisco in 1967. With each album they released, their success grew. Early in their career, the band backed legend Chuck Berry at the Fillmore West in a show that was recorded and released under the title "Live at Fillmore Auditorium" (1967).

SONG TITLE: "Joker"

LYRICS: I'm a joker, I'm a smoker, I'm a midnight toker, I get my lovin' on the run.

Stuff Smith & His Onyx Club Boys

Smith was a prominent violinist during America's swing era. Born in Ohio, he spent time in Texas playing with Alphonse Trent's band, then moved to New York in 1935 where he performed with his sextet at the Onyx Club.

Song title: "Here Comes the Man With the Jive"

Lyrics: Whenever you're feeling small, don't care for this life at all, light up and get real tall. Here comes the man with the jive!

Nugget: Stuff Smith is responsible for many other marijuana songs, including "You'se a Viper."

Sublime

Hailing from Long Beach, California, Sublime came on

the music scene with a blend of punk rock, ska, and reggae. The late lead singer/guitarist Bradley Nowell had an inherent sense of melody and rhythm. Nowell passed away in 1996 just before the release of the group's third self-titled album, which would go on to achieve national acclaim. The band re-formed with new singer Rome Ramirez in 2009.

SONG TITLE: "Smoke 2 Joints"

LYRICS: I smoke two joints in the morning, I smoke two joints at night. I smoke two joints in the afternoon, It makes me feel alright.

TOM PETTY

This American musician knows how it feels, and thinks another joint might just do the trick. He was a founding member of the supergroup The Traveling Wilburys alongside Dylan, Orbison, Lynne, and Harrison. He was also in

Mudcrutch, played with his band The Heartbreakers, and has had a successful solo career.

SONG TITLE: "You Don't Know How It Feels"

LYRICS: So let's get to the point, let's roll another joint. Let's head on down the road.

WEEZER

Guitarist/lead singer Rivers Cuomo leads Weezer in its sometimes sarcastic brand of alternative rock music.

SONG TITLE: "Hash Pipe"

LYRICS: Oh, Come on and kick me. You've got your problems, I've got my ass wide. You've got your big G's, I've got my hash pipe.

WHAT CELEBRITIES ARE SAYING

People are talking about weed. Not just your usual freaks and troublemakers, but famous people, like actors and comedians and other entertainment types. They are singing the praises of marijuana, extolling its medicinal value, and advocating for its legalization. Here's what they're saying.

JUDD APATOW (b. 1967)

He has produced some of the funniest modern stoner movies out there. His hits include *Pineapple Express, The 40-Year-Old Virgin, Super Bad, Get Him to the Greek, Walk Hard,* and many others. For creating such cult classics you would think he's be a big pothead. Guess again. In an interview with Geoff Berkshire for Metromix, he had this to say about *Pineapple Express,* "No, I'm not a pot guy... When I smoke pot I just wind up laying in the corner, sucking on my fist, crying, saying 'When's it going to end? When's it going to end?' I'm the guy who thinks this is an anti-pot movie. I see it as an example of what could happen to you if you smoke pot: You have Asian assassins coming after you."

NUGGET: Judd Apatow and Adam Sandler were once roommates in New York City.

DOUG BENSON (b. 1964)

From his stand-up comedy routines to his podcasts, "Doug Loves Movies," to his amazing documentary *Super High Me*, Doug Benson is bringing marijuana into the mainstream spotlight. Pot is a subject that Benson has always held close to his heart and waxes about in most of his dialogues. He has hosted High Time's Stony Awards, released several comedy records, and performed on the Marijuana-Logues, an off-Broadway comedy show.

QUOTE FROM BENSON'S MARIJUANA-LOGUES SET: "I recently cut back on my pot smoking, severely. I rarely smoke it anymore. Now the only time I smoke pot is when it is given to me by strangers, after the show, tonight. That's the only time."

LENNY BRUCE (1925–1966)

Stand-up comedian Lenny Bruce knew how to push the limit and from an early age understood the power of words and how to play on people's fears. After dropping out of high school, Lenny joined the Navy, which he soon realized was a mistake. Before long, he had gotten himself discharged by telling Navy psychologists he had been acting on homosexual desires. His first break was an appearance on *Arthur Godfrey's Talent Scouts* TV show in 1948. As he developed his act, it became clear he was different from most comedians of his era. His routine was intense and he was not afraid to use a lot of curse words that moderators found objectionable. In 1961 he was arrested on obscenity charges after performing at the Jazz Workshop in San Francisco. The jury found him not guilty. He died of a drug overdose (not marijuana) at the age of forty.

QUOTE: "Marijuana will be legal someday because every law student I know smokes it."

GEORGE CARLIN (1937–2008)

Stand-up comedian George Carlin is most famous for his "Seven Dirty Words" routine. The first of his fourteen stand-up specials was filmed in 1977 for HBO. His dark humor covered topics such as idiosyncrasies of the English language, politics, religion, and psychology. Carlin's "Seven Dirty Words" played a primary role in the 1978 U.S. Supreme Court's F.C.C. v. *Pacifica Foundation* case. In a very close vote of 5-4, the court deemed that the government did have authority to regulate what they deemed to be indecent material on the airwaves. Carlin on the ruling: "There are 400,000 words in the English language, and there are seven you can't say on television. What a ratio that is! 399,993 to 7. They must really be bad. They must be OUTRAGEOUS to be separated from a group that large. 'All of you words over here, you seven….bad words.' That's what they told us, right? …You know the seven, don't ya? That you can't say on TV? Shit, piss, fuck, cunt, cocksucker, motherfucker and tits."

QUOTE: "I'm not a big drug user anymore, but I have always a joint somewhere near me."

DAVID CHAPPELLE (b. 1973)

The man that brought us the films *Half Baked* and *Block Party* and the sketch TV series *Chappelle Show* holds a special place in Dr. Kindbud's heart. Chappelle has given the people of the world an insurmountable stash of quotable lines and some of the funniest scenes in sketch comedy.

Here are a few lines to get you started:

- *From a stand-up special:* "Weed's not as bad as everything else…'cause weed is a background substance. You know what I mean? You can smoke some herb and still function. You ain't crisp… but you'll function."

- *From a stand-up special:* "All white people talk about when they get high is other times that they got high."

- *From the movie Half Baked:* "I don't do drugs, though. Just weed."

- *From Chappelle's Show:* "I'm Rick James, Bitch!"

Chappelle's parents divorced and as a child he lived with both—his mom in Maryland during the school year and his father in Ohio for the summers. In the end he backed away from *Chappelle's Show*, chose to step out of the spotlight and return to his home state of Ohio to live with his wife and kids. Here's Chappelle on his decision: "Turns out you don't need $50 million to live around these parts, just a nice smile and a kind way about you. You guys are the best neighbors ever... That's why I came back and that's why I'm staying."

ROBERT CLARKE

Robert Clarke is a member of the International Hemp Association and Director of Pharmtex Consultants. He studied cannabis in the United States and in Amsterdam in the Netherlands and is working to develop reproducible strains for medicinal cannabis producers. In 1993 he published *Marijuana Botany: Propagation and Breeding of Distinctive Cannabis.*

MILEY CYRUS (b. 1992)

Teen pop sensation and daughter to Billy Ray, Miley isn't the good girl she's cracked up to be. After a home video of her smoking what she claimed to be the legal herb Salvia divinorum out of a bong went viral, her game was up. Upon receiving a Bob Marley birthday cake at her nineteenth birthday party, she said, "You know you're a stoner when your friends make you a Bob Marley cake. You know you smoke way too much fucking weed!"

CAMERON DIAZ (b. 1972)

Cameron has a reputation for liking a little grass. A photo was taken of her smoking a joint with Drew Barrymore in 2007 while in Hawaii. In an interview she also admitted to "probably" buying weed from Snoop Dogg while attending the same high school.

MELISSA ETHERIDGE (b. 1961)

Melissa Etheridge became an advocate of medicinal marijuana legalization after she used marijuana during her breast cancer treatment.

QUOTE: I don't want to look like a criminal to my children anymore. I want them to know this is a choice that you make as a responsible adult.

ZACH GALIFIANAKIS (b. 1969)

This American actor lit and smoked a joint on live television! As a guest on *Real Time with Bill Maher* on HBO, Zach produced a joint from his pocket and proceeded to light and smoke it during the interview. In a later interview on CNN, Bill Maher stated that it was not a real joint (although we have our suspicions). Either way, Zach is doing a great job bringing pot into the political spotlight.

QUOTE: I smoke so much pot sometimes I forget to smoke it.

WOODY HARRELSON (b. 1961)

You may know him as Woody Boyd from the sitcom *Cheers,* a lovable naive bartender, or from some of his later roles in movies such as *Natural Born Killers, Kingpin,* and *The People vs. Larry Flint.* Besides being a stellar actor, Woody sits on the advisory board of National Organization for Reform of Marijuana Laws (NORML) and is a cannabis lover at heart. In 1996 he was arrested in Lee County, Kentucky, after planting four hemp seeds to symbolically protest state laws that did not differentiate industrial hemp from weed.

MITCH HEDBERG (1968–2005)

Mitch Hedberg was an American stand-up comedian with

a genius for comic delivery and an approach to one-liners and short stories all his own. He died from a heroin and cocaine overdose on April Fool's Day 2005.

QUOTE: I love my FedEx guy 'cause he's a drug dealer and he don't even know it . . . and he's always on time.

JACK HERER (1939–2010)

Jack Herer is so famous on the stoner scene he's got a strain of weed named after him that has won the Cannabis Cup. He was an activist and book author who had the strain named after him in honor of the work he did fighting to get cannabis accepted as an important source of medicines and fuels.

GIL SCOTT-HERON (1949–2011)

Gil Scott-Heron was an American poet and singer most famous for his song "The Revolution Will Not Be Televised." His drug of choice was cannabis. According to Martin Johnson, a writer who interviewed him at the Blue Note in New York City in 1991, he chained smoked marijuana during the interview.

MARTIN LAWRENCE (b. 1965)

Martin Lawrence has made a name for himself as a stand-up comedian, an actor, film director and producer, and screenwriter. He has starred in movies such as *Blue Streak*, *Big Momma's House*, *Do the Right Thing*, *House Party*, and had his own TV show (*Martin*) from 1992 to 1997.

QUOTE: Black people and white people get high differently. I mean, you hit the joint, but if effects up differently. See a brother hit a joint and shit he like, "yeah mothafucker, yeah nigga, this is some good shit…" White people, y'all scare me. I don't know. You mother fuckers hit a joint and decide I'm on some other shit. "Woe, do you hear that man? It says kill four people!"

STEVE MARTIN (b. 1945)

Steve Martin can do it all. He's won Emmy, Grammy, and American Comedy awards, is a book author, stand-up comedian, and one hell of a banjo player. He's starred in such classic films as *The Jerk* (1979) and *Dirty Rotten Scoundrels* (1988) and wrote and starred in *L.A. Story* (1991).

QUOTE: I used to smoke marijuana. But I'll tell you something: I would only smoke it in the late evening. Oh, occasionally the early evening, but usually the late evening—or the mid-evening. Just the early evening, midevening and late evening. Occasionally, early afternoon, early midafternoon, or perhaps the late-midafternoon. Oh, sometimes the early-mid-late-early morning. . . . But never at dusk.

JIM MORRISON (1943–1971)

Jim Morrison embodied what it was to be a rock star in the

1960s. His lyrics often referenced drugs, and he lived the lifestyle to back it up. Marijuana was not his only vice, and alcoholism and other substance abuse led to his premature death. He also published books of poetry and made a film, *HWY: An American Pastoral,* which most have not seen. Here's what Morrison said when a fan tossed a joint onto stage while The Doors were playing in New York City: "Man that's what I call a New York joint. You can pick your teeth with a New York joint."

BILL MURRAY (b. 1950)

Bill Murray is an American actor who has played some of the funniest roles in film including roles in *Ghostbusters, Stripes, What About Bob?,* and *Rushmore.* A toker at heart, he played a groundskeeper at a golf course who rolled huge joints in *Caddyshack* and a pot-smoking ship captain in *The Life Aquatic with Steve Zissou.* In 1970 he was busted with a large quantity of pot and got kicked out of school.

This may have been the best thing for him since he soon followed his brother Brian to Chicago, where he ended up meeting John Belushi, Dan Aykroyd, and Gilda Radner.

WILLIE NELSON (b. 1933)

First and foremost a respected Grammy Award–winning American musician, Willie Nelson is also one of the most prolific spokesmen for the legalization of marijuana. After his arrest for possession, he formed the Teapot party, a political party that "leans a little to the left." Since its inception, there have been Teapot parties formed in all fifty states.

QUOTE: Tax it, regulate it, and legalize it, and stop the border wars over drugs.

MICHAEL PHELPS (b. 1985)

Phelps is an American swimmer with sixteen Olympic medals, fourteen of which are gold. In 2009, the *News of the*

World, a British tabloid, published a picture of him smoking a bong. This causes all kinds of trouble for an Olympic athlete. He stated that his behavior "was regrettable and demonstrated bad judgment." But you know, he had to say that. He was suspended from USA Swimming for three months and Kellogg's cereal did not renew his endorsement.

RICHARD PRYOR (1940–2005)

Best known as an amazing storytelling comic and hilarious actor, Richard Pryor contributed so much to the world of entertainment and enlightenment. He did not candy-coat his act as he candidly spoke his mind on topics such as racism. His stand-up specials include "Richard Pryor: Live & Smokin'" (1971), "That Nigger's Crazy" (1974), and "Richard Pryor: Live on the Sunset Strip" (1982). He appeared in many films, including *Superman III* (1983) and *Brewster's Millions* (1985). In 1980 Pryor accidentally set himself on fire while drinking 151-proof rum and freebasing cocaine. He ended up running down the street ablaze, until the police were able to put him out. He spent six weeks in recovery with burns over half his body. In 1986 Pryor was diagnosed with multiple sclerosis and used cannabis to treat his pain.

SARAH SILVERMAN (b. 1970)

As an American comedian, actress, writer, and musician, Sarah Silverman has her hands in many facets of the entertainment industry. She began her career as a writer on *Saturday Night Live* and moved on to have her own show, *The Sarah Silverman Program* (2007–2010), on Comedy Central. Silverman is not afraid to use her comedy to bring up issues and get people talking about religion, racism, and gay rights. She said, "And I like that people sometimes get more out of it… if it instigates thoughts about race, or sex, or something." She also loves her weed!

Lyrics from "I Love You More": "I love you more than the white stuff in a zit, I love you like Gary Busey, I love you more than dykes love pussy, I love you more than my after-show monster bong hit."

Howard Stern (b. 1954)

Howard Stern is an American radio personality who pushes the limits of talk radio. His controversial on-air personality got him labeled as a "shock jock." In addition to his radio career, Stern's book *Private Parts* spent twenty weeks on the New York Times Best-Seller list and was made into a film. Howard has a huge audience at his command, and he's never been afraid to speak up in defense of cannabis.

Quote: I'm for legalizing marijuana. Why pick on those drugs? Valium is legal. You just go to a doctor and get it and overdose on it—what's the difference? Prozac, all that stuff. So why not marijuana? Who cares? It's something that grows out of the ground—why not? Go smoke a head of cabbage. I don't care what you smoke.

JUSTIN TIMBERLAKE (b. 1981)

Justin Timberlake's first forays into the limelight were as a contestant on the television show *Star Search* and on *The New Mickey Mouse Club* on the Disney Channel. His fame accelerated as a member of the boy band 'N Sync. Since his departure from 'N Sync, Timberlake has released solo records and become a respected actor. When asked if he smoked weed, Timberlake stated, "Absolutely. The only thing pot does for me is it gets me to stop thinking. Sometimes I have a brain that needs to be turned off. Some people are just better high." He also claimed that legalization "would cut the crime rate in half. All the stoners I know are too paranoid to do anything stupid." Very true, Justin, very true…

TOWELIE

A pot-smoking weed-lovin' towel from the Southpark series. That's right a towel, like a bath towel. Perhaps the most prolific stoner towel in all of history, or… wait… maybe the only one. Known for mumbling such memorable lines as: "You wanna get high!" *[long awkward pause]* "Well, I'm gonna get a little high."

WAVY GRAVY (HUGH NANTON ROMNEY) (b. 1936)

A truly spectacular unique individual, Wavy Gravy is famous for dressing like a clown to both help children and soften his appearance at political protests. His moniker was given to him by blues musician B.B. King at the 1969 Texas International Pop Festival.

QUOTE: I think that, you know, that the herb should

be legalized because there is, as I say, a big difference between smack, crack, and smoking flowers.

SHAUN WHITE (b. 1986)

Shaun White is an American snowboarder and skateboarder most known for winning two Olympic gold medals. He is also known for the controversy surrounding him testing positive for marijuana and losing his metal. An unnamed source was quoted as saying, "We keep trying to tell Shaun that he's just one bust away from stocking the salsa bar at Baja Fresh."

QUOTE: My friends, I'll admit, most of them do ... and now, because it's Olympic time and everybody's getting tested for drugs, you see them just sweating bullets, man. I'm like, "Ah, whatever."

RICKY WILLIAMS (b. 1977)

American football running back Ricky Williams is a two-time All-American and received a Heisman Trophy in 1998 as the most outstanding player in college football. That's not why he's in this book though. He's in here for his notorious history of failing the league's drug tests for marijuana. After failing two (possibly three) drug tests, Williams announced his retirement from the NFL. He played in Toronto for a bit and has now returned to the NFL.

MONTEL WILLIAMS (b. 1956)

Would you believe that the former daytime TV talk show host is actually a medicinal marijuana activist? Montel Williams, who has been diagnosed with MS, has been able to find some relief from his pain by means of ingesting marijuana. Since his retirement from *The Montel Williams Show*, he has taken on activism for the cause as his main objective. He states, "For immediate cessation, I smoke it. Most of the time I eat it at night because I suffer from extreme tremors in the evening and I also suffer from extreme neuralgic pain in my feet."

ROBIN WILLIAMS (b. 1951)

American actor and comedian Robin Williams performs a unique style of fast-paced comedy filled with animated impressions and off-the-wall behavior. He has starred in many films, including *Mrs. Doubtfire* (1993), *The Birdcage* (1996), and *Good Will Hunting* (1997). At a 1986 stand-up performance at the Met Williams joked, "…and the horrible thing is people who get stoned try to get their animals stoned to make them feel better. It's not bad enough that you proved that Darwinism is wrong, you're going to take the whole family with you!"

QUOTE: Do you think God gets stoned? I think so… look at the platypus.

BAKED BOOKS

For your enlightenment, I made this list of books that are full of fact and fiction about weed and the pleasures of being high. Many delve into topics in-depth that we can only touch on in this book.

Alice's Adventures in Wonderland
(Macmillan and Co, 1st printing, 1865)

AUTHOR: Charles Lutwidge Dodgson (aka Lewis Carroll)

SYNOPSIS: Alice is a curious girl with a penchant for the psychedelic. Curious, she follows a hurried rabbit down a whole and the adventure begins. Don't forget about the sequel, *Through the Looking Glass*, which Disney partially combined with the first book when making its 1951 animated film.

Ask Ed: Marijuana Gold: Trash to Stash
(Quick American Archives, 2002)

AUTHOR: Ed Rosenthal

SYNOPSIS: This is a great resource demonstrating methods to turn your leftover scraps, parts of the plant with less THC content, into concentrated gold. The stems and leaves are not appetizing to smoke, but when concentrated can really pack a punch.

Aunt Sandy's Medical Marijuana Cookbook: Comfort Food for Mind and Body
(Quick American Archives, 2010)

AUTHOR: Sandy Moriarty, Foreword by Denis Peron, Preface by Richard Lee

SYNOPSIS: This book includes a cannabis butter recipe as well as delicious comfort food recipes to get you all warm and high on the inside. Check out the mac and cheese and the Buffalo wings.

Baked!: 35 Marijuana Munchies to Make and Bake (Ten Speed Press, 2010)

AUTHORS: Chris Stone and Gordon Lewis

SYNOPSIS: A great compilation of great stoner recipes to will take your meals to a new high! There are health benefits to eating your weed rather than filling your lungs with smoke, so don't be afraid to give it a try. Be sure to check out the hash brownies and spaced cakes.

The Bong Bible (Cider Mill Press, 2011)

AUTHOR: Dr. Seymour Kindbud

SYNOPSIS: A Do-It-Yourself MacGyver book to building bongs and pipes of all shapes and sizes. Everything one needs can be bought with a trip to the grocery and hardware store. The fun never stops.

Bongwater (Grove Press, 1996)

AUTHOR: Michael Hornburg

SYNOPSIS: This story, set in Portland, Oregon, and the East Village of New York City, is set through the eyes of a group of twenty-somethings as they search for meaning in their lives. David, who narrates the Portland portion of the book, is a lackluster filmmaker with a penchant for booze, drugs, and sex. A great read that was also adapted into a film. New Musical Express (UK) had this to say about it: "Ridiculously well written, a roller coaster ride through slacker sleaze and druggy romance, which is never less than riveting. Touching poetic stuff."

Botany of Desire (Random House Trade Paperbacks, 2002)

AUTHOR: Michael Pollan

SYNOPSIS: Take a walk through the world from the perspective of a plant. Programmed with the same drive to prosper on earth and evolve to succeed as humans, plants are pretty amazing. This book recounts history through the eyes of four plants; the apple, the tulip, the potato and… marijuana. Pollan uses each of these to demonstrate how domesticated plants and humans have evolved to a mutually beneficial symbiotic relationship. The apple satisfies our desire for sweetness, the tulip our desire for beauty, the potato our need for control, and marijuana our desire for intoxication. In exchange, humans have helped these plants prosper by spreading them across the globe, planting them and caring for them, ensuring their survival. Also check out the film of the same title.

The Cannabible (Ten Speed Press, 2001)

AUTHOR: Jason King

SYNOPSIS: A beautiful book featuring a collection of photos and descriptions of the top 200 strains personally captured by the author from locations around the world. More than 400 stunning photographs of buds from Hawaii to Europe! Don't forget to check out volumes 2 and 3 as well.

The Cannabis Breeder's Bible: The Definitive Guide to Marijuana Genetics, Cannabis Botany and Creating Strains for the Seed Market (Green Candy Press, 2005)

AUTHOR: Greg Green

SYNOPSIS: This book includes professional techniques for breeding 60 of the most popular strains, new hybridization techniques, and interviews with seed-bank pros and breeders. It also includes a section on international seed laws and best practices as well as photographs and instructive illustrations.

The Cannabis Companion: The Ultimate Guide to Connoisseurship (Running Press Book Publishers, 2004)

AUTHOR: Steven Wishnia

SYNOPSIS: Author Steven Wishnia, former senior editor of *High Time Magazine,* delves into the upscale side of cannabis. You will find sections on the history of cannabis, the best growers and their "vineyards," and some great joint-rolling techniques. Also included is a list of his top 20 strains complete with tasting notes.

Dr. Kindbud's Weed-O-Pedia
(Cider Mill Press, 2012)

AUTHOR: Dr. Seymour Kindbud

SYNOPSIS: Yeah, you know…the book you're holding. It's an encyclopedia of weed.

The Emperor Wears No Clothes: The Authoritative Historical Record of Cannabis and the Conspiracy Against Marijuana (AH HA Publishing, 11th edition, 2000)

AUTHOR: Jack Herer

SYNOPSIS: This book, first published in 1985, holds the title of the #1 selling hemp book of all time, eleven editions later. Author Jack Herer, a man so notorious in cannabis culture he has a strain of weed named after him, puts it all on the table and argues against hemp prohibition. The book, backed by several organizations including H.E.M.P and Sensi Seeds, offers $50,000 to anyone who can disprove the books claims.

From the back cover: "If all fossil fuels and their derivatives, as well as trees for paper and construction were banned in order to save the planet, reverse the Greenhouse Effect and stop deforestation, then there is only one known annually renewable natural resource that is capable of providing the overall majority of the world's paper and textiles; meet all of the world's transportation, industrial and home energy needs, while simultaneously reducing pollution, rebuilding the soil, and cleaning the atmosphere all at the same time... and that substance is—the same one that did it all before—Cannabis Hemp... Marijuana!"

Eye Voltage: A Stoner's Book of 40 Mind-Blowing Optical Illusions (Cider Mill Press, 2012)

AUTHOR: Dr. Seymour Kindbud

SYNOPSIS: Vibrant colors, classic optical illusions images, and other stoner brain games will have you seeing 3-D bongs and hemp leaves from the comfort of your couch (or bean bag chair).

Fear & Loathing in Las Vegas
(Random House, 1st printing 1972)

AUTHOR: Hunter S. Thompson

SYNOPSIS: This tale depicts the amazing drug-fueled adventure of journalist "Raoul Duke" and his attorney/accomplice Dr. Gonzo as they travel to and from Las Vegas. The first appearance of "Fear and Loathing in Las Vegas" by "Raoul Duke" was in the November 11, 1971 issue of

Rolling Stone magazine. It was accompanied by drawings by Ralph Steadman whose classic interpretations of Thompson's story were included when the book was later published.

Green Weed: The Organic Guide to Growing High-Quality Cannabis
(Cider Mill Press, 2010)

AUTHOR: Dr. Seymour Kindbud

SYNOPSIS: *Green Weed* contains everything one needs to know about how to cultivate indoor and outdoor cannabis crops organically. This book covers everything from a very "green" perspective, providing its readers with the knowledge and know-how to grow sweet green buds without the use of chemicals.

Grow Your Own Organic Weed!: Everything You Need... Except the Seeds
(Cider Mill Press, 2011)

AUTHOR: Dr. Seymour Kindbud

SYNOPSIS: This kit provides you with everything you need to start your farm—except the seeds. A full-color manual complements the kit and guides the reader with detailed step-by-step instructions and fixes to common problems.

The Little Green Book (Cider Mill Press, 2010)

AUTHOR: Dr. Seymour Kindbud *(shameless self-promoter)*

SYNOPSIS: A resource and a journal that includes amazing featured strains hand-picked by yours truly gathered from the leading producers from Amsterdam to California. Also included is a journal-formatted section for the logging your personal experiences and preferences.

Handbook of Medicinal Herbs

(CRC Press, 2nd printing, 2002)

AUTHOR: James A. Duke

SYNOPSIS: A tremendous catalog of uncommonly used medicinal herbs. With more than 800 herbal entries, including cannabis, this book is a great resource that includes data such as proven indications, folk indications, and dosage data.

The Marijuana Chef Cookbook

(Green Candy Press, 2007)

AUTHOR: S. T. Oner

SYNOPSIS: An amazing cookbook featuring recipes that may leave you hungrier than before you ate. A look through this book will leave your mouth watering and your stomach jonesing for some tasty THC. Check out their recipes for Nutter Butter and Primeval Pasta.

The Official High Times Pot Smoker's Handbook: Featuring 420 Things to Do When You're Stoned (Chronicle Books, 2008)

AUTHORS: David Bienenstock and the Editors of High Times Magazine

SYNOPSIS: *High Times* magazine has been a staple in the pot community and subculture since 1974. This collection draws from their vast library of past knowledge and pools it into one comprehensive field guide.

The Pot Book: A Complete Guide to Cannabis (Park Street Press, 2010)

AUTHOR: Edited by Julie Holland M.D. with contributions by Andrew Weil, Michael Pollan, Lester Grinspoon, and Allen St. Pierre

SYNOPSIS: A compilation of information gathered from the leading experts to create a comprehensive collection covering all aspects of cannabis including historical, political, medicinal, and cultural. Comedian/actor/activist Tommy Chong said this about the book, "Are you a lover or hater of the pot world? In either case this book is for you, if you want to be enlightened. I knew the book was a winner as soon as I held it and felt the good vibrations. Read it and tell your friends."

Pot Culture: The A-Z Guide to Stoner Language & Life (Abrams Image, 2008)

AUTHORS: Shirley Halperin and Steve Bloom

SYNOPSIS: A great collection of all things pot and stoner-related with a stellar introduction by the man himself, Tommy Chong. This book highlights stoner subculture's path through the ages as well as new slang and how-to tips.

Pot Stickers (Cider Mill Press, 2010)

AUTHOR: Dr. Seymour Kindbud

SYNOPSIS: A book filled with useful stickers of every kind. It contains everything from "My Munchie" labels to keep your roommates away from your food to an "Organic Oregano" sticker for your weed jar. Also included are stickers to signal your stoner peers that you're down such as "Have you seen my girlfriend, Mary Jane?" and stickers to label different strains such as "White Widow" and "Kush."

The Quotable Stoner (Adams Media, Inc., 2011)

AUTHOR: Holden Blunts

SYNOPSIS: A great collection of weed-related and weed-inspired quotations. Take a minute to learn a few before a party and make your friends laugh or impress them with your wit.

Reefer Movie Madness: The Ultimate Stoner Film Guide (Abrams Image, 2010)

AUTHORS: Shirley Halperin and Steve Bloom

SYNOPSIS: A compilation of stoner movies of all shapes and sizes. Also included are contributions from actors, directors, and musicians. Great for finding a film for a doobie date night or just relaxing with friends.

The Savage Detectives: A Novel (Picador, 2008)

AUTHOR: Roberto Bolaño

SYNOPSIS: Two young exiles, Ulises Lima and Arturo Belano, go on an adventure in search of a poet they admire. Their travels take them through Mexico City, Barcelona, Israel, Liberia, and eventually the desert of northern Mexico. And it's all funded by the pair selling Acapulco

Gold, a high-grade marijuana strain, to Mexico City artists and students.

Spliffigami: Roll the 35 Greatest Joints of All Time (Ten Speed Press, 2008)

AUTHOR: Chris Stone

SYNOPSIS: A guide to rolling joints and blunts of all shapes and sizes. From perfecting the standard joint to multi-pronged masterpieces, this book covers the bases and will have you rolling in no time.

Stoner Coffee Table Book (Chronicle Books, 2001)

AUTHOR: Steve Mockus

SYNOPSIS: This colorful collection of art is filled with eye candy sure to keep you and your stoner friends intrigued for hours. Light up a joint and pass it around (the book—pass the book!). Gaze upon worlds unseen to the sober eye, and frolic in the pages of fine details and wondrous images.

Wonder Boys: A Novel (Random House Trade Paperbacks, 2008)

AUTHOR: Michael Chabon

SYNOPSIS: Grady Tripp is a professor whose life is not going exactly as planned. His second book is never ending (even at 1,000 pages), he's sleeping with his boss's wife right under his nose, and his talented writing assistant, James Leer, may in fact be mentally unstable. A little weed never hurt anyone trying to take the edge off, especially not in Hollywood! A great look into the American fame machine.

POTHEAD POETS

MAYA ANGELOU (b. 1928)

Maya Angelou is a groundbreaking African American female poet, author, and social activist. In her autobiography *Gather Together In My Name*, she references "grifa," a slang term for marijuana.

From *Gather Together In My Name:*

"You like grifa?"

"Yes. I smoke." The truth was I had smoked cigarettes for over a year, but never marijuana. But since I had the unmitigated gall to sit up cross-legged in a lesbian apartment sipping wine, I felt I had the stamina to smoke a little grifa. Anyway, I was prepared to refuse anything else they offered me, so I didn't feel I could very well refuse the pot.

JIM CARROLL (1949–2009)

Jim Carroll was an author, poet, and innovator in the punk music scene. His 1978 autobiography *The Basketball Diaries* was his most famous work and featured stories of his troubled youth, including sneaking around to smoke marijuana.

From the poem *Dealers:*

Polaroid filter...clandestined drop-offs

Substituting the twigs of Thai

for the weeds of dill... cautious

ALLEN GINSBERG (1926–1997)

A prominent figure of the Beat Generation in the 1950s, Ginsberg was a poet and social activist. His legendary poem "Howl" was the subject of an obscenity trial in 1957, when prosecutors argued it contained "filthy, vulgar, obscene, and disgusting language." Though shocking to some of the culture at the time, the judge ruled that the poem was not obscene, saying, "Would there be any freedom of press or speech if one must reduce his vocabulary to vapid innocuous euphemisms?"

From *America* (1956):

... I'd better consider my national resources.

My national resources consist of two joints of

marijuana millions of genitals an unpublishable

private literature that goes 1400 miles an hour

and twenty-five-thousand mental institutions ...

JACK KEROUAC (1922–1969)

One of the great America poets and novelists, Kerouac was a pioneer of the Beat Generation.

From *American Haiku*:

Wash hung out

by moonlight

Friday night in May.

The bottoms of my shoes

are clean

from walking in the rain.

Glow worm

sleeping on this flower —

your light's on.

JOHN SINCLAIR (b. 1941)

Poet, writer, music scholar, political activist, and pioneer of marijuana activism. Sinclair was arrested in 1969 for providing two joints to an undercover narcotics officer. Though sentenced for ten years, protests and performances from Allan Ginsberg, John Lennon, and Stevie Wonder and many others during the "John Sinclair Freedom Rally" in Ann Arbor, Michigan, helped prompt Sinclair's release. Ann Arbor's pro-legalization "Hash Bash" still occurs annually.

From *Sendin' The Vipers:*

Way back in the day

when marijuana was something

people smoked in Mexico

or Mexicans brought with them

to the United States

& smoked quietly amongst themselves

there were musicians

in New Orleans & Los Angeles & Chicago

who were introduced to weed

by their Mexican friends

& began to apply its magical properties

to the shaping of the new music...

SHEL SILVERSTEIN (1930–1999)

Shel Silverstein was most famous for his children's books and poetry including, such classics as *A Light In The Attic* and *The Giving Tree*. He was also a skilled cartoonist and musician who wrote comedy songs for a more adult/pot-friendly audience. Songs include "I Got Stoned And I Missed It" and "The Smoke-Off," a song about a joint-rolling contest.

Lyrics from *The Smoke-Off:*

... In the laid-back California town of sunny San Raphael

Lives a girl named Pearly Sweetcake you probly know her well

She's been stoned twenty-one of her twenty-four years and the story's widely told

How she still can smoke 'em faster than anyone can roll

While off in New York City on a street that has no name

There's the hands of the Calistoga Kid in the Viper Hall of Fame

And underneath his fingers there's a little golden scroll

That says "Beware of Bein' the Roller When There's Nothin' Left to Roll"

FUN AND GAMES

Time to sit back on a Friday night and enjoy some stoner games with your friends. The next section highlights the best stoner and weed-related games. Grab a beer and the bong and let the games begin.

GRASS CARD GAME

This game, first packaged in 1979, includes a deck of cards in a real hemp bag and will keep you entertained for hours.

Now published by Eurogames and Ventura International, it is available from a variety of retailers including funagain. com and Amazon.com.

1,000 WEED GAMES

This bundle of board games will liven up your party. It features some original games as well as some reworked classics

that are geared toward smoking. It is available from WildPartyGames.com.

STONER GAMES

Stonergames.net website has a ton of animated online games all about pot. Don't forget to check out Weed Wizard in which you are a wizard flying on a dragon made out of smoke coming from your bong trying to avoid munchies and collect pot. Another classic is Who Wants to Smoke My Honey Bear?, an adaptation of *Who Wants to Be A Millionaire?* with trivia about weed.

STONER TRIVIA

Have fun with your buds playing this card game that includes trivia in categories such as Stoner Movies, Music, History, Paraphernalia, Law, Medicine, Sports, Television, Unjust Bust, World Culture, and Horticulture. www.StonerTrivia.com.

CHAPTER 3

420: THE CANNABIS SUBCULTURE

What's happening in the world of cannabis? It's everywhere you turn, it seems, and in places you'd never expect it to be. These fun facts and wild tales will amaze you and help you win stoned arguments with your buds.

BOB DYLAN AND THE BEATLES

Bob Dylan smoked The Beatles up for the first time. When Dylan met the Beatles I'm sure they were both excited to be in each other's company. Dylan may have been one step ahead of his British peers and takes the credit for introducing them to the ganja and most likely influencing the direction of rock music history.

The Brain's Automatic Synchronization of Audio and Visual Input

The brain is a powerful instrument. Though we understand very little about many of its functions, we observe certain phenomena, one of which is our brain's ability to make acoustic sound input appear to synchronize with visual input. Have you ever put on a cartoon turned down the sound, and put on a record? Before you know it, your brain will begin making connections and linking sounds to the visual. A classic example of this phenomenon is synchronizing Pink Floyd's *Dark Side of the Moon* with *The Wizard of Oz*. Far out.

CANNABIS CUP

In 1987, Steven Hager, editor and chief of *High Times* magazine, founded the Cup, which takes place each year in Amsterdam. Judges and growers come from around the globe to participate in the contest in the cannabis capital of the world. Judges get to sample each strain, then an overall winner is selected as well as winners of subcategories such as best hash, best glass-blown piece, and best new product. They also induct honorary members each year. Past inductees include Bob Marley (1997), Louis Armstrong (1998), William S. Burroughs, Allen Ginsberg, and Jack Kerouac (1999), Bob Dylan (2002), Jack Herer (2003), Tommy Chong and Cheech Marin (2007), Peter Tosh (2008) Tom Forcade (2009), and Coke La Rock (2010).

Check out the strains that took the Cup home in years past:

- 1st Cup 1988—Skunk #1 from Cultivator's Choice
- 2nd Cup 1989—Early Pearl/Skunk #1 x Northern Lights #5/Haze from the Seed Bank
- 3rd Cup 1990—Northern Lights #5 from the Seed Bank
- 4th Cup 1991—Skunk from Free City
- 5th Cup 1992—Haze x Skunk #1 from Homegrown Fantasy
- 6th Cup 1993—Haze x Northern Lights #5 from Sensi Seed Bank
- 7th Cup 1994—Jack Herer from Sensi Seed Bank
- 8th Cup 1995—White Widow from the Green House
- 9th Cup 1996—White Russian from De Dampkring
- 10th Cup 1997—Peace Maker from De Dampkring
- 11th Cup 1998—Super Silver Haze from the Green House
- 12th Cup 1999—Super Silver Haze from the Green House
- 13th Cup 2000—Blueberry from the Noon
- 14th Cup 2001—Sweet Tooth from Barney's

- 15th Cup 2002—Morning Glory from Barney's
- 16th Cup 2003—Hawaiian Snow from Green House
- 17th Cup 2004—Amnesia Haze from Barney's
- 18th Cup 2005—Juicy Mango Haze from Barney's
- 19th Cup 2006—Arjan's Ultra Haze #1 from Green House
- 20th Cup 2007—G-13 Haze from Barney's
- 21st Cup 2008—Super Lemon Haze from Green House United
- 22nd Cup 2009—Super Lemon Haze from Green House United
- 23rd Cup 2010—Tangerine Dream from Barney's
- 24th Cup 2011—Liberty Haze from Barney's

D.A.R.E.

The Drug Abuse Resistance Education organization was founded in Los Angeles in 1983. It educates youth on the harms of drugs, which in and of itself is not a bad thing.

But the approach to cannabis has been less than satisfactory to many. D.A.R.E. is led by police officers, police officers follow the law, and marijuana is against the law, therefore it is a harmful drug. It's that simple.

Death by Doobie

According to Martin Booth's book *Cannabis: A History* (London: Doubleday, 2003), it would take 800 joints to kill a person and the cause of death would be carbon monoxide poisoning. Pull out that nugget next time someone's giving you the old "pot kills" spiel.

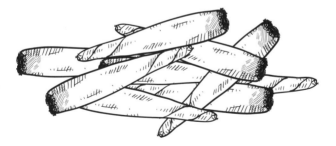

Grand Theft Auto Videogame

Rockstar Games release of Grand Theft Auto brought pot dealing to mainstream gaming. You can also run over pedestrians, kill hookers, and a whole plethora of other sins, so it may not necessarily be your cup of tea, or maybe it is. With a whole catalog of Grand Theft Auto games there's a lot of fun to be had.

High Times Magazine

One of the most powerful voices behind cannabis culture, *High Times,* started in 1974 by Tom Forcade, has been and continues to be the voice that fights for debate and reason in the battle to discuss and legalize marijuana. It is said that the magazine started as a parody of *Playboy* with cannabis substituted for women. However, the magazine became widely popular in stoner subculture. *High Times* does so much for the cannabis community, including the Stony Awards, the

High Times Freedom Fighters, and let's not forget, publishing an amazing magazine that has the balls the stand up for what its contributors and so many of us believe in.

Holy Smoke

Prisoners in Vancouver, B.C. have been known to uses pages of the Bible to roll their joints. Hard times.

Kindbud Koalas

In Australia, legend has it that koalas are drawn and addicted to eucalyptus leaves due to their narcotic effect on them. Koalas and stoners may have more in common than previously thought. Hmmm.

Marijuana, the Origin of the Term (or marihuana)

The term *marijuana* came to the United Stated in the late 1800s from Mexico. It is believed that Mexicans had adapted it from the Spanish pronunciation of the name *Mary Jane* that has also become a common term for the herb.

The McGurk Effect

The mysteries of nature and the human condition never cease to amaze. The McGurk effect states that the visual cortex has the ability to override auditory input. In one study a man stands before a camera and repeatedly speaks the syllable "ba." The viewer hears "ba" as they see it spoken. Next the man repeats the syllable "fa" in front of the camera while the original audio is stilled played. You may not believe it until you see for yourself, but Dr. Kindbud promises you, you will hear "fa." Seeing the man's lips pronounce "fa" makes the human mind hear "fa" and seeing the man pronounce "ba" with the exact same audio makes us hear "ba." No matter how many times you go back and forth the effect remains. Go on… YouTube it.

Passing the Drug Test

Since the invention of drug testing in 1972 by Manfred Donike, people have been trying to beat it. Common methods of circumvention include the chugging of different liquids such as water, cranberry juice, and even vinegar leading up to the test, exercise that induces sweating, and even smuggling in someone else's clean urine to pass off as their own. However, as technology got more sophisticated, other factors came into play such as the sample's temperature and in some cases even monitored sample collection. But just as there have been advances with the test giver's technology so have there been advances in test circumvention techniques. These days you can even buy a realistic prosthetic penis that can be used to pass a monitored test. Check out http://www.ureasample.com. Another option is a powdered clean urine and test tube heat-strip kit that provides clean results. Kits can be purchased at http://www.testclear.com.

The Pot vs. Alcohol Debate Method

Some people still shudder when they think about the horrors they've heard about relating to cannabis consumption. From the days of *Reefer Madness* there has often been much propaganda surrounding the earthly herb that so many find pleasure in ingesting. Take note of the debate points below. Hopefully one of these should put an end to the debating and a beginning to the toking.

Debate Points:

1. **Death Rate.** No one ever dies from smoking weed. According to the 2007 National Vital

Statistics Reports, 23,199 people died from alcohol-related causes. Granted some of these were accidental poisonings, but the report does not include unintentional injuries, homicides, or infant deaths from fetal alcohol syndrome. How many lives did weed claim in 2007? Marijuana is not even listed in the report.

2. **The Aggressive Stoner?** When is the last time you heard your friend tell a story about how he was sooooo stoned hanging in a club when a guy at the bar made a crack at him and he ended up getting in fight? How many news stories can you recall where a man was high on cannabis and was arrested for being abusive to friends or family?

3. **The Hangover.** Next time your friend is hanging over the toilet in the morning from too much sauce after the night before and you

rise slightly hazy (at worst), feel good that you have not tortured your body to such a great extent. A weed stupor is nothing compared to an alcohol hangover.

Prices Across America

Depending on what region you reside in North America you may be allocating more or less of your budget to your smoking habit than others. Typically (as of 2011) the West Coast of the United States and all of Canada has the cheapest weed. Centrally located states in the United States such as Kansas are known for steep prices, as well as much of the East Coast. Check out the website www.priceofweed.com for up-to-date polling statistics.

The Sink Saver

Yes, your mom may have noticed that those little metal

screens inside the faucet keep disappearing, but will she ever really catch on? These screens also sold in many tobacco shops are one of the best tools in a smoker's arsenal. Place one inside your bowl to ensure no one will be eating ash and also to prevent good bud from going down the "drain" prematurely.

The Stony Awards

An annual event sponsored by *High Times* magazine where awards are presented for the very best stoner films and television. It began as an article written by *High Times* Senior Editor Steve Bloom, and when it was suggested that a public event be held to celebrate they went for it. The first Stony Awards took place in New York City and continued to do so until moving to Los Angeles in 2007. They don't happen every year, just most years (this is *High Times!*). There's no shortage of celebrities on hand, from Snoop Dogg to Doug Benson.

Tie-Dye

Ken Kesey and his Merry Pranksters had just indulged in some LSD by a lake when a prankster decided to float oil-based paints in the water. To mess with a friend, they grabbed his last clean white T-shirt and submerged into the paint-filled water swirling it around. The result… the first tie-dyed t-shirt, a huge hit with hippies of the past and present, and most likely future.

WAMM

WAMM stands for the Wo/Men's Alliance for Medical Marijuana. This collective of patients and caregivers is based in Santa Cruz, California. For patients with a doctor's recommendation, this community provides organic medicinal marijuana on a donation basis. Check them out at www.wamm.org.

THE WORD

Across the globe, stoners rejoice, relax, commiserate, and celebrate in a variety of styles and settings. Due to the illicit nature of cannabis in many countries, unique slang has evolved in communities around the world. Some terms have grown to national recognition while others are used on a local level. Some are scientific in origin and some are just plain goofy. New terms are constantly being created. The following section is a compilation of lingo from across the globe. If you and your friends are looking for some new code words to throw the parents off your scent, bring back a classic from Harlem in the 1920s (unless your family grew up in 1920s Harlem). Maybe you were always too embarrassed to ask what exactly a percolator is? Fret not, this section will get you up to speed.

Terms:

- ¼. Refers to one quarter of an ounce, a common quantity sold at consumer level.

- ⅛. Refers to one eighth of an ounce, a common quantity sold at consumer level.

- 420, 4:20, ⁴⁄₂₀. Many myths and legends claim to be the true origin of 420. Is it a police code for smoking? Could it be a hidden message from a Dylan song referring to pot? As the term has gained popularity in pot subculture, it has come to mean a lot of things to a lot of people. The following is the true story of the slang's origin as first reported by Steven Hagar for *High Times* magazine. The term was created and first used by a group of five San Rafael High School students dubbed the Waldos, who were named for their hangout spot, a wall outside of their high school. In the fall of 1971 the five students heard a rumor that a Coast Guard service member had to leave and abandon his crop. They decided to meet up after athletic practice at 4:20 by a statue of Louis Pasteur and go search for the crops. Originally the full term they would exchange when passing in the halls was 4:20-Louis, but eventually the Louis was dropped. They never did find the crop but had some great times searching, and a slang term was born. They are credited with the creation because they have provided proof in the form of dated letters in which the term was used and is, to date, the earliest written appearance of "4:20." Today it is a time of day when people gather and smoke; April 20 has become a national holiday in pot subculture where large groups gather in parks and city centers to celebrate; and 4:20 is an all-around code word for weed-related activities.

- Aunt Mary. A term for cannabis. Doesn't she sound sweet?

- Ash Catcher. (1.) A secondary water-filled chamber that slides in and out of the main chamber providing extra filtering and prevention of ash entering the main chamber. (2.) A cone that allows joints to be smoked hands-free without ash falling on the floor.

- Baked. A term for being high.

- Blaze. A verb meaning *to smoke*. "Let go blaze!" Blazed may also be used as an adjective to describe someone who is high.

- Blunt. A hollowed-out cigar filled with cannabis and smoked like a joint.

- Bogart. To mindlessly hold onto a smoking device without regard to others anxiously awaiting their turn.

- Bodega. A corner convenient/liquor store. The term comes from the Spanish word for grocery store. Bodegas may also covertly sell pot.

- Bong. A term brought back to the United States in the 1970s by soldiers returning from Thailand who had taken up the locals' practice of smoking cannabis out of *baung* pipes. These pipes, also known as water pipes, are made up of three simple components: the bowl/stem, in which you put your smoking product, the main chamber, which is partially filled with liquid, and a mouthpiece, from which you inhale. There are many variations, upgrades, and additions available to the standard bong such as additional chambers, ice catchers, and sliding male and female bowl/stem pieces (used to act as a carb). The physics of a bong are fairly simple. As your mouth draws air through the mouthpiece, air is pulled through the bowl, through the slide (or other connector), into

the water in the main chamber and up to your mouth.

- Boom. A slang term for marijuana.

- Bud. The flower of the female cannabis plant that is dried and consumed.
Also a general term for marijuana.

- Buddha. A term for marijuana.

- Burn-out. Occurs when a user becomes unresponsive in
speech or action.

- Bush. A British slang term for weed.

- Cannabis. Oh where to begin? If not for this mighty
flowering herb this book wouldn't even exist. Canna-
 bis, when smoked in dried
flower form, produces a high
primarily induced by one of
its psychoactive molecules tetrahydrocannabinol, or THC.
Besides producing a great high,

cannabis also can be used to produce hemp. Hemp can be used to manufacture a plethora of resources including paper, clothing, rope, and even hemp milk.

- *Cannabis Indica.* One of the two strains of psychoactive marijuana. Two good examples of varietals that are 100 percent indica are Afghani Kush (A-K) and Double Whammy.

- *Cannabis sativa.* The scientific name used around the world for the plant we know as marijuana and hemp. It has two strains: sativa and indica. (Learn about the taxonomy of Cannabis in the Far-Out Science chapter.)

- Carburetor or carb. A secondary air supply into the main chamber of a bong used to clear smoke out of the pipe.

- Cashed. A bowl whose contents have been completely used.

- Chamber. A component of a water pipe, or bong, where the smoke collects before inhalation. Some bongs have multiple chambers to filter the smoke.

- Cheeba. A term for marijuana.

- Chillum. A small pipe usually used for covert smoking. Generally chillums are a straight shot from the bowl to the mouthpiece with no added extras. Also known as a Oney, One-Hitter, Bat and Dugout.

- Chronic. A term for superior quality marijuana.

- Clear. A verb meaning to draw fresh air into the chamber in order to clear all the smoke out of the pipe through the mouthpiece.

- College. A verb derived from the phrase "to give it a college try." Used when asking the next smoker in a rotation if they would like to try to get one last hit off a joint that is almost finished.

- Diffuser. A slide with a sealed bottom with made tiny holes in it. This serves to break the smoke in smaller bubbles within the water. This provides more smoke filtering and cooler smoke.

- Dime bag. Ten bucks' worth of weed.

- Dispensary. A U.S. state-certified retailer of cannabis for medicinal use. States where you can find a dispensary include California, Rhode Island, and Colorado.

- Doob-age. One or more doobies or joints.

- Doobie. A slang term for a joint. Sounds fun doesn't it?

- Dopamine. A chemical in one's brain that is released upon intake of THC. Dopamine is responsible for many functions in the body and brain including that great feeling of being high.

- Dope. A term for marijuana.

- Drag. A single inhalation from a joint.

- Fried. Someone who has smoked a large quantity of marijuana and has become momentarily unintelligent. This term is also commonly used to describe a person tripping on a hallucinogen such as LSD.

- Fuming. The process in which a glassblower allows ions from burning gold and silver to penetrate the glass which creates a "color changing" piece.

- Gage/gauge. A term for marijuana.

- Ganja. A term for marijuana.

- Grass. Slang for marijuana.

- Green. Did you think green only referred to money? Nope! Green is also slang for marijuana.

- Grifa. A term meaning marijuana used by Maya Angelou in her autobiography *Gather Together In My Name*.

- Hashish/Hasheesh or Hash. A concentrated resin created from the flowers of the female cannabis plant. The resin may either be smoked or chewed.

- Hash oil. Resinous oil made by extracting THC into a solvent. It is known for having a very high THC content and may be smoked and ingested orally.

- Headshop. A store where pipes and tobacco-related

accessories are sold.

- Herb. Slang for cannabis.

- Hemp. The tough fiber created from the cannabis plant that can be used for cordage, fabrics, paper, fuel, and more.

- Hempster. An individual who is a proponent of the legalization and mainstream use of hemp as a resource.

- High. The state of being intoxicated from THC.

- Hippie. A term originating in the 1960s meaning a person who rejects the corporate atmosphere; projects love, compassion, and understanding; and is not fearful diving into the expanded consciousness. The movement and attitude developed in the '60s largely was a reaction and protest to the Vietnam War. Hippies are easily distinguished by their simple comfortable clothing, their free-love attitude, and their openness to others (at least that's how it should be!). Although not as prominent today, hippies still have their place, especially in cannabis

subculture. Keep your eye out for persons wearing Birkenstocks, beaded jewelry, and recycled garments.

- Hit. A verb meaning to take a single inhalation from a joint. May also be used as a noun meaning a single hit.

- Hootie-hoo. A call used to alert others that police have been spotted made popular by Outkast in the song "Slump" on the album *Aquemini*.

- Hybrid. A cannabis plant created by breeding multiple strains.

- Jazz cigarettes. Slang for a joint, paying homage to the jazz and blues musicians of the 1920s and '30s.

- Jive. A term for marijuana used by early jazz musicians.

- Jonesing. A verb meaning to have a strong craving or urge for a substance usually related to drug use.

- Kaya. A slang term for marijuana brought into pop culture by Mr. Bob Marley himself.

- Kief/Keef/Kif. The word *kif* derives from the Arabic word *kayf,* meaning pleasure or well-being. The trichomes, which are the resin glands of the cannabis plant, contain a concentrated amount of THC. Kief can gather at the bottom of weed sacks and jars or be removed from cannabis buds with a mesh screen or sieve. Many marijuana grinders have a kief collector compartment. Kief can be smoked, vaporized, or made into hashish.

- Kind or kind bud. A high-quality top-notch strain of cannabis.

- Marijuana. The dried flowers from the female cannabis plant.

- Marijuana County. A nickname for Medocino County, where pot is grown and smoked in quantum proportions.

- Marijaweed. A joining of two great words to create an even greater word that means exactly the same thing the words meant individually!

- Mary Jane. Everyone's favorite lady (that you can smoke). A term for pot.

- Medicated. The official/legal term used for a stoned person after smoking medicinal marijuana.

- Medicinal marijuana. Pot prescribed by a physician for a variety of ailments including cancer and multiple sclerosis.

- Mellow. A slang term used in the 1920s and '30s as an adjective meaning high.

- Muggles. A slang term for marijuana used by jazz musicians in the 1920s and '30s.

- The munchies. The compulsion to eat anything and everything while stoned.

- Nickel bag. Five dollars' worth of weed.

- Nugget (or nug). A bud from the flower of the cannabis plant, dried and ready to smoke.

- Perculator. A secondary chamber of a bong filled with water that purifies the smoke as it filters it through a second stage of water.

- Piece. An alternate name for a marijuana pipe.

- PoPo. Slang for a police officer.

- Pot. A term for cannabis.

- Prop 19. A California proposition to allow persons to grow 25 square feet of marijuana for personal use. It did not pass.

- Psychedelic. A mental state of conscious awareness described as a sense of intensified perception and emotions, hallucinations, and profound thoughts. Often used to describe an LSD or magic mushroom trip.

- Puff. An inhalation of smoke from a joint or alternative smoking device.

- Reefer. A term for cannabis. Also can refer to a joint.

- Resin. A sticky black substance that results as a byproduct of burning herbs. After a few uses, resin buildup will be noticeable in a pipe, eventually leading to clogging if not scraped or cleaned.

- Roach. The leftover butt of a smoked joint. There are four options: (1.) Smoke the joint in its entirety using a roach clip. (2.) Save it to be scavenged through at a later date when you're hurting for weed. (3.) Eat it! (4.) Discard it.

- Rolling filter. A cardboard strip that is rolled into the mouth end of a joint. This method is particularly popular in Europe.

- Rotation. The order in which the smoking device is passed around. As in, "Don't mess up the rotation!"

- Sack. Slang for a bag of weed.

- Shwag. A slang term for poor grade marijuana.

- Screen. The small circular screen that is used to put in the bowl component of a pipe to stop marijuana shake from being sucked through prematurely.

- Stems and seeds. Many stoners find themselves nearing the end of their bag, reach in to pack a bowl and find that all that remains are stems and seeds. These are the least potent sections of the cannabis plant. But don't necessarily dispose of them! Stems do contain some THC and can be great for making THC butter or oil.

- Session. A group of people enjoying a smoke together.

- Shake. The broken-up bud fragments, hairs, and crystals that inevitably end up falling off big weed flowers in a sack or jar. Usually the buds are the first to be smoked leaving behind a stash of shake (which is great for rolling joints and can be very potent).

- Shotgun. An exchange between two or more smokers. Smoker #1 takes a hit off a joint, then before exhaling places the lit end of the joint carefully in his mouth. He then exhales his hit through the joint into the mouth of smoker #2.

- Sieve. A woven mesh or net screen often used for sifting flower. May also be used for removing kief from marijuana buds.

- Sinsemilla. Marijuana buds from the female plant that contain a very high THC content.

- Skunk. A variety of weed known for its skunky smell. Pee-Yew!

- Slide. A slide is made up of two parts, a male and a female. The female piece secures to pipe while the male easily slides into it creating an airtight seal. The slide is very useful because it serves as a carb to clear the smoke as well as the bowl piece.

- Smoke. As a verb, it means to inhale. As a noun, it may be used as slang for cannabis.

- Smoke up. To smoke pot.

- Smoking circle. A group of smokers gathered in a circle passing weed around. Every stoner knows the circle is the most efficient shape for smoking pot.

- Space cake. Street name for a brownie or cake that has been baked with THC butter or oil.

- Splif or spliff. A joint rolled with a mixture of cannabis and tobacco. It some circles, it can also refer to a joint rolled from just cannabis.

- Stash. A bag of pot hidden in a location known only by the owner (and maybe a few stoner friends).

- Sticky-icky. Snoop Dogg uses this word to refer to high-quality marijuana buds that are extra sticky.

- Stoned. High on THC.

- Stuff. Slang for pot.

- T or tea. A term for marijuana mainly used by musicians in Harlem in the 1930s and '40s.

- Tea pad. Slang for a Harlem jazz club where musicians would gather late into the evening. Used in the 1930s and '40s.

- Tea party. A term used by blues and jazz musicians of the 1920s and '30s.

- THC. Acronym and street name for Tetrahydrocannabinol, the main active ingredient in marijuana.

- Toke. As a verb, it means to smoke weed. As a noun, it means a single hit of weed.

- Trees. Slang for marijuana.

- Viper. A term used in the 1930s by jazz musicians for a marijuana smoker.

- Wake and bake. The practice of waking up and partaking in a smoking session. This usually leaves the brain in a fog, which some people enjoy, since the brain hasn't had time to sufficiently wake up.

- Weed. Slang for marijuana. You already know this, of course.

- Zip. Street term for one ounce of marijuana.

Tools and Accessories:

- Color-changing glass. Glassblowers often use a process called "fuming" to create a color-changing pipe. They burn gold and silver alloys and let the vapors pass through the hot glass. Metal ions attach to the glass. As smoke passes through the pipe, resin is deposited. The resin, which is black in color, provides a backdrop for the ions within the glass and the colors emerge. Want to start the process over? Just clean the pipe.

- Glass jar. Many smokers prefer to keep their stash in a glass jar because it keeps the herb fresh and also is better at keeping the weed smell contained while traveling or in public.

- Grinder. A plastic or metal container that has teeth fixed to the inside walls that break nuggets of weed apart.

- Kief box. A compartment in a grinder that uses a silk-screen to scrape off the bud's resin glands, or crystals, and collects them for potent smoking.

- Nag Champa. Famous incense used by stoners across the globe. Just one whiff of this incense makes many stoners feel right at home.

- Purple Power 420 Cleaning Solution. A liquid cleaning

solution for glass pipes and bongs.

- Roach clip. A pair of tweezers, or similar device, used to hold a joint once it has gotten too small and hot to hold with bare hands. Some have used a matchstick with the cardboard split in half.

- Tobacco rolling machine. Most self-respecting smokers believe the skill and art that goes into rolling a joint is a matter of honor, a part of the habitual nature of pot smoking. But for those who prefer not to, a rolling machine will give you solid smokable joint. Also great for mass production for a party.

- Rolling filter. Usually made from a curled up strip of cardboard or thicker paper and rolled into the unlit end of a joint. There are several benefits to using a filter, including keeping a clear airway for inhalation and avoiding the need to have a bunch of roaches lying around stinking up the place.

Etiquette:

- Puff, puff, give. There are different customs and practices across the world, but in the United States many practice the puff, puff, give method. This means that each smoker should feel free to hit the joint or bowl two times and then pass it on to the left.

- Pass to the left. The first known instance of this rule is found if the song "Pass the Kutchie" by the Mighty Diamonds, later adapted and popularized by the group Musical Youth. If you're standing in a smoking circle, pass to the left.

- Keep your glass clean. No one wants to come over and smoke through crusty old resin-filled glass. It tastes bad, it blocks airflow, and it's just not polite.

- Don't bogart the joint. When the joint comes to you enjoy it, take your time with it, but do NOT overdo it. Don't start telling a story while your holding the joint, or step outside the circle. You'll make everyone else nervous.

- Paying it forward. If someone smokes you out, make sure you get them back at some point. You don't want your friends thinking you're the stoner mooch in the group.

- Stepping in on an existing smoking circle. Don't just barge in on a smoking circle without being invited. If you have a friend in the group, approach them first and check out the vibe. Otherwise, just get close enough that someone in the group notices you. If they offer, you're in, if not wander around for a bit.

- The sneaky smoke. Don't think the party doesn't notice when you and your select friends sneak off to some remote location to enjoy your herb in peace. Retreat one at a time by route of a restroom and avoid hurting people's feelings.

WAYS TO GET BAKED

The Classic Pipe

A classic pipe is made up of three components. First there

is the bowl, which is a receptacle open on one end that is connected to a chamber with a mouthpiece at the end. Herb is placed in the bowl and a flame is held over it as a smoker inhales. Many pipes have additional features such as a carb or color-changing glass.

The Bong

- The classic bong. The classical bong is made up of a vertical tubular chamber that is partially filled with water, a bowl whose stem goes into the water, and a mouth piece or opening at the top of the tube.

- The slide bong. The slide bong is the same as the classical bong except that the bowl is attached to a glass slide that is used to clear the pipe.

- The bubbler. The bubbler is another

variation on the classic bong that a carb is used to clear the pipe. Many bubblers are horizontal in design.

- Gravity/waterfall. A gravity bong uses water and gravity to draw smoke into a container. These can be made in many variations. The basic physics involve submerging a container in water and then displacing the water out a secondary hole in it to create airflow through a smoking bowl. A waterfall bong is a variation on a gravity bong where the water is released as a waterfall out the bottom of the container to draw smoke into the chamber.

- Hookah. A hookah is a tobacco pipe originating from the East. Smoke is drawn through a chamber with water in it and into a long tube with a mouthpiece at the end. Some hookahs have multiple tubes so that more than one smoker may partake at the same time.

Alternate Smoking Methods

• Rush tube. A rush tube is a long cylindrical tube that is used to inhale large amounts of smoke quickly. You can use anything you can get your hands on, even a didgeridoo!

• Vaporizer. A vaporizer uses a precision-controlled heating element to heat herbs to the point when THC is extracted in vapor form. The herbs are not actually burned, thus saving the smoker inhalation of carcinogenic matter. The heating element is attached to a bowl that fills a bag or receptacle with the vapor.

- Hot knives. Hot knives is a method used to smoke hash. Two knives are heated on a stove (or other heating element). Once the knives are hot, a piece of hash is placed on one knife and then covered with the other. The sandwiched hash will begin to smoke and is usually just inhaled by holding the knives close to the mouth.

Alternate THC Consumption Methods

- THC alcohol. THC is alcohol-soluble. In some countries, this drink is produced freely.

- THC tea. Although there's not nearly as much THC content in cannabis leaves, they may be brewed into teas and may have a mild effect. For a bigger punch you may use nuggets, but remember THC is not very soluble in boiling water. If you want it to pack a bigger punch add a little oil or butter to soak up the THC.

- Hashish. A purified resin that is made from the cannabis plant and either smoked or chewed.

- THC med-strips. These medicinal beauties look just like a Listerine breath strip. The only difference is that these are packed with 625mg of THC. Convenient, covert, and tasty!

- THC breath spray. Available at medicinal dispensaries, this method of THC intake is a portable, convenient method many prefer.

Stealth Pipes

- The Highlighter (or Hi-Liter) Decoy. A functioning but hollow "Hi-Liter" with a removable base that reveals a small metal bowl. It is easily concealed and perfect for traveling. Available online at http://www.jupitergrass.ca/.

- The Car Lighter Decoy. Portable, convenient, and super covert, the car lighter fits right into your car's outlet.

Simply pull it out for a toke and stash it securely. Available online at http://www.pipesguru.com/.

Types of Joints

- The basic. This is a simple joint consisting of marijuana rolled into a single paper.

- The cone. The cone is a variation on the basic joint in which the weed is placed in the paper it is rolled on an angle so the mouth end is smaller than the sparking end.

- The cross joint. Made famous from the stoner flick *Pineapple Express* this joint illustrates a mastering of joint rolling (and perhaps a little too much free time). This joint is fabricated by intersecting three joints into the shape of a cross and lighting them all at the same time. Stoner friend required!

- The filtered joint. This joint's name is a little misleading. The smoke is not actually filtered but a rolled-up strip of cardboard is rolled into a hollow cylindrical shape and placed into the mouth-end of the joint. This cuts down on waste and does away with the need for roach clips.

Ways to Hide Pot Smoke

• Burn incense. A little incense, such as Nag Champa, can really do the trick and throw others off your scent. It is a pleasant-smelling alternative that shouldn't bother the neighbors.

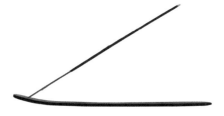

• Dryer sheet filter tube. It's time to sneak into the laundry room and snag a few scented dryer sheets. Then it's down to the kitchen to grab a discarded cardboard paper towel roll. Shove the dryer sheets into one end of the paper towel roll. After you take a hit, exhale through the other end of the tube. Mmmmm… smells like fresh laundry.

- Exhale tube. You will have to get some sort of long hollow cylindrical tube with holes on either ends such as a lacrosse stick or some broom handles. Hopefully it's not too cold outside. Crack a window and extend one end of the tube so it's sticking outside. Exhale through this tube, capping it with your hand after you blow out. All the smoke will end up outside. Just be careful you're not shooting it right into your neighbor's window.

- Towel the door. This simple task can save your ass. Twist a towel up and use it to seal the small air gap between your floor and the door. Also make sure if it's windy that you don't have any windows open creating a draft flowing out of your room.

HOW TO MAKE HASH

Bubble Hash

Throughout the world, hash is made and sold in large quantities. In many European countries as well as Morocco, India, and Thailand, it is more readily available than fresh green cannabis. This is partly due to the fact that it doesn't smell as much, is easier to transport, and many crops are grown specifically to produce hash. These strains generally produce a lower-grade marijuana, and the crops are easier to care for.

In countries such as Amsterdam, Canada, and the United States, smaller growers generally tend to put the quality of the crop first to be sold locally, and the hash becomes a potent by-product shared with close, trusted friends. The actual makeup of hash is simply crystallized resin (trichomes) separated from the plant material. These crystals are concentrated THC.

Making hash is not a very hard process to learn but can be very tedious and messy. You will need the right tools and access to fresh cannabis leaf trimmings. For a couple hours of work, one can be rewarded with a small amount of the finest extract limited only by the quality of the trimmings.

Here's what you need:

- Extractor bags. These can be purchased at a local hydroponics store (used for extracting lavender oil and such) or online. They generally are sold in three or eight bags per set for $50 to $100. The eight-bag set will produce more refined hash, but for starting the three-bag set is sufficient.

- 5-gallon bucket

- Electronic mixer with paddles, rather than blades. A paint mixer attached to a drill can also work.

- About 10 pounds of ice

- A workspace. Generally a bathtub will work, or a garage.

- Fresh water. A detachable shower head or hose with a shower head is best.

- 90% isopropyl alcohol

- A plastic card. An old driver's license or credit card will work.

- A razor blade

- 4 ounces or more of fresh frozen plant trimmings. The larger leaves (sun leaves) can be left out or done in a separate batch but will not produce nearly as much as the leaves grown closer to the buds.

To start:

- Each bag has a silkscreen with micron grades. The higher the number, the fewer particles that will pass through the bag. Place the bags inside the 5-gallon bucket, one at a time, beginning with the highest micron grade. Fold the top portion of the bags over the top of the bucket. The top bag is called your "work bag" and will allow almost all particles through, including dirt and some small plant material.

- Fill the bags and the bucket ¼ full with cold water.

- Add about 4 to 6 ounces of trimmings.

- Fill the bucket with ice, leaving a couple inches at the top. Top off with more cold water.

- Stir the solution with your mixer for about 20 minutes. A foam or bubbles should appear. You can rinse off the mixer paddles and pop the bubbles with the spray nozzle on your shower head or garden hose.

- Let the mixture sit for 5–10 minutes. At this time most of the frozen trichromes have broken off of the plant material from the mixing and are sinking to the bottom of the water.

- Mix again for 10–15 minutes.

- Let the mixture sit for a final 30 minutes.

- Pull up your work bag and rinse the leftover material and insides of the bag. Gently squeeze out remaining water.

- Pull up the other bags one at a time, also rinsing the insides. At the bottom of each bag will be a clump of what looks like wet sand, which is your hash! Each bag will have a separate grade. Most trichromes are around 110 to 130 microns, which is where you should find most of your hash. The blonder hashes have less dirt and plant material, and therefore are more potent.

- Gently scrape the hash from the screen using the plastic card. Your bags should have come with a small press screen. You can wipe the hash on this and press out the remaining water with paper towels.

- Place on a plate or piece of glass to dry for several days or weeks, depending on humidity. The hash can also be pressed into shapes or wafers at this point. While drying, some oxidization will occur with any hash exposed to air, which will darken the color. The potency will not be affected.

- Clean up using the razor blades and isopropyl alcohol. Any bits scraped with the alcohol can be used; just wait until the alcohol has evaporated and the hash dried out. Do this in a well-ventilated area.

Enjoy a hit from a nice clean bong with a new screen. Examine the ash left on the screen. Whiter ash = purer hash!

CHAPTER 4

COOKING WITH CANNABIS

In this section, we aim to give you an understanding of how and why to cook with marijuana. While there is no denying the pleasure that one can attain from a more traditional joint, bowl, bong, blunt, or even vaporizer (sorry to all those that we left out), the benefits and uniqueness of the high from eating marijuana are at least as positive. First and foremost, it is one of the best ways to stay high without having to kill your lungs with smoke or smell like a dead skunk. The only way that eating marijuana will compromise your cardiovascular health is if you never leave the couch. At the same time, you no longer have to worry about being the "smelly pothead" at the party because there's no more stinky weed smoke sticking to your clothes.

Many people claim, in addition, that the high that you get from eating pot tends to be much more mellow and long-lasting than one experienced from smoking the plant. I say "tends to be" because you most definitely can get *very* high from eating marijuana, and it can, at times, be more intense than smoking. This depends on a number of variables that come up when cooking that will be discussed in greater detail below.

Applying heat or flame to cannabis causes the flower to release the plant's THC in the form of vapors or smoke. When you breathe these vapors in, the THC is absorbed into your bloodstream through your lungs, and it is then able to bind with the cannabinoid receptors in your brain, causing you to feel high almost immediately. The way that you get high from cooking marijuana is completely different and, therefore, so is the high itself. THC is itself an oil, which means that it is soluble in other fats and oils. **If you want to get high from eating marijuana, you need to first cook it in something oily or fatty. Eating a bud will not get you high, and if it does, you are still wasting a lot of good THC!**

Even if you do eat the marijuana that you've cooked in butter or oil, it will not be absorbed into your blood as quickly as it is when you smoke it. This is because you need to begin to digest the oil/butter, and, in short, means that it will take longer for the high to kick in. Depending on the strength of the butter/oil, the metabolism of the person, and a variety of other factors, the exact amount of time that it does take to kick in could be anywhere between 15 minutes and an hour and a half (usually closer to the latter). BE PATIENT! There are countless stories of people who ate more and more and more brownies because "they didn't feel anything" and later ended up curled up in a ball sucking their thumb in the corner for twelve hours straight. Don't be that person!

When you do finally start to feel high, it may be very different than what you are used to from smoking. The intensity depends largely on the potency of your butter, something that will be discussed later in this chapter. But you can expect anything from a nice warm feeling in your belly and the giggles to something that feels closer to an acid trip than your usual high.

SPREAD THE SMILES

DESSERTS TEND TO BE A FAVORITE, BUT REMEMBER YOU CAN MAKE ANYTHING THAT CALLS FOR BUTTER OR OIL SPECIAL. SPREAD IT ON YOUR MORNING TOAST TO MAKE THOSE OFFICE BLUES DISAPPEAR! MAKE LINGUINI WITH MUSSELS FOR YOUR LOVER AND SEE WHERE IT TAKES YOU! HAVE FUN, LIVE LIFE WITHOUT FEAR, AND REBEL WITH THE WHOLESOMENESS THAT IS OUR HUMAN SPIRIT!

Butter and Oil

Oil and butter are the easiest and most common ways to extract the THC from your marijuana. Which of the two you choose to make should depend on what exactly you are cooking. That is, if you want to make a very special salad dressing, weed oil would make more sense because olive oil is a base ingredient in so many dressings. If you are baking weed cookies, on the other hand, butter would probably be more effective because so many cookie recipes call for butter. If the proportions in your butter or oil are to your liking, you should be able to replace the butter or oil in any recipe with the same amount of your special butter or oil.

Before we offer our recipes for butter and oil, there are a couple of variables that need to be discussed that might

cause your homemade concoction to come out differently from ours:

Potency/percent THC of the marijuana that you are using. This will not only affect the strength of the butter or oil that you make but it will also affect the type of high that you get when you consume your tasty treats. Due to the fact that you are able to extract so much more THC from your marijuana by cooking it than by smoking it, many people prefer to use cheap, low-grade weed for their culinary experiments. The argument goes: "If I can get real high from cooking a bag of shwag, why not just smoke the good stuff and save some money on the butter/oil." Just like smoking, though, the quality of the high that you feel completely depends on the quality of the weed you're cooking. Not only will you have to use more weed to make up for the lower THC content, but you might also get some of the same nasty side-effects that you do from smoking low-grade (e.g., headaches, paranoia, general stupidity).

The part of the plant that you are cooking in the oil or butter. We have a few different options here:

• Buds. This is where all the THC is concentrated, so you won't need as much to make a good strong oil or butter. One disadvantage to using buds is that this is also the best part of the plant to smoke or vaporize. Bigger, denser nuggets typically mean more THC, so if you are going to cook with buds, it might be better to use smaller, less dense ones that are not as good for smoking but will still do the trick in the kitchen.

• Shake. This is a great option for people who get big jars of weed that collect shake, keef, and dust at the bottom between each re-up. Shake is as good for cooking as it is for rolling joints and is typically very potent because the bottom of the jar or bag is where THC crystals tend to settle. It's also already pretty finely ground, so there's no need to worry about breaking or chopping it up before adding it to the butter or oil.

- Leaf trimmings. This option is really only for the home growers out there, but it is a great way to waste as little of your plant(s) as possible. Leaf trimmings from close to the buds have much more THC than leaves that are further away from the flowers, which means that they are much more potent and that you will need less to make a strong oil or butter. These trimmings are also good for making hash because they become caked with the THC crystals that the nearby flower produces in the blooming process. Leaf trimmings that did not directly touch the buds can still have THC crystals on them, even if they are not visible with the naked eye. Cooking these leaves in oil or butter will extract this THC and, even though you will need to use more than any of the other options above, the effect will still be the same.

Disclaimers. Before you start cooking, there are a couple of things you should know.

- When you are cooking your oil or butter to start

and every time that you cook something with it after, your kitchen will inevitably smell like pot. You won't have an apartment full of smoke or the stench stuck to your clothes and body when you leave, but don't expect the weed to somehow lose that beautiful stink just because it's not being smoked!

- You should **test the strength** of your butter or oil **and be patient** when doing it. It can be tempting to spread two or three tablespoons of butter on a bagel as soon as it has finished hardening and cooling, but **be careful**! As stated before, the high takes longer to kick in, sometimes up to an hour and a half, so eat a little bit at a time, wait a couple of hours, and try a little bit more if the first bit did not have the desired effect. This very scientific process might take a week of solid experimentation (Weed-heads: write your quantities down so you don't forget), but it will be worth it in the end when you know exactly how much oil or butter it takes to get you as high as you want to get.

- Preferences are different for everybody... We recommend that you should be able to use the same amount of weed butter or oil in a recipe that you would use of normal butter or oil for that same recipe. If you want to get real high, make your butter a little stronger instead of using a half a cup in a

recipe that only calls for a quarter cup of butter (for example). That way, your food will come out the way you're used to it but with a slight taste of your favorite plant.

"GREEN" BUTTER

INGREDIENTS AND SUPPLIES

1–2 pounds of butter (*this number depends on the variables discussed above and your personal preference for how strong you want the butter to be)

1 ounce of chronic (*this means the best marijuana money can buy [or at least in that ballpark])

A large pot

Cheesecloth

Strainer

Spoon or mixer

Bowls for straining

Tupperware to store butter

Funnel

DIRECTIONS

1. Weigh your weed and grind it up as finely as you want (whole buds, leaves, or even stems are fine, grinding it can just make it a little easier to work with).

2. Place a cooking pot ½ to ⅔ full with water on high heat. Add weed to the water as it comes to a boil. Stir for 5–7 minutes.

3. Reduce heat and simmer for 45–60 minutes, stirring occasionally. This will begin to break down the THC.

4. Add the butter to the mix. Because THC is *fat-soluble,* we need something fatty for it to bond with. We add the butter so that the cannabinoids that we crave so much and that have been breaking down for the last hour have something to bond with. Stir until all the butter melts, and simmer for as long as you want, stirring occasionally (we recommend 1–3 hours).

5. Clear a table or counter space for your straining bowl. Put a cheesecloth inside of the strainer and place it into the bowl. Dump the concoction through the cheesecloth and strainer and into the new bowl. Squeeze the remaining liquid out of the cheesecloth and into the bowl that should now be free of leafs and buds and filled only with a buttery, watery liquid. Once you've gotten all the liquid out of the cheesecloth, you can throw away the green (all the THC should already be extracted!).

6. Refrigerate your butter-water for 24 hours so that the butter can harden.

7. After 24 hours, remove the bowl from the fridge and dump out the excess water. Place chunks of butter on paper towels and pat off excess water. Place these chunks of "green" butter (once they have been patted down and touched-up to your liking) in a pan and melt until you have a liquid again. Using your funnel, carefully put the melted butter in containers for storage. Let them cool without lids on the counter until they are cool enough to refrigerate. Then, of course, cover and refrigerate.

"GREEN" OIL

INGREDIENTS AND SUPPLIES

1 ounce of chronic semi-finely ground pot (careful not to make it too fine, or it won't strain)

6 cups of canola oil

1 large pan or medium-size pot (an electronic slow cooker works best because it allows you to keep the temperature low)

Strainer/cheesecloth

Large bowl

Empty bottle

Funnel

DIRECTIONS

1. Place 6 cups of oil into pan/pot and heat on low heat.

2. Add chopped marijuana after the oil has had some time to heat up. Try to keep the temperature of the oil relatively low. You don't want to sauté the marijuana; you want it to slowly cook in the oil so that the THC can be extracted and absorbed by the fat.

3. Simmer on low heat constantly stirring for 15-30 minutes. Let the mixture cool, then reheat and repeat as many times as you'd like. This is a many-day process for some people. Be patient and allow the mixture to cool and reheat completely each time.

4. Strain out the remaining leafy materials and carefully pour the green oil into a jar or bottle using your funnel. Shake well before each use!

Recipe Examples

Unless you're embarking on your own crazy culinary adventure, once you have the butter made, the hard part is over. You can now substitute it in any recipe. Be careful though! If you made 1 tablespoon to be the perfect potency, stick to that within your recipes! (In other words, use recipes that require 1 Tbl of butter per portion.) I like to add it to chocolates; they are easy to transport, last a long time in the refrigerator, and can be made many different ways. My favorites are chocolate mint, honey sesame, and peanut butter cups.

How to Temper Chocolate

Tempered chocolate is the secret behind making molded candies. Chocolate that has been tempered has a smooth consistency and a shiny finish. The easiest way to make chocolates it to buy pre-tempered chocolate from a baking or cooking store. It is a little bit more expensive than regular semi-sweet chips but saves you a lot of time when preparing the mixture. Your other choice is to temper the chocolate by hand using a double boiler and candy thermometer. This is more difficult but can also be a fun learning experience. If you have pre-tempered chocolate, you can skip all these steps.

1. Use chocolate that is in block or bar form. Chips have additives that allow them to retain their shape at high temperatures, so will not temper properly. Chop your chocolate.

2. Melt ⅔ of the chocolate, stirring gently and steadily as it heats using a rubber spatula. Occasionally wipe

the condensation from the bottom of the bowl to prevent water from entering the mixture, which will cause it to seize.

Bring the chocolate to 110 degrees, 115 for dark chocolate. Do not overheat!

3. Remove it from the heat, wipe the bowl and add the remaining chocolate and stir. This will bring down the temperature of the mixture. Cool to 84 degrees.

4. Melt the butter in a separate container, taking care not to cook it.

5. Reheat the chocolate to 88 degrees. Your chocolate is now tempered. Careful not to heat past 91 degrees.

Once you get the tempering down, you can let your creativity take over. Add whatever you like, but in moderation. The chocolate will not hold together if there is too much of another ingredient, including butter.

HAZELNUT RUM CHOCOLATES

Chocolate, rum, and weed… can it get any better than that?

INGREDIENTS

2 lbs. of chocolate (can be white, dark, or milk but block or bar form only!)

1 cup of prepared butter

Rum flavoring

⅔ cup hazelnuts toasted

DIRECTIONS

1. Start with pre-tempered chocolate or follow the instructions for How to Temper Chocolate (page 403).

2. Slowly add the melted butter, rum flavoring, and hazelnuts, stirring until thoroughly mixed.

3. Keep the mixture around 88 degrees while pouring into molds.

4. Place in refrigerator until completely cooled. The chocolate should easily pop out of the molds, ready to eat!

PEANUT BUTTER CUPS

Makes 3 dozen friends.

What You Need

4 cups milk chocolate

1 cup peanut butter

¼ cup weed butter (or less, depending on your butter's potency)

Chocolate molds or cups or cupcake liners

DIRECTIONS

1. Use pre-tempered chocolate or follow the instructions for How to Temper Chocolate (page 403).

2. In a saucepan, combine the peanut butter and weed butter over medium heat. Stir until it has melted completely. Remove from heat and set aside to cool.

3. Spoon a quarter-inch of chocolate into each mold, and coat the sides. Refrigerate to cool. This will prevent the peanut butter from sinking.

4. Spoon about a tablespoon (maybe a little less) of peanut butter into the molds. Try to keep the peanut butter away from the sides.

5. Cover the peanut butter with another quarter-inch of chocolate, and cool.

LICE KLISPIE TLEATS

Be sure to serve these with a lisp.

INGREDIENTS AND SUPPLIES

6 tablespoons of special butter

6 cups of crisped rice cereal

1 package (40) marshmallows

Large cooking pot

Mixing spoon

DIRECTIONS

1. Melt butter over low heat in a pot or saucepan.

2. Add marshmallows and stir until they melt and mix with the butter (this should make a nice cleamy gleen mix).

3. Remove from heat and stir in cereal so that the marshmallow is dispersed evenly.

4. Spread out or cut out as you like and enjoy!

CHOCOLATE CHIP COOKIES WITH WALNUTS... AND WEED!

The ultimate comfort food. Makes 20–30 cookies.

INGREDIENTS AND SUPPLIES

1 cup very special butter

1 cup white sugar

1 cup packed brown sugar

2 eggs

2 teaspoons vanilla extract

1 teaspoon baking soda

½ teaspoon salt

3 cups all-purpose flour

2 cups semisweet chocolate chips

(you could make your own weed chocolate chips, too if you were so inclined!)

1 ½ cups chopped walnuts

Electric mixer

Mixing bowl

2 cookie trays

DIRECTIONS

1. Preheat oven to 350 degrees.

2. Using the electric mixer, blend together the butter and both types of sugar until smooth. Beat in the eggs and vanilla, then add baking soda and salt after dissolving them in a tiny bit of hot water. Stir in flour, chocolate chips, and walnuts.

3. Plop 20–30 large spoonfuls on cookie trays and cook for 10–12 minutes, making sure to stare at them through the oven door because they definitely cook faster that way.

4. Let cool and enjoy!

LINGUINI WITH GARLIC WEED BUTTER WINE SAUCE

The ultimate dinner date meal for two. Yum!

INGREDIENTS

½ lb. linguini

2 tbl. weed butter

1 tbl. olive oil

1 tbl. garlic

¼ onion minced

⅛ cup white cooking wine

1 tbl parsley chopped

1 egg yolk

Salt and pepper

Parmesan cheese

DIRECTIONS

1. Cook your pasta al dente in boiling water, don't forget to salt the water, and add a bit of weed butter, reserving some for later.

2. Saute the garlic and onion in the olive oil until it is slightly brown. Add the al dente pasta and saute for a few minutes.

3. Deglaze the pan (if needed) with white wine and a bit of pasta water.

4. Add the parsley and simmer for another minute or two. I like to cook the pasta in the sauce so it soaks up the flavor.

5. Add the butter and the egg yolk. This is an old cook's trick, many might not like or use; it thickens the sauce, just enough, and coats the noodles perfectly.

6. Salt and pepper to taste, and top with fresh Parmesan.

CHAPTER 5

LIGHTING UP AND THE LAW

Cannabis had been freely grown and used for food, fiber, medicine, and intoxicant for five thousand years. In the early twentieth century, lurid stories of violent cannabis users spread through the Western world. Governments began to regulate its growth and ban its use for healing or recreation. It remains a crime in most countries to use cannabis for fun. But in a growing number of U.S. states and in countries around the world, medical marijuana is being approved for treatment of a variety of ailments, with a doctor's prescription and purchased from licensed growers and dispensers. Law enforcement at all levels still aggressively pursues large-scale distributors in even the most tolerant of countries, where discrete users are usually left alone.

This section is full of information on the many legal matters related to cannabis, but I want to be sure right up front that you don't mistake me for a lawyer—please don't use what you read here as professional guidance or advice. Just file it all under "Fun to Know."

WHO IS ENJOYING MARIJUANA?

95 million Americans over the age of 18—40 percent of the U.S. population—have tried it.

22 million Americans in the past year.

8 million Americans more than 100 times a year (including today, most likely).

162 million people worldwide in an average year.

3.8 percent of people ages 15–64.

29 percent of people in Micronesia.

21 percent of Ghanaians.

18 percent of Zambians.

17 percent of Canadians.

Sources: The Substance Abuse and Mental Health Data Archive (SAMHDA), funded by U.S. Department of Health and Human Services, and 2007 World Drug Report by the United Nations Office on Drugs and Crime.

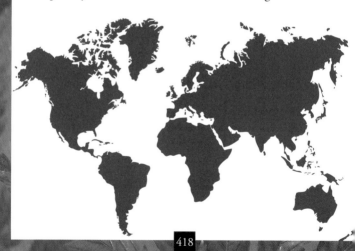

HOMEGROWN PRODUCT

Increased border surveillance, growers' ingenuity, and breeding of varieties adapted to indoor and outdoor conditions in the United States have dramatically increased domestic cannabis production.

Conservative estimates value the domestic cannabis crop at about $10 billion annually, making it one of the nation's top five cash crops.

An estimated 22 million pounds of marijuana were produced domestically in 2006. Cannabis is the most valuable cash crop in twelve states, including Alaska, Alabama, California, Connecticut, Hawaii, Kentucky, Maine, North Carolina, Oregon, South Carolina, Tennessee, and West Virginia.

About 35 percent of the marijuana consumed in the United States is grown domestically. That's up from less than 5 percent in 1974.

The U.S. Department of Justice estimates that in 2008 law enforcement officers destroyed 450,000 plants growing indoors and 8 million growing outdoors as

compared to 200,000 indoors and 3.2 million outdoors in 2004. In 2008, nearly 4 million plants growing on federal lands were eradicated by officers from the Forest Service and U.S. Department of Interior.

The former chairman of the Mendocino County (California) Board of Supervisors, Jim Wattenburger, has stated that up to 60 percent of county residents are involved in the marijuana industry.

NORTH AMERICAN TRADE

Cannabis is cultivated in 172 countries around the world, mostly for local or regional use, according to the United Nations World Drug Report of 2007. "For the North American market, the U.S. and Mexico are the biggest producers," the report states, followed by Canada. North America produces one-third of the marijuana used in the world, according to the international police organization, Interpol.

Mexico has long been a major supplier of marijuana

to the United States. According to the U.S. Department of Justice, Mexico's marijuana production increased an estimated 59 percent between 2003 and 2008, reaching 21,500 metric tons. At the same time, production increased within the United States and Canada, the Justice Department reports. While much of the marijuana from Mexico is grown outside, the vast majority from north of the border grows inside.

Canada's national police force (the Royal Canadian Mounties) estimates that the country's marijuana trade generates about $7.5 billion annually.

PROHIBITION ERA

While you could not legally purchase alcohol in the United States in the late 1800s and early 1900s, you could buy cannabis as an over-the-counter medicine in drug stores. In the 1920s and '30s, newspapers stirred public fears with

reports of violent, sex-crazed Mexican "marihuana" smokers, and states began to pass laws prohibiting its use sale and use. (You can get the whole story starting on page 48.)

The Bureau of Narcotics (part of the U.S. Treasury Department) proposed taxing and regulating the distribution and use of the cannabis plant. Congress passed The Marihuana Tax Act in 1937, requiring that anyone who dealt commercially in marijuana—hemp producers were exempt—pay one dollar to the federal government. It did not criminalize the possession or use of marijuana; you just had to report that you'd done it and pay your dollar tax. Violators were threatened with up to $2,000 in fines and five years in prison.

The American Medical Association lobbied against the law because it affected physicians who prescribed cannabis medicine and pharmacists who dispensed it. Its leader, Dr. William C. Woodward, testified to Congress that "The American Medical Association knows of no evidence that marihuana is a dangerous drug," and that any prohibition "loses sight of the fact that future investigation may show that there are substantial medical uses for Cannabis."

The law was enacted and enforced almost exclusively against those involved in recreational use, often as a political weapon. The cannabis medicines were soon replaced by new, more lucrative drugs. The U.S. Supreme Court ruled the law unconstitutional in 1967 (*Leary v. United States*).

NUGGET

"SINCE THE USE OF MARIJUANA AND OTHER NARCOTICS IS WIDESPREAD AMONG MEMBERS OF THE NEW LEFT, YOU SHOULD BE ON THE ALERT TO OPPORTUNITIES TO HAVE THEM ARRESTED ON DRUG CHARGES."

—FBI DIRECTOR J. EDGAR HOOVER IN A TOP SECRET MEMO TO AGENTS IN 1968

BUSTED

KILOGRAMS (2.2 POUNDS) OF MARIJUANA SEIZED BY THE DEA IN 2010: 722,476

KILOGRAMS OF MARIJUANA SEIZED IN 2000: 331,499

KILOGRAMS OF MARIJUANA SEIZED IN 1990: 127,792

SOURCE: U.S. DRUG ENFORCEMENT AGENCY DATA

LOCKED UP

Police arrested an estimated 872,721 people for marijuana violations in 2007, according to the FBI's Uniform Crime Report. Of those charged with marijuana violations, nearly 90 percent were charged with possession only. The remainder were charged with "sale/manufacture," which includes cultivation offenses.

Marijuana violations comprise nearly half of all drug arrests in the United States.

The total number of marijuana arrests exceeds the total number of arrests for all violent crimes combined, including murder, rape, armed robbery, and aggravated assault.

Since 1992, approximately six million Americans have been arrested on marijuana charges. That's more than the entire populations of Alaska, Delaware, the District of Columbia, Montana, North Dakota, South Dakota,

Vermont, and Wyoming combined.

Marijuana arrests have more than doubled in the last twenty years.

New drug policies have especially affected incarceration rates for women, which have increased at nearly double the rate for men since 1980. Nearly one in three women in prison today are serving sentences for drug-related crimes.

LEAP AHEAD

Many police officers, prosecutors, judges, and others in the criminal justice profession have concluded that the "war on drugs" in the United States is wasteful, ineffective, and misguided. Some of them are willing to stand up and say so. In 2002, a group of them formed Law Enforcement Against Prohibition (LEAP), an international organization that advocates for "repeal of prohibition and its replacement with a tight system of legalized regulation, which will effectively cripple the violent cartels and street dealers who control the current illegal market."

TEST CASES

In 1986, President Reagan signed an executive order that prohibited federal employees from using drugs, on or off the job, as a condition of their employment. Two years later, Congress passed the Drug-Free Workplace Act and established a Federal Workplace Testing program. The program's mandatory guidelines apply to executive agencies of the federal government, the uniformed military, and contractors or service providers under contract with the federal government. Many state and local governments passed similar statues and enacted their own drug testing guidelines.

The federal law also requires that employees in security operations and those that might put public safety at risk must be tested for drug use. Many states have also mandated drug testing for applicants and employees in health-care, operators of heavy machinery, and professional drivers.

The federal and state Drug-Free Workplace programs allow:

- Testing of existing employees and job applicants.

- The use of urine, blood, saliva, and hair samples.

- Random testing before hiring, "upon reasonable suspicion" or "for cause," after a workplace accident, and/or following a treatment program.

- Screening for cannabis as well as for opiates, amphetamines, cocaine, hallucinogens, inhalants, and anabolic steroids.

Drug testing programs raise a concern about the U.S. Constitution's protection against unreasonable search and seizure, codified in the Fourth Amendment. In the 1989 case of *Treasury Employees v. Von Raab*, the U.S. Supreme Court ruled that requiring employees to produce urine samples constituted a "search" within the meaning of the Fourth Amendment. Therefore, all such testing must meet the Constitution's "reasonableness" requirement. The Court also ruled that positive test results could not be used in criminal prosecution without the employee's consent.

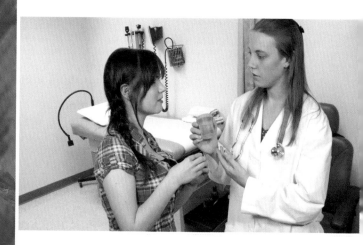

Employees may be tested whenever their employers have "reasonable suspicion" that they are using drugs. Many state laws limit or prohibit random testing of employees unless the job warrants it.

Learn more about drug tests and how to try to pass them on page 524.

HEMP RULES

Hemp and marijuana both come from the *Cannabis sativa* plant. Hemp contains compounds that block the psychoactive effects of the plant. Instead, its value is as a source of food and fiber, for which it has been grown throughout the world for thousands of years.

At this time, more than thirty nations (including the United Kingdom and Canada) permit industrial hemp farming. In fact, the European Union subsidizes farmers who grow the crop. Current hemp varieties grown in

Canada and Europe are certified to have THC levels below 0.3 percent. The certification system originally developed in Europe to allow for the commercialization of industrial hemp. Current law in the United States prohibits commercial hemp production without a federal license.

Still, you will find an increasing number of hemp products available even in the United States, from apparel and shoes to food products and even vitamins. Just not the plants.

SUPER SMUGGLER

Like a lot of high school kids in the late 1960s and early 1970s, Bruce Perlowin started selling nickel ($5) and dime ($10) bags of marijuana to his classmates in South Florida. It was a small but profitable business for him, but he moved on to a variety of other jobs. A few years later, Perlowin was in need of income to support his wife and infant son, so he helped a friend market about fifty pounds of grass to hippies and other local users. Before long, he was transporting suitcases packed with 100 pounds of marijuana on flights he took from Florida to California.

In 1976, Perlowin, by then 26 years old, was moving hundreds of thousands of dollars of marijuana smuggled in from Jamaica. When two of his associates were arrested and charged with smuggling in Florida, Perlowin moved his operations to northern California. Between 1979 and 1983, he became the largest pot smuggler on the West Coast. He had a fleet of boats larger than most countries' navies and had developed a new smuggling route from western Colombia to San Francisco. Law enforcement estimates that over four years Perlowin's operation brought 300,000 pounds of marijuana right under the Golden Gate Bridge to a pier he owned in Richmond, California. His worldwide network encompassed several hundred growers (including an entire village in Colombia), smugglers, and distributors. He claims to have deployed "a motor home with over a million dollars of sophisticated communications and surveillance equipment that tracked every Coast Guard boat in the Pacific Basin (800,000 square miles of ocean) from South America to Alaska to the PAC Rim countries." He said, "by the time I was 30 I had made over $100 million in profits."

The hammer came down in March 1983, when Perlowin was arrested by federal agents and charged as a marijuana smuggler, allegedly based on information gleaned from a notebook he had lost containing details of his operation. He served nine years in the Federal Correctional Institution in Pleasanton, California, a minimum-security facility that was the last co-ed prison in the United States.

After his release, Perlowin got into a business selling long-distance phone cards and other facets of the telecommunications business. After he was featured in 2008 in a documentary called "Marijuana, Inc." that aired on the CNBC TV network, Perlowin became a kind of celebrity, the so-called "King of Pot." He also developed an interest in medical marijuana and hemp. Now he's back in the business—but as an aboveboard player, this time. He proclaims that one of his companies, Medical Marijuana, Inc. (stock symbol MJNA), does "everything in the industry except medical marijuana dispensaries and growing medical marijuana."

BIG-TIME BUSTS

About 150 miles south of San Diego, in the desert of Baja California, a black screen shielded a 300-acre plantation not only from the blistering sun but also from prying eyes flying overhead. But in July 2011, the Mexican military discovered the plantation—the largest marijuana farm yet found. The commanding officer estimated that the crop would have yielded about 120 tons of marijuana, worth about 1.8 billion pesos or about $160 million. He said that crude buildings on the site indicate that about 60 people worked there.

In October 2010, Mexican authorities made their

largest ever seizure of marijuana packaged for sale, a record 148 tons (134 metric tons) found in a number of tractor trailers and houses in Tijuana.

A month later, U.S. and Mexican investigators found two long, sophisticated tunnels under the border, along with more than 40 tons of marijuana in and around them. The tunnels ran about 2,000 feet from Mexico to San Diego and were equipped with lighting, ventilation, and a rail system for moving the drugs swiftly and easily.

UNDERGROUND FARM

In April 2005, the Tennessee state police raided a luxurious home on a wooded property in rural Trousdale County. Inside the house, they found no furniture, appliances, or normal signs of people living there, but they did discover a hidden door in the garage. It led to a network of caves that was nearly 250 feet long and equipped with sleeping quarters, bathrooms, offices, and a discretely covered exit. It also included two lengthy rooms with elaborate watering and ventilation systems, each home to nearly 600 marijuana plants.

The police arrested three men for setting up and managing this extraordinary grow house. They were able to produce 12 to 14 crops each year, according to the police investigation, earning about $500,000 per crop. When they needed extra help to process their large crops, they hired men from faraway cities and kept them blindfolded until they were in the cave.

How did this ingenious operation get busted? The house had an extra-large transformer installed when it was built, but the growing operation must have needed more power. Rather than arouse suspicions by requesting more power from the utility company, the growers found a way to splice directly into the grid and siphon off the energy they needed. Eventually, the lost power did attract attention from the utility company. An employee sent to investigate

438

saw in the windows that the house appeared vacant, and notified police of his suspicions.

A year after the three men were arrested, the house burned to the ground.

LEGAL TIMELINE

1906

Pure Food and Drug Act required for the first time that patent medicines sold in the United States, including those made with cannabis, provide complete ingredient lists on their labels.

1911

South Africa banned the consumption of cannabis as medicine, sacrament, or intoxicant. Its use had been spreading among its "colored" population (Indian workers) and the black native Africans.

1925

The International Opium Convention, signed in 1912, was the first worldwide drug control treaty. When it came up for renewal in 1925, Egypt, China, and the United States argued for including cannabis among the regulated drugs, but objections from India and other nations softened the final rules.

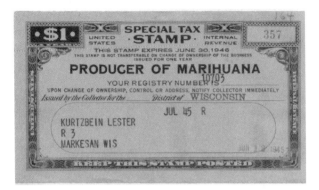

1937

The Marihuana Tax Act passed by Congress required those who grow and distribute cannabis to pay $1 for a federal stamp.

1951

With the Boggs Act, Congress increased the penalties for violations of a 1922 law banning the import and export of narcotics and the marijuana tax law, and for the first time legally linking cannabis with drugs such as heroin and cocaine. The Boggs Act established mandatory minimum prison sentences for violators. Simple possession would be punished with two years; a second offense, with five years.

1956

The Narcotics Control Act increased mandatory sentences for violations of the existing drug laws.

1961

The United Nations adopted the Single Convention on Narcotic Drugs. Signatory countries, which included the United States, agreed to actively prevent the "possession, use, trade in, distribution, import, export, manufacture, and production of drugs," including cannabis.

1967

The Harvard professor turned LSD evangelist Timothy Leary challenged his arrest for failing to pay the marijuana tax when he was busted in California with a couple joints.

The U.S. Supreme Court unanimously agreed with his argument that the Marihuana Tax Act violated his Fifth Amendment right against self-incrimination and declared the law unconstitutional.

1970

The modern war on drugs began with the Comprehensive Drug Abuse Prevention and Control Act. It classified drugs into five "schedules" depending on their medicinal value and likelihood of abuse. Cannabis was included in Schedule I with heroin and LSD—drugs deemed to have no medicinal purpose and prone to abuse. The Justice Department drew up a Uniform Controlled Substance Act for state legislatures to enact to be consistent with federal law.

1973

The Drug Enforcement Administration was established as mandated by the 1970 law, and the Treasury Department's Bureau of Narcotics and Dangerous Drugs was disbanded.

1977

President Jimmy Carter proposed that Congress decriminalize the possession of less than an ounce of marijuana. "Penalties against possession of a drug should not be more damaging to an individual than the use of the drug itself," he said.

1978

A lawsuit brought by glaucoma patients compelled the federal government to allow them to test medical marijuana under the Compassionate Use of Investigational Drug program.

1986

The far-reaching Anti-Drug Abuse Act re-established stiff mandatory minimum sentences for drug-related offenses, empowered law enforcement to seize all of drug traffickers' assets, funded collaboration with foreign governments to eradicate and interdict drug traffic, lowered the threshold quantities for advanced felony charges, and prohibited interstate commerce (i.e., mail-order) in drug paraphernalia.

1988

The United Nations Convention Against Illicit Traffic in Narcotic Drugs and Psychotropic Substances established international controls over drug trafficking, including marijuana.

The U.S. Office of National Drug Control Policy is created as a cabinet-level agency, with the so-called "Drug Czar" reporting directly to the President.

1993

Surgeon General Joycelyn Elders urged that the federal government consider legalizing drugs to reduce crime and to foster the development of treatment options. A few months later she was fired by President Clinton for expressing this and other controversial opinions.

1994

Cannabis cultivation—even hemp strains—had been prohibited in the United States since 1970. But hemp was designated as a strategic crop when President Clinton signed Executive Order 12919, the National Defense Industrial Preparedness Order.

1996

California Proposition 215, or the Compassionate Use Act of 1996, was enacted by statewide ballot initiative (55 percent of voters were in favor). It authorized physicians to prescribe cannabis as medication and their patients to cultivate, possess, and use it.

1997

The American Medical Association officially recognized the credibility of the research in support of marijuana's medical value, recommended that doctors and patients should not be punished for discussing it as a treatment option, and urged the federal government to fund further research.

1998–1999

Oregon, Washington, Alaska, and Maine voters approved ballot measures allowing patients with specified conditions and doctors' prescriptions to cultivate, possess, and use cannabis. Patients are required to register with their state health departments.

2000

Medical marijuana law was passed by the state legislature

(not just a ballot initiative) in Hawaii.

2001

Voter initiatives in Colorado and Nevada approved use of cannabis as medicine.

2003

The governor of Maryland signed a medical marijuana bill passed by the state legislature.

2004

The state assembly in Vermont and the voters of Montana approved medical marijuana laws. Richard Durbin (D-Ill.) introduced a medical marijuana bill in the U.S. Senate for the first time.

2006

The Rhode Island state legislature overrode the governor's prior veto of a law authorizing physicians to prescribe cannabis to their patients.

2007

A record 870,000 people were arrested for marijuana violations. That was 5 percent more than the previous year.

2008

A ballot initiative that decriminalized possession of one ounce or less of marijuana was passed by Massachusetts voters. In Michigan, voters approved a measure granting terminally ill patients permission to cultivate, possess, and use cannabis.

2009

Congress passed legislation allowing the District of Columbia to implement its medical marijuana law, which voters had approved ten years prior.

In an online campaign launched by the Obama Administration, respondents selected "legalize marijuana" as the top first initiative they'd like the new president to undertake.

2010

Voters in Arizona approved a ballot initiative legalizing medical marijuana and establishing licensed dispensaries.

2011

Delaware's Governor Jack Markell signed the law approved by the state legislature allowing registered patients to

obtain three ounces of marijuana every 14 days from state-regulated compassion centers.

AROUND THE WORLD

Here is the legal status, as of this book's publication, of cannabis in countries around the world.

Argentina

Marijuana is classified as a controlled drug, and large-scale growers and distributors are prosecuted. But possession for personal consumption has been decriminalized and is largely ignored.

Australia

Possession of cannabis has been decriminalized, but an expanding industry of hydroponic growers has prompted enforcement of limits on cultivation.

Brazil

The penalty for possession or cultivation of marijuana for personal consumption is a warning, community service, and drug-abuse education.

Cambodia

Cannabis use is illegal, but many urbanites openly smoke it, and rural people treat it as a sacrament. So-called "Happy Herb" restaurants in several cities season pizza and other food with cannabis.

Canada

You may think of Canada as a level-headed nation with great tolerance for any private behavior that does not affect other people. But marijuana remains illegal and possession arrests are common (yes, even in B.C.). Several federal-level courts have declared the marijuana laws unconstitutional, but they remain in effect. The national health-care provider, Health Canada, does allow registered and approved patients to use medical marijuana.

Chile

Cannabis is illegal, but cultivation and possession for personal consumption is tolerated. Medical marijuana is accepted but not regulated.

China

The Chinese people have a 5,000 year history with "ma hemp" but its use as an intoxicant is prohibited and the law strictly enforced.

Colombia

Once a leading producer and exporter of high-quality marijuana, Colombia prohibits its cultivation and sale, but does not prosecute for possession of one gram or less.

Costa Rica

Possession and use of marijuana is illegal but almost never prosecuted. Costa Ricans are among the world's top users.

Egypt

Recreational use of cannabis is prohibited, but smoking hashish is still a popular pastime at coffee shops and other gathering spots and is tolerated.

Ethiopia

Possession and use are illegal and are often punished with prison sentences.

France

Marijuana possession and use are banned and violators are prosecuted. France has pressured other members of the European Union to enforce cannabis laws more strictly.

Germany

Even personal use amounts of marijuana or hashish are illegal, but northern cities such as Hamburg do not prosecute for possession of five grams or less. Southern cities, including Munich, are said to be less tolerant.

Indonesia

Citizens may be forced to submit to urine tests if police suspect they have been using hashish or other forms of cannabis. Prison sentences may be up to four years for basic violations.

India

Cannabis is a sacrament used in some Hindu rituals, and

government-owned shops in cities where religious pilgrims gather sell bhang. Private sale and possession are illegal but almost never prosecuted.

Iran

Cultivation for seeds or food-grade oil is legal, as is possession of up to 15 grams of hashish.

Ireland

Sale, possession, and use of cannabis are prohibited and the law enforced. Use continues to grow in popularity and head shops are proliferating around the country.

Israel

The Health Ministry grants permits for medical use of marijuana, and THC is being tested as a treatment for the widespread problem of post-traumatic stress disorder. Recreational use is illegal.

Italy

Cannabis in all its forms is illegal, but use is growing among the rapidly increasing population of immigrants from North Africa and the Middle East.

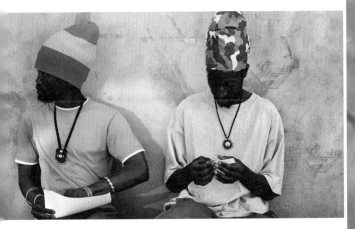

Jamaica

Don't believe the tourists—ganja sale, possession, and use are illegal, even if you sport natty dreadlocks. The laws are loosely enforced, but tolerance is lower for non-residents.

Malaysia

Those caught with more than seven ounces of marijuana are considered drug traffickers. Convicted drug traffickers face the death penalty.

Mexico

Possession of up to five grams of marijuana is not a felony, but any cultivation or sale is.

Netherlands

Sanctioned coffee shops sell a wide variety of cannabis products—a selection that would dazzle just about any American connoisseur—but outside sales and consumption are illegal and violations are prosecuted. Some municipalities have announced plans to restrict tourists from visiting their coffee shops. (See "The City of Amsterdam" on page 463.)

New Zealand

No cultivation, possession, or use of marijuana is

permitted, but an estimated 14 percent of people ages 15 to 64 consume it regularly—a higher rate than all but eight countries.

Norway

Possession of fifteen grams or less is punishable by fine; holding greater amounts and sales are subject to long prison sentences.

Peru

Citizens may possess up to eight grams, but when caught in possession of other drugs with it, the punishment is more stringent.

Portugal

Any drug user caught with less than a ten-day supply submits to an administrative—rather than criminal—process. The user must meet with a committee from the Commission for the Dissuasion of Drug Addiction, made up of a social worker, psychiatrist, and attorney. They develop a treatment, punishment, and rehabilitation plan for the violator.

Russia

Arrest with just the personal use limit of six grams of marijuana or two ounces of hashish is punishable by fine. Those caught with more may be sentenced to lengthy prison sentences.

Saudi Arabia

Recreational use of cannabis can be punished with imprisonment. Execution has been the penalty for some large-scale distributors.

Spain

Cultivation on private property for personal use is protected by the Constitution. Selling marijuana is a crime; consuming it in public is a misdemeanor.

Sweden

Any possession or consumption of cannabis is illegal and subject to fines and imprisonment. The Swedish government does not recognize a medicinal value for cannabis, though some citizens have sued for the right to use it to treat their debilitating illnesses.

United Kingdom

A Class B drug (moderate risk), marijuana is illegal to possess or consume. Possession of less than three grams on a first offense results in confiscation and a written warning.

United States

Though sixteen states and the District of Columbia have established medical marijuana programs and eight have decriminalized possession of marijuana, it remains a federal crime to distribute, possess, or use it.

THE FRANKFURT RESOLUTION

In 1990, representatives from several European cities, including Amsterdam, Hamburg, and Zurich, met in Frankfurt, Germany, to discuss drug policy. They concluded their meeting with a resolution declaring that attempts at eliminating drugs and drug consumption are a failure. "At its best," the signers stated, "drug policy can regulate and limit the results of drug use only." They proposed Europe-wide legislation to decriminalize possession and consumption of cannabis and urged European leaders to establish legal trade of it.

The Frankfurt Resolution had no binding authority, but it did encourage those cities participating and others to explore alternatives to arresting and prosecuting users.

THE CITY OF AMSTERDAM

The Netherlands (aka Holland) has always been a bit different than its neighbors. Even before the American Revolution, the Dutch king was elected to an office that was not hereditary. For centuries, the small country was a haven of tolerance for people of many unpopular faiths and sects.

In 1970, the Netherlands launched an experiment in

law enforcement. Prostitution and cannabis consumption were legalized and strictly regulated by the government. In the years since, the country and more specifically its largest city, Amsterdam, have attracted a growing tourist industry serving cannabis enthusiasts from all over the world. The annual Cannabis Cup alone draws thousands to the city each fall. (Learn all about the event on page 336.)

HASH MARIJUANA & HEMP MUSEUM IN RED-LIGHT DISTRICT OF AMSTERDAM
AIJA LEHTONEN / SHUTTERSTOCK.COM

Under Dutch drug law, licensed coffee shops are permitted to sell up to five grams of cannabis to each customer over 18 years old with valid identification. Customers are typically presented with a menu that offers a wide selection of cannabis products, including joints of varying degrees of potency, often with detailed genealogy, hash by the gram, sweets made with cannabis "butter" and flavored teas.

The coffee shops may not sell alcohol or permit the use of hard drugs, though Holland does have a needle exchange program and treats addiction like a health problem rather than just a crime. In 2008, the Netherlands, like many countries, banned smoking tobacco in the workplace. Customers who like "spliffs," or joints with cannabis and tobacco mixed, are limited to designated smoking areas.

Experienced visitors warn newbies not to choose the strongest items on the menu, because they can be a lot more potent than the cannabis available elsewhere. For instance, Nederwiet is a popular Dutch variety with a THC-content double that of average varieties.

A Dutch journalist has estimated that the government collects 400 million euros (a little more than $600 million) a year in taxes from the country's 700 licensed coffee shops. Their annual sales are about at 265,000 kilos (583,000 pounds) of cannabis, with gross revenue of about $3.2 billion.

In 2011, some municipalities in the Netherlands announced changes to their policies, in response to complaints from citizens about cannabis tourists. The smaller cities banned smoking cannabis in public—it is permitted only inside licensed coffee shops and private residences. Most significantly, cities such as Maastricht enacted regulations limiting access to coffee shops to those carrying a permit or membership card. Those would go first to natives and to regular customers from the neighboring countries of Germany and Belgium, in effect limiting the number of tourists who could access the shops. These laws don't yet affect Amsterdam or Rotterdam, but the Dutch government has decided to explore the idea taking these measures nationwide.

RESOURCES

The Cannabis Law Institute (cannabislawinstitute.com)

Law Enforcement Against Prohibition (LEAP.org)

"Mandatory Guidelines for Federal Workplace Drug Testing Programs" (workplace.samhsa.gov)

Marijuana Policy Project (MPP.org)

National Organization for Reform of Marijuana Laws (NORML.org)

CHAPTER 6

FAR-OUT SCIENCE

Before there's a smoldering bud in your bong, there's a plant that botanists know as *Cannabis*. It's one of the world's most unique and interesting species. It grows in a wide variety of conditions—in most of the world's temperate zones it behaves like a weed, sprouting up all on its own, though it gets plenty of help from people on nearly every continent. Cannabis produces both male and female plants, and the differences are absolutely critical to your buzz. The species has two distinct strains, only one of which belongs in a bowl, though the other is highly valued, too. The plants are loaded with uncommon compounds that create the pleasurable effects that we enjoy.

Today scientists are documenting what traditional healers have known for centuries: Those compounds can have powerful health benefits, too, especially for people suffering from debilitating diseases.

In this section, you'll get insight into the amazing plant from how it grows and produces buds to up-to-date research on the effects it has on your mind and body.

WHAT'S IN THE NAME?

Remember back in middle school when you learned how all living things are classified? Kingdom > Phylum > Class > Order > Family > Genus > Species. *Cannabis* is obviously part of the Plant Kingdom (as opposed to the Animal or Fungi kingdoms) and belongs to the Phylum of flowering plants (as opposed to those that only produce leaves). It is part of an Order that includes mulberries, elm trees, and nettles. The Family Cannabaceae has two members: *Cannabis* and *Humulus*, which includes hops, a plant long used as a natural painkiller by herbalists and as a key ingredient in beer.

The most important classification of *Cannabis* for you to know is its Genus and Species, which is *Cannabis sativa*. Within that species, botanists generally agree (though there are some disputes about this because that's what scientists do for fun) that there are three subspecies: *Cannabis sativa ssp. sativa, Cannabis sativa ssp. indica,* and *Cannabis sativa ruderalis.* The first two—sativa and indica—have long been cultivated, selected for their most appealing attributes, and cross-bred into the countless varieties available today. Both include strains that are potent enough to

raise your consciousness as well as strains that are fibrous enough to make into canvas.

Ruderalis was identified in the Soviet Union in the mid-twentieth century as a unique species developed from plants that escaped cultivation. No, they didn't run away from farms; their seeds were carried by wind and birds and sprouted up where no one intentionally planted them. Ruderalis, now found wherever *Cannabis* has been cultivated including most of the United States and Canada, was once dismissed by marijuana breeders because its potency was low. More recently, ruderalis plants have been cross-bred with sativa and indica plants because they flower earlier than the others, which is a highly desirable trait in northern climates where the growing season is short. Now you will find hybrids with traits from all three subspecies. Mighty Mite is one of the most widely grown early varieties with ruderalis in its mix.

"ALL HUMAN CULTURES EXCEPT THE INUIT USE PLANTS TO ALTER CONSCIOUSNESS."

—MICHAEL POLLAN, AUTHOR, *BOTANY OF DESIRE*

SATIVA AND INDICA

The two most common cannabis subspecies, sativa and indica, are so similar that some scientists argue they are really strains of the same subspecies with slight differences based on the influences of where they grow. From the point of view of the professional and amateur breeders, who are creating the many marijuana varieties you find on the market, sativa and indica do have variations in their attributes.

Sativa grows readily outdoors in areas near the

Equator, such as Mexico, Jamaica, and Thailand. The plants tend to be fast-growing, tall (up to twelve feet high), and quite leafy. Those leaves are light green and even tend toward gold. The buds are long and thin and turn red as they mature. They smell sweet, have a fruity taste, and the smoke is mild. The high you get from sativa is said to be stimulating and cerebral. Haze and K2 are two common sativa varieties.

Indica plants are found in more northern climates, such as Afghanistan and Pakistan, and they are typically shorter and bushier than sativas. The skunky-smelling buds, which turn purplish as they mature, were once more often used to make hashish or kef than smoked themselves. Indica varieties are reputedly more soothing and calming to mind and body than sativas. Northern Lights and Kush are popular, very mellow indicas.

Most of the varieties grown and sold are now hybrids bred using strains from both sativas and indicas, which in scientific nomenclature would be *Cannabis sativa sp. sativa X indica*, with the "X" indicating a cross between the species.

RED, GOLD, BROWN, AND GREEN

In the early 1970s, when I first began my personal research into the miraculous properties of cannabis, my neighborhood supplier talked up the qualities of varieties known as Panama Red and Colombian Gold, which tasted better and were noticeably more potent than Mexican Brown. Occasionally, Afghani Black would be available. The Red, Gold, and Black varieties were *sativa* strains, and they almost always had some seeds in the buds.

By the 1980s and '90s, those varieties were no longer commonly available—perhaps because U.S. law enforcement became more aggressive at targeting the supply coming in from Central and South America.

That's when all the good pot turned green—first, as Maui Wowie and other so-called Hawaiian varieties, and later coming from California, Florida, and other spots within the United States. These very potent and tasty *sativa* and *indica* hybrids tend to be seedless and are called sinsimilla. That's the good smoke most people grow and want in the twenty-first century.

HOW IT GROWS

You know your buds come from a plant, but if you've never grown it yourself, you likely don't know much about how it gets from the ground to your bowl. Cannabis is classified as an "annual" plant, which means that it lives out its full life cycle each growing season. Tomatoes and most other vegetables, and flowers like marigolds and zinnias are other familiar annuals. They all come up in spring from new seeds, grow to their mature height, flower, are pollinated, produce seeds of their own, and then die when the growing season ends, in most cases from a hard freeze.

Just so you know the difference, perennials may appear to die above ground, but their roots survive from year to year, so the plant continues to come up in the same place. Trees and shrubs are obvious perennials, but so are asparagus and raspberries, daisies and irises. Perennials may produce seeds, but they may also reproduce in other ways.

SIMPLE ANATOMY

Stalk. The thick stem of a cannabis plant has two primary components: the bast and the hurd. The bast is the layer just below the outer "bark" and is used to make fibers that are woven into fabrics, such as canvas, or blended with others such as cotton. Just below that layer is a pulpy center, or hurd, that is used to make paper or pressed for oil. The stalk's main value to the plant is to transport water and nutrients from the soil to the leaves and flowers.

Leaves. The foliage on a cannabis plant has little psycho-active THC—that's why smoking leaves is more likely to give you a hard cough than a smooth head. But the leaves do the critical work of capturing sunlight and photosynthesizing it into vital nutrients for the plant's growth. The leaves typically emerge in pairs and each has five, seven, or nine "fingers."

Node. The node is the crotch where branches and leaves connect to stems.

Calyx. Immature flowers emerge in the nodes of both male and female plants. They are enclosed and protected by a sheath or envelope called a calyx (*KAL-icks*). As the flower buds inside develop, the calyx opens and allows pollen either out or in.

Pistil. A slender, red or yellowish tube called the pistil grows out of the calyx on the female plant. It snags pollen and guides it to the ovary. THC helps pollen stick to the pistil.

Trichome. A plant gland, or trichome, produces compounds essential to the plant's reproduction, notably THC and other cannabinoids.

Raceme. A cluster of many tiny flowers is known as a raceme. Queen Anne's lace, which you've probably seen in fields and untended lots, is one example. Your buds are another. Technically speaking, they are a panicle, or a cluster of branched raceme. Each plump little sheath, on every red hair, represents a flower.

HETEROSEXUAL AND HERMAPHRODITE

Smoking bud contributes to a healthy sex life whether you

like boys, girls, or both. The cannabis plant, though, is naturally heterosexual or, as the guys in the lab coats like to say, "dioecious" (DI-oh-ee-shus). Some hybrid varieties produce hermaphrodites, which have male stamens and female ovaries on the same plants. Cannabis plants that are grown under artificial light for inconsistent photoperiods are prone to becoming hermaphroditic, too. Dioecious species are not uncommon among plants—your garden-variety tomatoes are hermaphrodites. They, um, self-pollinate.

LIFE CYCLES

Cannabis plants start their lives as seeds. (It is also possible to start them with clones you make from existing plants. You can learn more about this in the How to Grow Your Own chapter.) To germinate, the seeds need moist soil and nighttime temperatures warmer than 65 degrees Fahrenheit. In about 7–10 days in these conditions, the seed will sprout up two round little embryonic leaves (just about every type of seed has these leaves). A few days later you'll see the plants' first true leaves—they have the long, fingered shape you recognize, and they emerge in pairs as the plant grows.

As the days get longer, the plant grows more and bigger leaves and a taller, heftier stalk. Under favorable

conditions, a cannabis plant can reach twenty feet tall in four to six months. While the daily amount of sunlight—referred to by scientists as "photoperiod"—remains more than ten hours, the plant continues rapid growth, adding more leaves and girth to the stalk. When the day-length begins to drop down to ten hours or less, cannabis reproduction begins. I grant you that plant reproduction isn't as thrilling to participate in or even watch as it is when humans do it, but you'll want to pay attention here because it has bearing on your buzz.

WHEN PLANTS MATE

Before the reproductive cycle begins, cannabis plants are like little kids with short hair: You can only distinguish the boys from the girls with very subtle cues. But when the plants mature and the light gets low, the differences show themselves and become very important.

Male and female cannabis begin their reproductive cycle with the growth of tiny flowers in the nodes where branches and leaves connect to the main stem. Male plants tend to show flowers first but the timing overlaps. The male flower first reveals its gender as it develops a curved, claw-like shape, while the female flower produces a swollen, symmetrical calyx, or sheath. Many hybrid varieties and plants that have been grown under artificial light are prone to produce hermaphrodites, or plants with both sets of reproductive organs.

As they grow, you'll see that females tend to have more branches but to be shorter than the males. If you have a magnifying glass, you can see that the female flowers appear as two long white, yellow, or pink pistils (or tiny hairs) protruding from the fold of a very thin membranous calyx. The calyx is covered with resin and has glandular trichomes. The calyx measures 2 to 6 millimeters long and contains the ovary.

Male flowers grow in pairs that hang down and have five stamens (approximately 5 millimeters long) that gradually emerge. The stamens consist of slender anthers (pollen sacs), splitting upwards from the tip and suspended on thin filaments, almost like little balls. The pollen grains are nearly spherical and slightly yellow, and are as small as 25 to 30 microns—to give you a frame of reference, about 600 microns will fit into the period at the end of this sentence.

As soon as male plants shed their pollen, which is called "dehiscence," they die. Meanwhile, the female plants can live for five months after pollination. Male plants produce pollen in stamens, which highly magnified look like a pair of tiny balls (yes, very similar to those you'd see on a human male). Within as little as a few hours and up to a week or so after daylight drops down to ten hours, the pollen sacs burst open. Around the same time, the ovaries on the female plant swell and begin to form little flowers.

When the pollen is carried by bugs and the wind onto the ovaries, conception occurs, and the female begins to make seeds for next year's plants. To capture as much pollen as possible and hang onto it, the female plants grow little red hairs that are covered with a sticky substance called tetrahydracannabinol, or THC. That's why, generally, the stickier the bud, the stronger it is. (See, I told you this science stuff would be good for your head.)

When the female plants are not fully pollinated, they continue to produce flowers (along with the THC) in the hopes of attracting some of the male's reproductive stuff. As the flowers grow, they form larger and larger clusters, which you know as buds. If they get a little pollen, a few seeds will form in the buds. If no pollen reaches the flowers, you get sinsemilla, or seedless buds. When a lot of pollen gets to the flowers, you have a lot of seeds and not much to smoke.

A few things you want to remember from all this icky

talk about cannabis sex: Don't waste your breath smoking male plants—they produce no buds or THC and will not get you high. And if you want to grow your own, you have to keep the boys away from the girls. In the How to Grow Your Own chapter, I explain how to do that, but bear in mind that the seedier the buds, the less THC they'll contain and the less potent they will be.

GOOD BREEDING

Every anonymous plastic bag of buds seems to come with a name. Back in the day, it was Columbian Gold, Panama Red, and Maui Wowie. In the twenty-first century, you hear about Super Lemon Haze, Northern Lights, and 4-Way. They all have unique characteristics—taste, smell, hue—though they're all the same species *(Cannabis sativa sp. sativa X indica)*. Where do all of the variations come from? People have been breeding them for centuries and, more recently, professionals and amateurs have been using the current understanding of genetics to produce buds with the most desirable traits.

The ideal cannabis would not be the same for everybody everywhere. Each of the different varietals—that's the wine expert's way of referring to the many types of grapes—have distinct attributes that growers and consumers want. Indica strains, for instance, are better adapted to cooler conditions than sativas. Indica plants are short, so they're well-suited to indoor growing. The fruity flavor of sativas balances the skunkiness of indica. And the variations go on and on. To create a varietal with specific traits, breeders rely on the same two methods that are used to create new types of many other plants like grapes and tomatoes.

Selection. The most basic breeding couldn't be simpler. You grow a crop of cannabis and allow at least some pollination. You keep the seeds only from the most robust and productive plants. Grow them the following year, again saving seeds from the best plants. By saving the seeds each growing season from the plants with the traits that you want, you are creating your own strain that is well-adapted to your particular growing conditions and with the attributes you value. This selection process is how people have been breeding plants since they first started growing them, and traditional farmers around the world continue to use this process for a variety of crops.

Cross-pollination. Now that science has explained how genes and the pollination process work, breeders can take a more direct role in improving a varietal's traits. They begin with two different strains that have desirable traits and grow them both. When the plants mature and show their gender, breeders separate the boys from the girls and collect the stamens, or pollen sacs, from the males, which they apply directly (with a thin paintbrush) to the ovaries of the females. Amateurs simply place the pollen in a paper bag and use it to cover a few females of the second variety.

After a day or so, the females will be pollinated.

The seeds from the cross-pollinated females will have traits from both sets of parents. By continuing to cross-pollinate each generation of plants that have the desirable traits, those attributes gradually become dominant. Each blend becomes a new varietal, which the breeders—or their employers—get to name. Now whether sellers along the supply chain keep the true name or go for one with a more coveted "branding," I can't say for certain.

NATURAL HABITAT

The archeological (fossils), anthropological (human culture), and DNA evidence all point to one region of origin for cannabis: Central Asia (e.g., Afghanistan) and South Asia (India and Thailand). You may have heard that Africa or South America is the native habitat of cannabis but the substantiated science does not concur. You can get

489

the facts about this in the chapter "A Long Strange Trip Through History."

Cannabis thrives in the rich, fertile soil found near forested regions. It grows best where the soil is slightly alkaline (pH 7.0–8.0) and well-drained. Acidic and sandy soils are less hospitable. The perfect temperature range is 80 degrees Fahrenheit during the day and 65 degrees Fahrenheit at night. Annual rainfall of 30 inches is ideal.

All that said, cannabis is a very resilient plant that thrives in a wide range of habitats. It has adapted well to—and been bred for—short growing seasons, artificial lights, and hydroponic (soil-less) growing systems. Indoor growing systems do produce potent cannabis, but the best (tastiest and most potent) crop always comes from growing it in rich, fertile soil with a long summer of direct sunlight.

LOOKALIKES

Maybe you think found an untended patch of wild weed. Or maybe you're sowing your own patch and you'd like to surround it with similar-looking plants so your weed won't be noticed. That's your business. But there are a few plants with leaves that look like cannabis. They even have a scent that could make you sniff twice. Of course, no other plant has flowers that look like primo buds. But before the flowering stage, these plants just might fool you and other people.

Cleome (*Cleome hassleriana*) also known as spider flower, grows tall, has "fingered" leaves and a distinct scent that will seem familiar to you.

Swamp hibiscus (aka Texas star, *Hibiscus coccineus*) reaches 5 feet tall or more and when it first comes up, its leaves look just like cannabis.

Chaste tree (*Vitex agnus-castus*) is a shrub or small tree that is also known as "hemp tree" because its foliage bears a strong resemblance to cannabis. It, however, has the strong aroma of sage.

Cinquefoil (*Potentilla pulcherrima x P hippiana*) is a low-growing garden plant with leaves that might fool the untrained eye.

THE OTHER CANNABIS

Hemp has long been used to make rope, canvas, and other

products, and its seeds are pressed for oil, or eaten raw or roasted. Today, you can find hemp milk and lots of other hemp products in natural foods stores and even in supermarkets. Hemp advocates love to trumpet its sustainability (it grows like a weed without any need for toxic fertilizers and pesticides) and its healthfulness. Hemp seeds are high in omega-3 fatty acids, which are critical to healthy heart functioning.

So why am I telling you about hemp in a book about marijuana? Because the plant that produces hemp is *Cannabis sativa*. That's right, botanically speaking it has the same DNA combination as your favorite smoke. Does that mean you can smoke rope and get high? Or that you will get buzzed when you eat hemp seeds in an energy bar? Unfortunately, no.

Cannabis plants contain unique compounds called cannabinoids. (Sorry to go all chemistry class on you, but this stuff is intense.) Tetrahydra-cannabinol, or THC, is the psychoactive ingredient, the one that gets you high. Over the centuries of cannabis cultivation, growers who wanted to smoke it selected the plants with the highest THC and planted their seeds, gradually creating strains with maximum amounts of the compound. At the same time, growers who wanted to raise the plant to make clothing or food from it, selected the ones with qualities they desired, such as strong fibers. These strains have developed a low level of THC (as low as .05 percent vs. 5 percent or more for average potency marijuana) and a comparatively high level of CBD, cannabidiol, which actively suppresses the effects of THC. It is in these molecular variations that you find the crucial distinction between marijuana and hemp.

HEMP PRODUCTS

Despite the difference between the two strains of cannabis, the U.S. government does not permit hemp cultivation. Nevertheless, an industry of imported hemp products

has sprouted up, and advocates have taken up the cause of promoting its benefits as a sustainable, healthy source of food and fiber. Hemp products are currently available in many forms.

Food. Hemp seeds are pressed into cooking oil or ground into flour, added to cereal and energy bars, and soaked into a milk substitute. You can eat the leaves in salad, too.

Fabric. You can find T-shirts, pants, socks, sweaters, and shoes made with hemp fibers, often blended with cotton and/or wool. Hemp requires no chemical

fertilizers or pesticides to produce a substantial batch of fiber, in contrast to cotton which is one of the most heavily treated agricultural crops. You can also buy canvas, linen, yarn, rope, twine, and other textiles made with hemp.

Body care. The oil from hemp seeds is very rich in essential fatty acids, critical components of healthy skin and hair. Many manufacturers are offering soap, shampoo, body lotion, and other preparations made with hemp.

FALSE HEMPS

Before scientific categorization of plants was standardized, people referred to many sources of fiber as "hemp." Plants that have held onto the name today include Manila hemp (abacá, *Musa textilis*), sisal hemp (*Agave sisalana*), Mauritius hemp (*Furcraea gigantea*), New Zealand hemp (*Phormium tenax*), Sunn hemp (*Crotalaria juncea*), Indian hemp (jute, *Corchorus capsularis* or *C. clitorus*), Indian hemp (*Apocynum cannabinum*), and bow-string hemp (*Sansevieria cylindrica*). You won't get a pleasant buzz from smoking any of these either.

ACTIVE COMPONENTS

Cannabis plants contain more than 400 compounds, of which eighty-five are "cannabinoids." Delta-9-tetrahydro-cannabinol (THC) is just one of these cannabinoids, but it's the chemical most often associated with the effects of cannabis. Many researchers are now concluding that while THC content is critical to the plant's psychoactive power, the balance of the many cannabinoids in each strain may be equally important. The concentration of THC and other cannabinoids is affected by the growing conditions, the plant's genetics, and how it is handled after the harvest.

Terpenes are a key component in the fragrance of cannabis. They're compounds that are found in the essential oils of many plants. Menthol and camphor are two familiar terpenes. Many cleaning products contain terpenes, which often have a "piney" scent. And, as you might guess, terpenes are in turpentine. Perfumes and colognes are made with the essential oils from a wide variety

of plants including cannabis. You can even buy cannabis fragrance products. I don't mean something to splash on to hide the bong-water reek or a bottle of *Eau de Smoke-Filled Van*. A few expensive cosmetics brands, such as Demeter and Malin + Goetz, are marketing colognes that include the essential oil from cannabis along with the lavender and rose water. There's even one called Black Afghano. All of them, I believe, are available to purchase by the ounce.

SCENT BE-GONE

The aroma of fresh cannabis ranges from piney and fruity to skunk- or musk-like. When you're growing it indoors, that scent is not only hard to conceal, it soon permeates the whole house. A filtered ventilation system can help keep the air fresh, but once the plants start flowering the scent gets stronger.

Even storing less than an ounce of the dankest of buds can make a house smell slightly skunky. Turkey bags, the plastic bags used for roasting turkeys, are most effective at trapping the potent smell emanating from a bag of buds. Tightly sealed glass jars and resealable plastic containers (that is, Tupperware) work almost as well as the turkey bags.

The smell of smoked cannabis is harder to suppress. It doesn't smell like tobacco smoke (unless you've packed it into a blunt), and it has a distinct, sweet aroma. All smoke is warmer than the air around it, so it rises and hangs over the room. The best you can do is try to vent it, mask it, or absorb it.

Blow it out. Most bathrooms, especially those with no window, have a fan designed to pull steamed air out of the room. You can buy a window fan that works the same way.

Homemade filter. You can filter smoke by blowing it through a wet washcloth or towel held across your mouth. The moisture in the cloth traps most of the particles in the smoke.

Cover up. Back in the day, we burnt incense to mask the smell of pot smoke; today, scented candles are a more popular choice. They work, though to me that seems like putting on cologne when you haven't bathed. Cigarettes and cigars seem like a waste of breath to me, but they can overwhelm the smell of smoked cannabis.

Absorbent spray. Standard air fresheners are too perfumed to blend well with cannabis smoke, and they always remind me of bathrooms. Ozium is an odor absorber that's so effective hotels use it to clean non-smoking rooms where guests have smoked. It's available at the major drugstores and many supermarkets.

The flavor, or rather the after-taste, of a nice pure hit of cannabis, is strongly influenced by its smell (just as aroma plays a strong role in the taste of food), but there are other factors. Sugars, alcohols, and fatty acids are all part of cannabis's natural chemical make-up and affect how it tastes. The plant's genetics play a key role in its flavor, as do the growing conditions, particularly the soil's make-up and the types of fertilizer used. When growing your own, go organic, I always say, to bring out the natural attributes rather than infusing it with the ammonia-like taste you get from synthetic fertilizers.

IN YOUR HEAD

Your brain is ready and waiting for you to ingest cannabis. Whether you do or you don't, there are cannabinoid receptors in your brain. Everybody has them, as do many other mammals, birds, fish, and reptiles. Most scientists once believed that cannabinoids were foreign substances that acted randomly in your body and could cause brain damage, but in 1988 researchers at the St. Louis University Medical School identified cannabinoid receptors in the brains of rats.

Let's talk a little anatomy so you really understand what's happening inside your skull. Your brain cells, or neurons, are able to communicate with each other and maintain your body's countless functions through chemicals called "neurotransmitters" that are released into the gap between the neurons. The gap is known as the "synapse." The neurons have receptors that are triggered by the neurotransmitters and hold onto their chemical messages. Neurons can have thousands of receptors for different neurotransmitters.

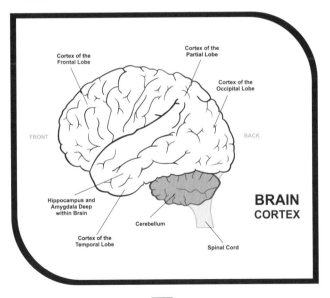

Cortex of the Frontal Lobe

Cortex of the Partial Lobe

Cortex of the Occipital Lobe

FRONT

BACK

Hippocampus and Amygdala Deep within Brain

Cerebellum

Cortex of the Temporal Lobe

Spinal Cord

BRAIN
CORTEX

Among those receptors are many that are triggered by cannabinoids, which are compounds produced by cannabis plants and in our bodies. The cannabis plant produces eighty-five distinct cannabinoids; tetrahydrocannabinol, or THC, is the one that scientists believe is the most psychoactive. The specific locations of the cannabinoid receptors explain many of the ways that THC and cannabinoids affect the brain.

The highest concentrations of cannabinoid receptors are in the hippocampus, cerebellum, and basal ganglia sections of the brain. The hippocampus is crucial for consolidating and preserving short-term memories. The cerebellum and basal ganglia control physical coordination and unconscious muscle movements. This information explains how after a few bong hits you can trip over the same spot on an uneven rug three times in a row.

Your body produces a neurotransmitter called anandamide, which is a naturally occurring cannabinoid.

Anandamide and the cannabinoid receptors interact and appear to play a central role in regulating your emotions and mood, as well as your appetite. Scientists now theorize that cannabinoids help our brains to manage anxiety in stressful situations and promote a sense of well-being and relaxation. They also seem to induce your thoughts to wander aimlessly or focus intently on a very specific object. You probably know the feeling.

If you don't, it may be because you are one of a small minority for whom THC does not bind to the right receptors, which can cause the opposite reaction—racing, scattered thoughts and anxiety. Other people report no effects at all from cannabis consumption. Scientists haven't yet identified the physical difference between people who enjoy the effects of cannabis and those who don't (though from my casual observations I surmise it could have something to do with a naturally uptight personality).

NUGGET

"THE DRUG IS REALLY QUITE A REMARKABLY SAFE ONE FOR HUMANS, ALTHOUGH IT IS REALLY QUITE A DANGEROUS ONE FOR MICE AND THEY SHOULD NOT USE IT."

—J.W.D HENDERSON, DIRECTOR OF THE BUREAU OF HUMAN DRUGS, HEALTH AND WELFARE, CANADA

NOT LIKE THE OTHERS

"Gateway drug." That's how law enforcement, mental health professionals, and others have long described marijuana. They argue that even if cannabis consumption does not cause brain damage or permanent harm to your body—as most of the research has demonstrated—people who enjoy it will be enticed to try more potent and destructive drugs, particularly cocaine, amphetamines, and heroin.

There's no debating that most hard drug users try marijuana before they are locked into their habits. But I'll bet that the vast majority of those users move on to stronger drugs because marijuana doesn't satisfy their craving, not because it stimulates their craving.

That's because those drugs—as well as alcohol and nicotine, it's worth noting—impact your brain in a very different manner than cannabinoids do. They affect the production of dopamine, a neurotransmitter that's directly linked to the most pleasurable sensations. Experts refer to it as the brain's "reward system," and it is most active in the limbic system, an area of the brain associated with the control of behavior. Cocaine and amphetamines (including crystal meth and Ecstasy) block the brain's absorption of dopamine, prompting massive overproduction of it. Heroin and other opiates mimic the brain's natural dopamine stimulants and inhibit the production of another compound that slows dopamine production when sufficient levels are reached.

How good does dopamine make you feel? Research animals will forgo food and drink, and even willingly suffer electric shocks, to stimulate their brain's dopamine production. Therein is the fertile soil of addiction.

No cannabinoid receptors have yet been found in dopamine-producing neurons. And there's another key difference between cannabis and addictive drugs. The medulla is the part of the brain that controls automatic functions, like heartbeat and breathing. While the medulla is affected by addictive drugs, it has no cannabinoid receptors. That explains why heart failure and other fatal breakdowns of the body's vital functions occur with overdoses of addictive drugs but not from marijuana consumption.

DON'T HOLD YOUR BREATH

The longer you hold marijuana smoke in your lungs, the

higher you get from the hit. That's what I was told when I first tried pot. So I would try to hold in my hits until the smoke forced its way out of my lungs. Most others I knew did the same. As we panted, our heads would be reeling from the "monster hit."

The truth is, we weren't absorbing any more THC or getting any higher than the lightweights who blew out their hit after just ten seconds. Two groups of scientists have studied this (and no, I don't know how you get on the list of people called for this type of research). The researchers found that test subjects who held their hits longer than about ten seconds had no more THC in their blood than those who blew out the smoke after twenty seconds. That is, the alveoli (tiny capillary sacs) in your lungs captured all the THC in about ten seconds. Also, the monster-hit holders performed no differently on specific cognitive tests nor reported stronger high sensations than those who held their hits for just ten seconds.

Holding your hits longer has two results, neither beneficial. First, your lungs have more time to absorb the tar and other contaminants in the smoke, which can irritate the lungs and lead to chronic bronchitis. Second, you may feel higher from holding in your hit, but in fact you are simply depriving your body and your brain of oxygen, which can make you feel dizzier but not truly higher.

BODY CONTACT

Within a few seconds after you inhale cannabis smoke or vapor, the THC has entered your bloodstream and is on its way to your brain. The most intense effects of THC expire after about two hours. You feel the effects of THC beginning about thirty to forty minutes after you eat brownies, lollipops, or other foods made with cannabis. Eating cannabis (as opposed to smoking or vaporizing it) has a subtler impact and tends to stay in your body rather than your mind. You feel relaxed and at ease, rather than buzzed in your brain.

WHY THE MUNCHIES?

Your body began producing its own cannabinoids (called "endogenous cannabinoids") from the time you were born and felt that first pang of hunger. Anandamide is a neurotransmitter—a brain chemical—that plays a pivotal role in regulating hunger. (The scientists who discovered it in 1992 named it from the Sanskrit *ananda*, meaning "inner bliss".) Cannabinoids you add to the existing mix seem to boost the reactions, so that you don't just feel hungry, you feel insatiable. Thus, the munchies.

It's worth noting that there's no evidence that using cannabis causes your blood sugar to drop or that it will lead to diabetes. Munching on a pint of ice cream several nights a week and sitting on your couch are the habits that lead to what is now known as "metabolic syndrome," or obesity and pre-diabetes. Take care of your body with lots of fresh fruit and vegetables, and you'll feel great before, during, and after your high.

MEDICAL REPORTS

There are no long-term studies linking cannabis use to the development of specific diseases, overall ill health, or shortened lifespan. No real case of marijuana overdose has ever been documented, because it doesn't affect your body's automated systems, such as your heart or lungs, as other drugs do. I probably don't need to tell you that an overdose is very unlikely because when people are too baked, they pass the next time the joint comes around.

This is not to say that frequent smoking doesn't have a cost. Smoking irritates your lungs and can lead to chronic bronchitis and hacking bong cough. And your heart rate can be elevated in the minutes after your first hit—this could be a heart-attack risk for people with certain heart conditions.

Your body has cannabinoid receptors in other areas besides your brain. They are abundant in white blood cells, the warriors of your immune system. These receptors are on the scene of every invader that comes into your body—infections and viruses—to fight them off. Cannabis use stimulates their activity, which may protect you from illness.

Even more extraordinary, a Spanish study found that THC killed brain cancer cells in a petri dish and shrunk brain tumors in laboratory mice. The Spanish team tested its hypothesis on two humans with aggressive brain cancer and recorded a dramatic decline in the cancerous cells and tumors after treatment with THC.

All the functions of cannabinoids are not yet fully understood, but researchers—and by that I don't mean customers of medical marijuana dispensaries—have documented its benefits in treating appetite loss and nausea in AIDS and cancer patients, reducing convulsions among sufferers of epilepsy and multiple sclerosis, and easing the eye pressure caused by glaucoma. Cannabis also has been shown to relieve pain and reduce stress.

The following are a few credible studies of cannabis that document its benefits as a therapy—for real ailments, not as a cure for a dull day or a bummer mood.

Nerve pain

Neuropathy is a difficult-to-treat nerve pain that often accompanies diabetes, cancer, AIDs, spinal cord injuries, and other serious conditions. Cannabis consistently reduces patients' pain levels as effectively or better than currently available medications, according to a 2010 report from the University of California Center for Medicinal Cannabis Research. It conducted a series of randomized, placebo-controlled clinical trials on inhaled cannabis—the rigorous type of studies the FDA requires of pharmaceutical drugs.

Rheumatoid Arthritis

In 2006, researchers at British Royal National Hospital for Rheumatic Disease reported that rheumatoid arthritis patients treated with cannabis extracts experience significantly less inflammation and pain and better sleep versus those treated with a placebo.

Multiple Sclerosis

A disease of the central nervous system, MS causes painful inflammation, weakening muscles, and a gradual loss of motor control. "Smoked cannabis was superior to placebo in reducing spasticity and pain in patients with multiple sclerosis and provided some benefit beyond currently prescribed treatment," reported researchers from the University of California at San Diego in 2008 based on a placebo-controlled, randomized clinical trial. Ironic, isn't it, that the same substance that causes you to stumble over the rug on your way to the fridge helps MS sufferers to retain their coordination?

MS patients may also find cannabis relieves another symptom—incontinence. British scientists reported in a 2003 issue of the journal *Clinical Rehabilitation* that "self-administered doses of whole-plant cannabinoids" improved bladder control and reduced episodes of incontinence versus placebo for MS patients. A 2006 randomized, double-blind study documented a 38 percent reduction in incontinence.

Glaucoma

Intraocular pressure—the result of fluids building up around the eyeball—is a symptom of glaucoma, which is among the leading causes of blindness. Studies all the way back to the 1970s have established that cannabis reduces intraocular pressure, which is why the U.S. government allowed a small group of sufferers to purchase and use cannabis from a licensed grower at the University of Mississippi.

Nausea and Lack of Appetite

You get the munchies because the part of your brain that triggers hunger is turned on by the cannabinoids in your cannabis. People enduring chemotherapy, suffering from AIDS, and struck with other diseases often lose their appetite. One review of studies published between 1975 and 1996 concluded that oral THC is as effective, or more effective, than commonly used prescription drugs for reducing nausea associated with chemotherapy. The reviewers also concluded that cannabinoids may be useful at low doses to improve appetite in patients with AIDS. Cannabinoid drugs containing concentrated THC have been approved by the U.S. Food and Drug Administration (FDA) for use in relieving nausea and vomiting and increasing appetite in people with cancer and AIDS.

Alzheimer's Disease

Short-term memory loss is a familiar side-effect of getting high on marijuana. So it would seem counterintuitive to consider it a treatment for the devastating loss of brain functioning that comes with Alzheimer's disease. But when researchers tested a THC extract on rats, they observed a reduction of inflammation in the rats' brains and the vigorous growth of new brain cells. And when the researchers tested the rats treated with THC, they found that those rats performed better on learning and memory tasks than the control group.

Tourette's Syndrome

Two small studies from 2009 tested the effects of cannabinoids on the symptoms of Tourette's syndrome, a neurological disorder that afflicts sufferers with tics and other compulsive behavior. The study subjects treated with cannabinoids had fewer and shorter episodes of their uncontrolled behavior.

DOCTOR'S PROGNOSIS

In 1967, Lester Grinspoon, M.D., a psychiatrist and researcher at Harvard Medical School, was concerned about the increasing use of marijuana. He says he "had no doubt that [marijuana] was a very harmful drug that was unfortunately being used by more and more foolish young people who would not listen to or could not believe or understand the warnings about its dangers."

Dr. Grinspoon began to study marijuana with the

goal of defining the risks of using it. But his research and dedication to scientific truth led him in the opposite direction. He concluded that it was not only less harmful than he had been led to believe, but it also had therapeutic value. He published a book with Harvard University Press in 1971 called *Marihuana Reconsidered*, in which he detailed his findings. With it, he became a leading expert on the benefits and risks of recreational and medicinal uses. In 1993, Dr. Grinspoon and James Bakalar (editor of the *Harvard Mental Health Letter*) published *Marihuana: The Forbidden Medicine*, which provided credible science-based information to the burgeoning medical marijuana movement. Dr. Grinspoon was also called to testify before Congress in the hearings about deporting musician John Lennon in 1972.

Today Dr. Grinspoon is a retired professor of psychiatry, but he continues to speak and publish articles about cannabis use and to share information with the community through his online effort (at rxmarijuana. com) to collect as many users' experiences as possible. Rumor has it that in his spare time the doctor enjoys the vaporizer most.

NUGGET

"CANNABIS IS REMARKABLY VERSATILE. CASE HISTORIES AND CLINICAL EXPERIENCE SUGGEST THAT IT IS USEFUL IN THE TREATMENT OF MORE THAN TWO DOZEN SYMPTOMS AND SYNDROMES, AND OTHERS WILL UNDOUBTEDLY BE DISCOVERED IN THE FUTURE."

—LESTER GRINSPOON, M.D.

PILL POPPER

The pharmaceutical industry has taken notice of the reports that THC has valuable healing properties. Its scientists synthesized THC in laboratories and got approval from the federal authorities—the FDA and the Drug Enforcement Agency—to market it in pill form. Marinol and Dronabinol are two of the drugs that can be prescribed for cancer and AIDS patients suffering from nausea or loss of appetite. Among the listed side effects are familiar responses such as "elevated mood," "sudden warm feeling," and "strange or unusual thoughts" along with the less enjoyable sounding "sleepiness," "memory loss," and "confusion."

HERBAL HIGH

In online advertisements and in many head shops, gas stations, and other outlets you will see so-called herbal products that claim to be legal ways to get a cannabis high. K2, Spice, Demon, and Genie are common brand names for products that sell for as much as $40 a gram, which are marketed as incense or "herbal smoking blends."

The products contain a variety of traditional herbs used for medicine that produce mild effects and, the manufacturers claim, when taken all together they give you a high similar to the feeling you get from marijuana. Herbs listed on the packaging of Spice include *Canavalia maritima*, *Nymphaea caerulea*, *Scutellaria nana*, *Pedicularis densiflora*, *Leonotis leonurus*, *Zornia latifolia*, *Nelumbo nucifera*, and *Leonurus sibiricus*.

In 2009, German scientists analyzed Spice and found that the actual ingredients are not those listed on the packaging. Subsequent analysis determined that the active ingredients are laboratory-synthesized cannabinoids, specifically cannabicyclohexanol, JWH-018, JWH-073, and HU-210.

Now I can't say personally whether these products really work, since I would not consider using them when high-quality, all-natural marijuana is so widely available. If you have or are planning to try them, you should know that those synthetic cannabinoids are controlled or even banned in many places, including the United States. So the promise that they are a legal way to get high is at best misleading. Further, though the synthetic cannabinoids do not produce positive results in drug tests for marijuana, their metabolites are detectable in your urine. Lastly, the American Association of Poison Control Centers logged 567 cases across forty-one states in which people had suffered a bad reaction to Spice during the first half of 2010.

PASS THE TEST

Drugs like cocaine and crystal meth are water-soluble, which means they are excreted through urine within 48–72 hours after you ingest them. THC, on the other hand, is fat-soluble and it doesn't wash out of your body for up to ten days after you smoke or eat marijuana.

However, if you enjoy cannabis more than five times a week, the metabolites of THC—the components left after your body breaks it down—are detectable by a blood or urine test for up to sixty days after the last time you ingest it. You read that right—up to two months after your last high, a widely used test can detect nonactive compounds and identify you as a marijuana user. Just 50 nanograms per milliliter of THC metabolites will cause you to fail a test.

If that causes you concern, what can you do? The best answer is to stay marijuana free for at least sixty days before the test. If you can't do that, you might be tempted to buy one of the "masking" products sold through shady Websites and head shops. Dr. Kindbud advises you not to waste your money on them—they are not effective. But you can try these strategies to increase your odds of passing.

Exercise more. Working your muscles speeds up your metabolism, so your body processes the by-products of cannabis faster. Hitting the gym or running are great, but surfing, bike riding, and even walking kick up your burn rate. They're also a good way to combat the urge to sit and vegetate after using cannabis.

Drink a lot. From the time you learn you will be tested until the day you get handed a cup, drink as many as eight glasses of water throughout day, especially leading up to and on the day of your test. Processing water keeps your cleansing systems active, and when you're ready to give your sample you want it as diluted as possible. Actually, drinking a lot of water is a healthy habit often overlooked by cannabis users. Headaches, dry mouth, and sluggishness are all caused by dehydration, the result of smoking and drinking diuretics such as alcohol and coffee.

Pre-pee. The first whiz of your day is the most concentrated. Be sure you've already flushed away the first pee (and probably the second pee as well), before you go in a cup.

Pop an aspirin. THC metabolites are masked from some types of tests by aspirin. You won't know for sure if you're taking one of those tests—unless you are asked not to take aspirin—but otherwise it couldn't hurt. Take the aspirin four hours before the test.

RESOURCES

Health facts

The National Institutes of Health, the government's research arm, is a generally trustworthy source of verified information. It operates the cannabis-unfriendly National Institute on Drug Abuse, and its website has lots of information about the impact of marijuana on your mind and body. More information is available at www.nida.nih.gov/

infofacts/marijuana.html.

The National Organization for the Reform of Marijuana Laws (NORML) is best-known as a lobbying group. It has assembled an in-depth and trustworthy guide to the latest science on cannabis as medicine. Look for "Emerging Clinical Applications for Cannabis and Cannabinoids" at NORML.org.

RxMarijuana.com is where users of marijuana as medicine can share their experiences and learn about others. The discussion is curated by two psychiatrists and members of the faculty of the Harvard Medical School with years of experience studying marijuana.

Fragrance

An online perfume merchant, Frangrantica (Frangrantica. com) offers several options for those looking for cannabis in their cologne, including the hard-to-find Nasomatto Black Afgano.

Variety reviews

Find regularly updates evaluations of many different strains and products, medical and legal reports, and basic cannabis botany at kindreviews.com.

Hemp

Food, fuel, and fiber is the mantra of hemp.com, where you will find news, history, and products from the non-psychoactive cannabis plant.

Home testing

Basic kits for testing the THC level in your urine at home are inexpensive, easy to use, and very accurate. Look for them at drugteststrips.com.

CHAPTER 7

HOW TO GROW YOUR OWN

Raising a small stash of buds is easy and fun, and can be very rewarding. You don't need a large plot of land or special equipment to grow outside—Mother Nature provides the most important resources for you, free of charge. But whether you plan to grow outdoors or indoors, it helps to understand the plant's unique life cycle and how to manage it to maximize your harvest. In this chapter, I'll explain all of that to you, share a few basics of good gardening, and give you pointers that will help you succeed wherever you grow.

Not to be a buzzkill, but before we get too far, I need to remind you that as of this book's printing, **growing marijuana for sale or personal use remains a federal crime in the United States and Canada**. A few states license growers and patients to cultivate it for medical purposes. No matter where you live, I must advise you to use the information in this section at your own risk.

GO ORGANIC

Marijuana is all-natural—a product of sunshine, fresh air, and the fertile earth. But because of anxiety, greed, or ignorance, a lot of cannabis growers today douse their crops with agrichemicals—synthetic fertilizers, pesticides, and herbicides. These chemicals taint your crop and threaten the health of you and every other living thing.

The information in this chapter tells you how to create the conditions in which your plants will thrive by providing for their needs and using smart techniques that mimic nature. The organic approach is simple, effective, and good for you and the environment. And your buds won't taste, smell, or burn like ammonia.

CHOOSING A VARIETY

How do you pick from among the hundreds, maybe even thousands, of varieties you could grow? When you're starting out, you're likely to just go with whatever you have access to. But if you have choices, these considerations can help you make a smart selection.

Outdoors or in. The sativa types grow very tall and need a long time to mature, so they're best for growing outside. The shorter plants and quicker life cycle of indicas make them more manageable for growing indoors.

Warm or cool. If you live where spring warms up quickly and the summers are long and hot, sativas will thrive in your conditions. Indicas are a better choice in cooler climates with shorter growing seasons, as are hybrids with Cannabis ruderalis in their genealogy.

Quality or quantity. If you want to grow the best-tasting, most potent buds, you should plant sativas. You get more buds with stronger (some say harsher) flavor from indicas.

Most of the varieties you come across today are sativa-indica hybrids—pure strains are uncommon. Each variety has a unique set of attributes and the more you research about the qualities of the hybrids you're considering, the more likely you will be to choose the one that is best adapted to your conditions. Plants growing in the right conditions need much less attention and are far less prone to problems than those out of their element.

You dramatically increase your chances for success if you can plant several different varieties. Diversity protects you from complete failure if one variety is not well-adapted to your conditions. Planting different varieties in your first years of growing allows you to compare the performance of each. Once you see which variety handles your conditions best and yields buds that suit your tastes, you can focus your future efforts on it. This is important for your long-term success.

Breeding the perfect variety for your unique conditions is surprisingly easy. Allow some of your best plants to bear seeds and replant those seeds the following season. Repeat for a few years and you'll have your own personal strain, adapted to your unique conditions.

GOING UNDERGROUND

The key to successfully growing bud-laden stalks of marijuana is under your feet. In healthy, biologically active soil, plants grow up healthy and productive with little care. No chemical, potion, or TLC can help a plant overcome poor soil.

What do I mean by "biologically active"? Consider this: There are more living organisms in just one teaspoon of healthy soil than there are people on Earth. Healthy soil is teeming with billions of microscopic bacteria and fungi. They break down organic matter—the remains of decayed leaves, stems, and roots—and turn it into the nutrients plants need. Over millions of years, plants evolved in a co-dependent relationship with those microbes. You want to nurture a robust population of soil microbes so they can support your plants' growth.

HEALTHY DIRT

The way to feed the microbes in your soil is with organic matter, or decaying leaves, stems, and other parts of plants. Worms and all the microscopic creatures in the soil's food chain break it down into nutrients for your plants. Think of it as feeding the soil to feed the plants.

You want to continuously add organic matter to your soil, before, during, and after growing your cannabis crop. The resources you need to replenish the organic matter in your soil are free and lying on the ground outside your door. Leaves and grass clippings are two readily available resources. If possible, shred the leaves first with a bagging lawn mower to get them started on decomposing. If you use grass clippings, be sure they come from a lawn that has not been treated with chemicals.

Compost is the most potent kind of organic matter. It feeds the microbes, kills soil diseases, and helps disperse water evenly, and it is so easy to make with ingredients you probably have on hand or can find easily. Pile up fallen leaves, grass clippings, kitchen scraps from fruits and vegetables (no meat or oils), dead garden and houseplants, straw, shredded paper, and (if you can get it) manure from herbivores like poultry, cows, horses, sheep, goats, and rabbits. Never put carnivore manure (or what is known as humanure) into your backyard compost pile.

Keep the pile moist, and when it gets to be three feet by three feet by three feet, the ingredients will begin decomposing fast. Every couple of weeks use a shovel or fork to turn the stuff that's decomposed in the center of the pile to the outside and move what's been on the outside to the center. In about three months, you'll have the best soil

conditioner and plant food possible. It will look like dark chocolate cake crumbs and smell earthy sweet. You may even feel a little pride that you've reduced your contribution to the gushing waste stream.

Mix a few inches of compost or organic matter into your soil before planting, and throughout the growing season, keep your soil blanketed with a 2- to 4-inch layer of shredded leaves and/or grass clippings. After your harvest, stir more organic matter into the top few inches of the soil to begin decomposing over the dormant months.

OUTTA SITE

Picking a spot for an outdoor pot plot can be tricky, especially if you need to keep it from view. It won't be worth the trouble, though, if you don't keep in mind these key factors.

Full sun. Cannabis plants need at least twelve hours of

sunlight (and preferably more) each day during the height of the growing season. Avoid sites that are shaded by buildings, fences, trees (especially short, dense types), or shrubs. Remember that the sun's angle changes as the growing season goes on—what might be sun-drenched in June may be in shadow most of the day when your buds are ripening in September. If the only options you have are shaded at least part of the day, go for one that gets afternoon sun. Afternoon sun lasts into the evening during the height of summer, as opposed to morning sun. All else being equal, beds facing south or west get the most light.

Shelter from artificial lights. While your plants need lots of sunlight, you want your plot shielded from street lights and other artificial lights to help you manage the reproductive process (see page 560 for an explanation).

High and dry. Don't plant in very low-lying or swampy areas—your crop will drown there. Also, stay away from creeks, ponds, and other bodies of water that could overflow after a heavy downpour.

The ideal location. You won't find a better site than a south-facing slope (picture a vineyard) with a wide variety of wild flowers and a few very tall trees on it.

The right size. Your whole plot can be as big as you want, but management is easiest if you break it up into a series of beds about 4 feet wide and 8–10 feet long, with pathways on all sides of each of them. This width lets you reach into the beds—to water or pull weeds—from one side or another without stepping on the soil, which can compress and squeeze out all the pockets where water and air move through.

MAKING YOUR BED

The easiest method for turning a lawn or uncultivated ground into a planting bed takes about three to four months, but you will be building the soil at the same time you are preparing the space for planting.

Start by spreading a layer of six to eight sheets of newspaper (just the black-and-white pages), or a single layer of craft paper or cardboard on top of the ground. Don't bother to dig up or remove the plants that are already growing there—the layers of paper will smother them. Be sure the sheets of paper overlap each other, so no sunlight gets through to the ground. Top the paper with an inch or two of peat moss and blanket that with an equally thick layer of the organic matter. Continue alternating layers of peat and organic matter until there's about 4 inches or more covering your plot.

Now you can kick back and wait. In twelve to sixteen weeks, the layers will have decomposed, blended together, and wiped out any vegetation growing on the spot. When you're ready to plant, just dig through the layers and make holes. The longer you can wait before planting, the better. In fact, this method works best if you cover the soil with the layers in fall and then plant the following spring.

If you can't wait three months or more to start planting, you can prepare the bed and plant the same day with either a little muscle and sweat or a gas-powered tiller. If you go with the machine, run it through the plot at least twice, and then use a rake to pull out large chunks of plants and their roots. Don't obsess about getting rid of every little bit. Smaller pieces decompose quickly and add valuable organic matter to the soil. Break up any large

clods of soil either with the rake or your hands.

You don't need a tiller, though. You can use a spade or carpet knife to slice into and peel back the top layer of vegetation on the soil. As you pull up each section, shake it over the bed so that any loose soil falls back onto it. If a lot of soil is clumped to the bottom of the section you remove, use your fingers to break it free and put it back onto the exposed ground. After using the spade or the knife to remove the sod or other ground-covering plants, work the shovel or fork into the soil and loosen it down about 12 inches (or as deep as you can). Remove any large stones. Mix organic matter into the soil.

PLANTING SEEDS

You can start your cannabis crop from seeds or cuttings, or clones, taken from existing plants. Cuttings are easy to work with and have a high success rate. But you need to find a grower with a healthy, good quality crop from which you can take a few cuttings. (See page 591 for details.)

If you don't have access to plants or clones, you can start with seeds. Just gather seeds from all the good buds you smoke and ask your friends to save theirs, too. Before long you'll have the few dozen you need to plant a manageable size crop. You also can buy seeds from online sources—check the "Resources" section at the end of this chapter for a few links.

Before you plant seeds, take the time to check their viability—their readiness to grow. In general, the ones that are dark, round, and feel solid are viable, and any that are pale or white, dented or crushed in any way, or seem light in weight are not. You can quickly check their viability by pouring them all into a bowl of water. Those that float are at least partially hollow and will not sprout. The sinkers are ready for planting.

SOWING OUTSIDE

Planting seeds right into the soil outside is the least amount of work and is safest if you don't want to have cannabis plants in your home. But you have to wait until the nighttime temperatures are warm enough (60 degrees Fahrenheit), and you need to plant a lot of extra seeds to compensate for those that fail to germinate or are lost to birds and other animals.

Plant your seeds after your last frost date (you can find out the date from your cooperative extension office—there's one in every county in the United States). But you want to wait until the ground is not too muddy. Right before you plant, spread a half-inch to an inch of compost on the soil. Use a hand shovel or a hoe to carve out a furrow (or shallow trench) about an inch deep. Moisten but don't soak the soil. Watering before rather than after planting the seeds protects them from being swamped, or washed up and out of the soil.

Spread the seeds down the furrow about 3–5 inches apart. Gently press each of them into the soil to be sure they have contact with it. Cover the seeds with the soil you dug out and firm the soil on top. Don't pack it down so hard that the sprouts can't come through it.

The soil must be kept consistently damp so that when the seeds sprout and put out their first roots, they have water available. Without it, they could come up and then die within just a few hours on a warm, sunny day. Until the seeds have sprouted and grown two sets of leaves, lightly sprinkle water on the seedbed whenever it's dry on the surface. When you see the little sprouts poking up, you should spread dried grass clippings, shredded fall leaves, or straw on the surface of the soil all around them. Having a 1- to 2-inch layer of these organic mulches keeps the soil from drying out too quickly, and it blocks sunlight from any weed seeds that might have landed on the exposed soil.

INDOOR START

Planting your seeds indoors and then transplanting them outside after they've grown in a protected environment for a month or two is the most reliable way to raise a crop unless you live in a semi-tropical climate (where the conditions are most hospitable for cannabis growing). The plants get a head start on the growing season, so they grow bigger and bushier—bigger, more mature plants produce more buds, and they're more potent. Mature plants are better able to withstand weather extremes and are less inviting to deer, rabbits, and other plant-eating wildlife. You don't have to check on and water larger plants daily as you do with sprouts that have just come up from seeds. This can be critical if you are trying to avoid drawing attention to your plot.

Raising cannabis seedlings indoors does not require expensive equipment—you can find everything you need in a hardware store or nursery. The following items will give you a good working setup:

Fluorescent shop lights. You want both "warm" and "cool" bulbs.

Seedling trays. Rectangular, plastic trays that contain removable planting cells.

Plastic wrap. Used dry cleaner bags work well, as will any brand of clear food wrap.

Soil-less mix. This is sometimes sold as seed-starting mix. It's a blend of peat moss or coir (coconut fiber) and either perlite or vermiculite, which are minerals mined and heated so they can hold and disperse water gradually. Pass on any mix that claims to have fertilizer added—it's sure to be synthetic and will tarnish your organic cannabis crop. Don't use soil from outside or even potting mix you can buy for houseplants; they hold too much moisture and are too heavy for starting seeds inside.

Liquid fish-and-seaweed fertilizer. Brands such as Alaska and Neptune's Harvest are widely available brands. Avoid any plant food that's bright green or blue liquid, powder or crystals; they're not organic, no matter what the packaging claims.

Compost. Either homemade or store-bought will do.

Timer. Get one that will turn your lights on and off at regular intervals.

Spray bottle. The best way to water seedling cells is to spritz them.

Small fan. Even cannabis wilts in the heat. Just kidding. The breeze helps the plants grow sturdier stems.

Choose the room where you will grow carefully. You want to be able to completely control the light the plants get—even moonlight—and to keep the temperature between 65 and 75 degrees Fahrenheit.

In a bucket or large pot, mix three parts of the soilless mix to one part compost. Dampen the mix. Pick up a handful and fill a cell in the seedling tray with it. Repeat until each cell is nearly but not completely full. Press the mix down, but don't pack it tight. Put two seeds into each cell, pushing them in to be sure they have complete contact with the soil. Sprinkle a little of the mix on top of each cell. Then cover the whole tray with plastic wrap.

The seeds do not need light to germinate, so keep them in a dark spot (though at this stage you don't have to shield them from any ambient light as you will later on). Check each day for condensation on the plastic, which indicates that the soil is moist. Before the mix dries out completely, pull back the plastic and use a spray bottle to mist the soil with water so that it stays constantly damp.

As soon as you see the first sprouts coming up—typically in ten days to two weeks—remove the plastic. Now set up the fluorescent lights so that you can sit the trays a few inches below them. As the sprouts grow, you want to always keep them no more than 2 to 3 inches from the lights. However you set up your lights, you want to be able to raise them and/or the trays to be sure you maintain that 2- to 3-inch distance between bulbs and plants all the way to the end.

If you're using a timer, attach it right away. Give the plants light for at least 14 hours each day. Be sure you are consistent with the amount of light the seedlings get—it has a critical impact on growing productive and potent female plants. Unless you use a timer, your best bet is to keep the lights on 24 hours a day at this stage.

Keep the soil consistently moist so that the sprouts

have a steady supply. They can dehydrate and die overnight. A week or two after the seeds sprout, they develop their first set of "true" leaves, which make them instantly recognizable as marijuana plants. When they develop their second set of true leaves, you can begin to feed the sprouts. Once a week, add a few drops of the liquid fish-and-seaweed fertilizer to the water you spray on the soil.

After the sprouts have two sets of true leaves, set up a small fan two or three feet away from the trays. Run the fan at its lowest speed so that it blows very gently on the sprouts. The light breeze helps the plant develop sturdier stems, which help them better withstand outdoor conditions once they move out. And the breeze also diminishes the risk of fungus forming on top of the constantly moist soil. (If you do see fungus on the soil, sprinkle cornmeal or a little peat on top.) The fan does not need to run all day—you can attach it to the same timer as the lights.

If you planted two seeds in each cell, many of them are likely to grow two seedlings in them. In the third or fourth week, pick the seedling in each cell with the thickest stem and the biggest leaves. Snip off the other one with scissors. I know, you hate to lose a potential plant, but the remaining one will grow bigger and more productive because it won't be competing for water and nutrients. If you don't do this, you'll have two smaller, weaker plants instead of one healthy one.

In a few weeks, the seedlings will be more than 6 inches tall and outgrowing the seedling tray. Your pot plants are ready to be "potted up." You can buy small plastic pots for this or ones formed out of peat and wood pulp, commonly called "Jiffy" pots. Get the 4-inch size. Or you can recycle used yogurt cups. Be sure to rinse them out well first and poke a few small holes in the bottom for drainage.

Get together the same mix and compost blend you used for starting the seeds, moisten it, and fill each pot about two-thirds full. Now lift up your packs of seedlings and carefully push one out from the bottom. Put it into one of the bigger pots and add more of the soil-less mix. Take the plastic cells out of the trays, then put the pots in the flat bottoms and set them beneath the lights (still just a few inches below the bulbs). Now you can add water to the tray rather than pouring it on the individual plants. They will grow roots down through the soil to absorb it. Once a week, let the tray dry out and give each plant a dose of diluted liquid fish fertilizer. Keep using the fan and watch how thick and healthy the stems grow.

MOVING OUT

The time to move your seedlings outside is the same as if you were planting seeds. That is, as soon as possible after your last frost date. About two weeks before that, begin preparing your seedlings for their life outside by the process called "hardening off." Take the plants outside and put them in a sheltered location—out of direct sun and wind—for a few hours, then bring them back indoors and put them under the lights again. Over the next two weeks, gradually increase the amount of time the plants have outside and how much direct sunlight they get. Be sure the soil stays damp—sunlight and wind dry out the soil a lot faster than fluorescent lights, and you want the plants to keep growing stronger during the hardening off period.

Late afternoon on an overcast day is ideal for transplanting. The planting hole should be as deep as and slightly bigger in diameter than the plant's container. Moisten the soil first, then tip the plant out of the pot (pushing a little from the bottom if need be), and set it into the hole. Backfill with soil and firm it up around the plant's stem, but don't pack it down hard.

For the first 24 hours or so after you transplant, the stems and leaves may appear a bit droopy. This is a normal symptom of "transplant shock." They should recover in a day or two. If a plant doesn't straighten up and look like it's adapted after a couple days, firm the soil around the stem with your hands to make sure it has solid contact with the roots.

THE SEX TALK

Cannabis, like most other annual (as opposed to perennial) plants, has a goal each and every season: to reproduce. It reproduces by flowering, pollinating, and bearing seeds. If you're like most cannabis lovers I know, you don't want many, if any, seeds in your weed. So you must perform cannabis interruptus.

You can learn all about the anatomy of cannabis plants on page 476, but right here you just need to know that there are males and females. When male plants pollinate female plants, you get seeds. The buds are clusters of female flowers that are mostly (or completely) unpollinated.

Males produce pollen and release it into the air. About the same time, the female's ovaries open and extend a tube that captures the pollen. Those tubes are the "hairs" that you see when you look closely at a bud. The nearly microscopic grains of pollen attach themselves to the tube and then travel up to the ovaries to make seeds. To get more buds with little or no seeds, you remove the males before the act of pollination occurs.

Separating the boys from the girls takes careful, regular attention. The two types of plants have some immediately visible differences. Female plants typically are shorter and have more branches than males do. Also, the females are generally leafier, especially at the top, while you see more stem and fewer leaves on the males.

Those are helpful early signs, but they're not conclusive enough to trust. You want to identify the reproductive organs. They appear along the plant's main stem at intersections where lateral branches connect to the stem. Botanists call these spots "nodes." At first, the two types of reproductive organs look very similar. But within a day or even a few hours you can notice differences.

Male organs develop a curved, claw shape, and then change into rounded balls hanging down from very thin filaments. The balls have five segments, or petals, which separate slightly at the top. They can be yellow or whitish, or fully green. Males growing outdoors begin showing their organs approximately three weeks before the females. Exactly when depends upon your climate, whether you started with seeds or transplants, and the strain. At northern latitudes males may first appear as early as mid-July. Strains adapted to growing in the South may start revealing the males as late as the middle of September. As soon as you see a male plant in an outdoor plot, cut it off at its base. As much as possible, avoid shaking the plant so that it doesn't shed its pollen near any female.

A few hours up to a couple days after the males show

their gender characteristics, the females develop long white, yellow, or pink "hairs," called the pistils, sticking out from a thin, fluted membrane called the "sheath." The pistils typically show up in pairs.

Growers who start their seeds indoors—either for planting outside or in—have even more control over the development of males and females. When your plants are about 4 inches tall with a few sets of leaves, reduce the light to just eight hours a day. In a few days to a week, the males will reveal themselves. Cull them all out, and then go back to giving your females 14 hours of light a day.

SEE THE LIGHT

That trick of changing the light pattern to get the males to reveal themselves tells you that light plays a critical role in the reproductive process of cannabis. When the dark periods last long enough, the reproductive cycle is triggered. The plant redirects its energy from growing more limbs and leaves to flowering.

With an understanding of "photoperiod"—the balance of light and dark—and its effects on cannabis's reproduction, you can influence the timing of when your harvest comes in, which is especially critical for growing outdoors where fall frosts come early. Growers everywhere can manipulate the photoperiod to increase the quality and quantity of buds they harvest. By making the nights artificially longer, you can set the budding process in motion when you want.

For instance, if you live in the north, you can start covering your plants for part of each day in early to mid-August. You want to do this while the weather is still mild enough for the plants to continue growing for another month after flowering. Cover them with anything opaque, like a tarp or two to three plastic trash bags. Any light that reaches the plants—from streetlights, car headlights, even flashlights—can disrupt the long-night cycle you are working on. Take extra care to be sure no light gets to your plants while they are cloaked. If you are growing your crop in containers, you can simply move the pots to a dark location where no light gets to the plants.

BULKIER BUDS

Now you understand how to kick off flowering, but you might just want the opposite—to inhibit your plants from flowering. This will give the plants time to grow bigger and put on more limbs (on which more buds will form) before they start to reproduce. This can dramatically increase the amount of buds you harvest—by as much as double for each extra month of growth the plant does before flowering.

You're probably already guessing how to prevent the plant from flowering—by interrupting the dark period with light. You can do this with artificial lights. You can use electric lights, car headlights, or an industrial-strength flashlight. The most reliable way to do this is to put up a string of lights attached to a timer.

Be sure the light shines on the entire plants. Any limbs kept in a shadow may start to bloom and spoil your effort to delay flowering. It doesn't take much light. On a clear night, the full moon emits about .01 foot-candles. Just .03 foot-candles is bright enough to do the job. The lights need to be on only for a few minutes to work. The ideal time is between midnight and 3 a.m., so that you break up the longest period of darkness.

When your plants are big and you are ready for them to flower, shield them from exposure to any light for at least ten hours each day. In just a few days, they'll start their reproductive process, and you can start looking forward to your harvest of big buds.

WATER WISE

For the first few days after you transplant young cannabis seedlings outside, give them a daily sprinkling to keep the soil around the roots damp at all times. But once you see the seedlings starting to grow again, you want to encourage them to build a deep and wide root system that can hold up a tall, bushy plant and scavenge in the soil for water and nutrients throughout the season. You accomplish this by watering less frequently but more deeply.

As your plants become established, cut back on the daily watering. Instead, push your index finger two knuckles deep into the surrounding soil whenever you check on your plants. Feel damp? If so, don't water the plants, no matter what they look like. They may appear to be wilting in high heat, but that does not mean they are dehydrated. Plants curl their leaves in the heat to slow down transpiration, which is the loss of water from the leaves.

When the soil is definitely dry, give each plant a gallon of water. Pour it on slowly so that it can percolate down deep into the soil, rather than running off your plot and leaving only the top few inches wet.

Water the soil, not the plants. They can absorb very little moisture through their leaves, so watering leaves, even when they look wilted, is wasteful and doesn't help the plant build a large root system. Pour the water in an area up to a foot away from the stem in all directions. Again, this entices the roots to grow wide rather than just below the stem.

For maximum efficiency and reliability, many small-scale farmers and home gardeners set up drip irrigation systems comprised of a network of tubes through which the water flows to emitters set at intervals chosen by the grower. They deliver water right to the plants' roots and nowhere else. By attaching the system to a timer, you can be sure the plants get exactly the right amount of water, exactly when they need it, so you don't have to find the time to do it each day. Timing does matter. The ideal time to water your plants is first thing in the morning. This gives them time to absorb the moisture and get it out to the leaves and buds before the sun evaporates it during the heat of the day. The next best time to water is in the evening, an hour or so before dusk.

Maintain a layer of mulch on top of the soil. Mulch is absolutely vital for keeping your crop evenly hydrated by shielding the soil from the sun and keeping weeds from sprouting up and stealing moisture from your plants.

HOLD THE CRYSTALS

You may have seen (in garden centers or online) special "crystals" that are touted to hold and disperse water to your plants. They may be sold separately or may be included in potting soil mix. For several reasons, I do not recommend these for your organic cannabis crop.

They are not natural "crystals," but rather are made of polymer, a plastic produced with petroleum. They are not organic or sustainable. They do nothing that compost doesn't do, and they don't nourish the population of beneficial microbes in the soil, as compost does. The crystals are likely to give you a false sense of security and upset the natural balance in the soil. Stick with compost and pass on the crystals.

FEEDING TIME

As I've stated elsewhere in this section, the key to growing a productive, high-quality organic cannabis crop is building healthy, biologically active soil. No matter what you've heard or read, there's no shortcut to get around building healthy soil. No "miracle" product or fertilizer can circumvent the need for it. You feed the microbes, and they nourish your plants with a healthy, well-rounded diet.

In contrast, synthetic fertilizers are high in salts. Persistent use of them raises the pH of your soil and dehydrates the beneficial microbe population you are nurturing. Chemical fertilizer formulas also rely on phosphoric acid, which research shows neutralizes other important trace minerals in the soil.

Building healthy soil takes time, and while you are waiting, you can use packaged organic fertilizers, made with ingredients whose names you understand, like *poultry meal* rather than *ammonium nitrate*. When you look at fertilizer packages, you see a ratio listed on the label. The ratio is always a three number set, like 10-5-

10. This refers to the proportions of nitrogen, phosphorus, and potassium, or N-P-K, in the fertilizer. All three are essential macronutrients plants need to survive. Nitrogen feeds leaf and stem growth, phosphorus supports root and flower development, and potassium (also known as potash) aids the plant in processing the other two. Nitrogen-rich fertilizers are most valuable early in the growing season, to help the plant build a sturdy stem and dense leaf cover. As the plant matures, you want to give it less nitrogen and more phosphorus to stimulate flower (that is, bud) production.

DOO FOR YOU

The classic, well-balanced organic fertilizer is manure from barnyard animals. If you live near a farm where cows, sheep, goats, chickens, or horses are raised, you can often get manure free if you'll shovel or haul it. Take the "stable bedding," too, which is the straw, wood chips, or other stuff on the ground. It adds healthy amounts of organic matter to your soil along with the nutrient-rich manure.

You can also use the waste from pet rabbits, guinea pigs, and other herbivorous (non–meat eating) animals. Rabbits' waste pellets are like little fertilizer pills, which gradually release their valuable nutrients. Leftover alfalfa rabbit food is not just for the bunnies; it nourishes plants, too. It contains a natural fatty-acid growth stimulant, tri-anconatol, along with a balanced supply of N-P-K.

Do you have a fish tank? Save the dirty water because the fish poop in it is nutrient-rich food for your plants. And if you happen to be at a zoo or circus, you can take home the droppings of their herbivores to use as fertilizer.

When using manure, remember this important caution: If it is fresh, do not apply it directly to your garden during the growing season. It can be very "hot"—or decomposing very rapidly—and can literally burn your plants. Spread it on your plot early in spring, about sixty days before you plan to plant. If you get a load (sorry) during the growing season, add it to your compost pile or let it sit and decompose for about two months before spreading it on your plot. Exceptions: The fish tank water can be applied immediately, but if it is very dirty, dilute it in an equal amount of water before using it on your plants. Rabbit dung can also be applied to your plot without waiting for it to compost.

FREE FOOD

Chicken eggshells are 93 percent calcium carbonate, making them a rich source of the essential mineral calcium. Dry your eggshells in a pan in the oven with either the pilot light or at the lowest temperature setting. Crumble them by hand and pulverize them in a blender or food processor, and then sprinkle over your soil. Ground clam and oyster shells serve the same purpose, as well as many other shells you can find on the beach.

You can find other troves of free fertilizer on the beach. Seaweed, particularly kelp, is loaded with potassium (approximately 20–25 percent). Gather kelp and store it in a large drum or plastic trash barrel filled with water. Cover and allow it to decompose for two months. You will be left with a concentrated solution, which you can dilute with water to make a spray you can use to fertilize your plants.

Growers living near mushroom farms can often ask for the "spent" compost that is discarded after each crop. It's high in both organic matter and phosphorus. Researchers have found that it turbocharges the yields of organic vegetable beds.

I want to mention one more easy-to-get, free source of fertilizer for your plot. Your liquid waste! That's right, human urine is 46 percent nitrogen and has higher concentrations of nitrogen, phosphorus, and potassium than most commercial fertilizers. Not only that, but these elements are in an extremely soluble and available form, which makes urine a great starter fertilizer. But don't go outside and pee on your pot patch; it needs to be diluted before you apply it to your plants. Mix it with ten parts water and distribute evenly.

WORMS' DOO

The most nutritious and quickly absorbed organic fertilizer you can give your plants comes from worms. Technically referred to as "vermicompost" or worm "castings," the semi-liquid stuff that worms excrete is the best food for seedlings and plants growing in containers. You can buy it (there's a business opportunity you probably haven't thought of!) or you can start a worm bin in your house, feed them your kitchen scraps, and collect the castings for your plants. You need a lot of worms and vegetable scraps to produce enough castings for an outdoor crop, but you can collect plenty for container plants or to blend with your soil mix when you're starting seeds.

Worm compost tends to be kind of costly, and is often sold in little boutique bags. If you want to make your own, it can be fun. You can buy a kit or you can also just get worms—red wrigglers are the best species—and a plastic-type storage bin (like Rubbermaid makes), add shredded newspaper for bedding and fruit and vegetable waste (carrot peels, apple cores, etc.) from your kitchen, and then let the worms do their stuff.

BUD TIME

Now comes the moment you've been waiting for—harvesting bagsful of your homegrown, pure and natural, organic, and very kind buds. While there's no reason not to sample a little of your harvest whenever you and it are ready, you also want to be patient to ensure that you get the majority of your buds at their peak and prepare them to be stored until you are ready to enjoy them.

As the amount of daylight diminishes and the nights grow cooler, your plants' growth slows and then stops completely. Only focused attention and experience will tell you when this moment comes. Take your time and be sure. The buds put on significant weight in the last final weeks of their growth. When they stop, the pistils, or "hairs" in the buds, become darker in color. Under ideal conditions—warm and dry for weeks on end—this is the moment to harvest your crop. In most parts of North America, the ideal conditions don't often occur at the end of the growing season. Falling temperatures and rain can push you to harvest sooner.

A mild frost does not kill cannabis plants, but most of the time it shuts them down for the season, ending their further growth and development. If a warm, sunny spell is forecast after the light frost, you can leave the plants in the ground, and they may continue to grow. But if the weather doesn't warm up after a light frost, pull the plants because they are finished growing. A hard frost, when everything freezes, almost always kills the plants and can damage the buds. You want to be sure to harvest before a hard frost strikes.

You can sometimes get a few extra nights or even a week or two for your buds to mature by protecting them from frost by covering the plants through the first few mild frosts. On nights when frost is forecast, gently drape old sheets or blankets over the plants about an hour before sunset. Watering the plants also helps reduce the risk of frost by increasing the humidity in the immediate area.

Watch the weather forecast, and if your buds are close to being ready before a rainy spell is predicted, harvest them before they get soggy. The drier the plants are when you harvest them, the better your buds will taste and the longer they will keep in storage.

CURING CANNABIS

Feel free to try out a few of your buds right after you harvest them, but don't judge their quality right away. In many cas- es, the buds ripen fully and keep better until you are ready to enjoy them if you take the time to cure them properly.

Start by pulling the whole plant out of the ground—roots and all. Hang the plants upside down for 48 hours in a cool, dry spot away from direct sunlight. Leave space between each plant, and, as much as possible, ensure that air can flow around them on all sides.

After a couple of days, clip the roots and stems up to the lowest set of leaves on each plant. Toss the trimmings into your compost pile. Put each top into its own paper grocery bag. Leave the bags wide open and store them in a cool, dry place away from direct sunlight. The best location is cool (60–65 degrees Fahrenheit is ideal), low in humidity, and protected from direct sunlight.

When the plants have been in the bags for four to five days, clip the buds from the stems and trim off large "fan" leaves. You could store the buds away at this stage, but if you can, spread them out of on a screen (an old window screen works great for this) and set them in your cool, dry location so that air can circulate around them on all sides. Leave them there for a couple days, and you can be sure they will be mold free.

After you have cured them thoroughly, put them in glass jars—old-school Mason canning jars work great for this. If you don't have glass jars, you also can use plastic containers (like Tupperware) or even plastic bags. Whichever you use, seal them tightly and keep them in—you guessed it—a cool, dry place away from direct sunlight. Check on them periodically, especially in the first few weeks, to be sure there's no condensation on the container (which can encourage mold to form) or worse, a musty smell that indicates mildew has already formed. If you do find condensation or mildew forming, remove the buds from the jar or bag and set them for two to three days on a screen to finish drying them out.

INDOOR CROP

Do you live in the Far North, where the growing season is too short for a cannabis crop to fully mature outside? Want to grow year-round? Are you in a city or other place where there is no available land? Do you need to keep your crop secure from unwanted attention?

A truly organic crop needs sunshine, rain, fresh air, and real living soil. Still, you can grow a healthy crop of cannabis indoors without using toxic chemicals, but you do need to pay special attention to lighting, ventilation and humidity, soil and containers, watering and fertilizing.

For starting seeds, ordinary fluorescent lights work well, but they're not powerful enough for growing mature plants. Incandescent lights (like your standard household light bulbs) are stronger, but they tend to get hot and, because you can't put the plants close without burning them, you get long stems that are spindly, weak, and prone to toppling over. For raising full-grown plants with lush foliage that eventually flower, you need to invest in lights designed specifically for raising plants inside.

You can get fluorescent bulbs for growing plants, which are strong in the red and blue ends of the light spectrum. Many growers find that they work fine. But for maximum

productivity, you want to use either metal halide or high-pressure sodium lamps. Metal halide lamps are strong on the blue side of the spectrum. If your growing room gets little or no natural light, metal halide is almost essential. The sodium lights work great as a supplement to natural light. Their strength in the red-orange end of the spectrum helps promote flowering and budding. If at all possible, get both types of lights—the extra cost will be paid back in a bigger, better harvest.

Artificial lights work best when they are as close to the plants as can be. When the lights are too far from the plants, they put all of their energy into growing longer stems to get closer. You want shorter plants that focus their energy on growing leaves and flowering, not lengthening their stems.

Controlling how much light your plants get is vitally important indoors because there is no natural cycle for the plants to follow. If you want to harvest buds with few if any seeds, you must pay strict attention to the light and dark periods. As the plants are building their stems, branches, and leaves, you want to give them as much light as possible—up to 24 hours a day, and no less than 14 hours daily. Give them the maximum amount of light for at least three months so the plant can make a dense canopy of branches and leaves. The older and bigger the plant is when it starts to flower, the more buds it will produce, and they will be more potent. When you're ready for budding to begin, increase the dark period to more than ten hours daily as I explained on in the "Bulkier Buds" section (page 562).

Attaching a timer to the lights is almost essential for managing this properly. If you are inconsistent with the amount of light, only some of the plants may flower. Some may become hermaphrodites, with both male and female reproductive organs. Make sure the room is sealed off from any ambient light and take care not to open the door during the dark part of the cycle.

Your grow room needs to be closed to light, but it cannot be shut off from air. Plants take in air, use the carbon dioxide, and emit oxygen. (People, you may recall, do the opposite.) A steady supply of fresh carbon dioxide is essential for healthy plant growth. In a closet or small room, a table-size fan and your respiration can be enough to meet your plants' needs. In a large room or greenhouse, a ventilation fan that draws in fresh air and pushes out the stale air makes a big difference. Plants that are not getting enough fresh air turn yellow and droop.

The ideal temperature for your indoor plants is between 68 and 78 degrees Fahrenheit, with a 10- to 15-degree drop during the dark hours.

Plants growing in the ground outside enjoy the benefits of a healthy, self-sustaining soil microbe population to nurture and nourish them. Indoors, you want to do all you can to mimic those conditions. Still you should not use soil from outside to grow plants in containers, indoors

or out. It is too heavy, holding so much moisture that the plants may drown. Instead, mix equal parts of peat moss or coir and fully decomposed compost.

One advantage indoor growers have over most out-door crops is in providing a constant water supply. Just be careful not to overwater, which can drown the plant or set up conditions for fungus to take hold. Rely on touch— your finger pushed in the soil—to determine when you plants need watering rather than irrigating on a schedule.

When you do need to water, the best place to deliver it is from below. Sit your pots in a dish of water, and then let the water wick up to the roots. When the soil at the bottom of the pot is damp, roots grow down to extract the water. The bigger the root system, the bigger the plant. The bigger the plant, the more buds you will harvest.

You can buy drip irrigation systems specifically for growing in containers. Add a timer and you have an al-most attention-free system that gives your plants a steady supply of moisture.

The compost in your soil mix provides a healthy dose of nutrients. But as your plant grows, it needs more. Get liquid fish-and-seaweed fertilizer, which you mix with water. Start with a dilute solution, as little as just a teaspoon in a quart of water, and gradually increase it to the proportions recommended on the package. Feed your plants with this just once a week—excess fertilizer disrupts the plants' natural growth pattern. When flowering begins, switch to a fertilizer that is higher in potassium—BioBloom is a widely available brand.

NUGGET

When growing indoors, take extra care to use grounded electrical cords and keep water away from them at all times. You don't want to lose your plants, your home, or someone's life because of carelessness.

HYDROPONIC ORGANIC—NOT

Hydroponics is the cultivation of plants in nutrient-rich water rather than in soil. You can use organically based liquid fertilizers rather than synthetic ones in a hydroponic system, and that would be better than pumping the plants full of manufactured nitrates. But a truly organic crop, however, can only be grown in soil. A hydroponic system is unnatural—the plants did not evolve to grow in water—and it does not include the beneficial microbes in the soil that have a symbiotic relationship with the plants. If you need to grow indoors, at least get your plants in soil.

FOUR-LEGGED FIENDS

The most troublesome pests for outdoor growers tend not to be the kind with six or eight legs or even wings. Wildlife including deer, woodchucks (aka groundhogs), and rabbits, do in some places munch on cannabis plants, especially in early spring when the plants are tender and other food is scarce. Protecting your crop from these critters does not, however, require a shotgun or poisonous chemicals.

A fence is the most reliable way to keep wildlife away from your crop. An electric fence works best of all—it will also impede any two-legged varmints with a mind to get at your crop. A fence needs to be at least eight feet high to be tall enough so that deer won't try to jump it. For woodchucks and rabbits, bury the fence a foot or two underground—otherwise, they'll tunnel under it.

If you're growing where a fence isn't feasible, you can try to scare wildlife away with whirligigs (which spin when blown by the wind), reflector tape, motion-detector lights, sprinklers, or just about anything else that moves or glitters enough to unnerve the animals. The more of these you use, the more effective they'll be. Over time the animals grow accustomed to them and are no longer spooked by them. At least, mix them up so that the change gives the marauders pause before they decide to eat your crop.

Certain aromas can also deter wildlife from your patch. Many gardeners find that hanging bars of strong-smelling soap, like Irish Spring, in low branches of trees around the plot discourages deer from walking through the area. Homemade sprays produced by blending hot peppers, garlic, and even rotten eggs and then applied to leaves can stop critters from chewing on them. You can buy specially formulated deer repellents that have the same effect.

Another product you can buy is fox urine (in liquid

concentrate or powder)—no, I am not making this up—that you sprinkle around the perimeter of your plot to scare off critters with the scent of a predator. If you have a dog, it might serve the same purpose. In fact, distribute a bit of your own "scent" around the area and it's likely to work, too.

I hate to be discouraging, but you sometimes have to accept what nature wants. If you're growing where the critter population is high and your plants are the best available food source, they will eat your plants no matter what you do. You need to find a new location for your plot if your plants have been munched to the ground more than once.

CLONING AT HOME

Planting your cannabis crop from seeds is smart when you're just starting out because seeds are accessible, and unless you saved them all from one stash, they are likely to come from different strains and varieties. After you've grown them, you will discover which perform the best in your conditions. When you have identified a variety that really suits your needs, you can clone it.

You don't need a lab or gene-splicing skills to do this. Simply snip off a limb from the top of the plant, cutting it cleanly at the juncture where the stem attaches to the main trunk. Then put the cut end of each cutting into a small pot filled with the seed-planting mix. Set the cuttings where they can get direct sunlight or put them under fluorescent lights about 2–3 inches away from the bulbs. Keep the soil mix consistently moist. Within a few days, the plant will start growing and within a week you'll notice it's taller and is beginning to add new leaves. The clones quickly catch up in size to the mother plants. In about three weeks, you can transplant them outside.

RESOURCES

Books

Green Weed, by Dr. Seymour Kindbud. Information you can trust (if I may say so myself) about how to grow a righteous crop of pure buds outdoors or in.

Seeds

I have never purchased seeds from any of these vendors nor do I have any relationship with them.

Buy Dutch Seeds (buydutchseeds.com)

Ganja Seeds (ganja-seeds.com)

Weed Seed Shop (weedseedshop.com)

Supplies for Organic Growers

Clean Air Gardening (cleanairgardening.com)
Compost bins, rain barrels, pest control

Composters.com
Compost bins, worm bins, rain barrels, season extenders

Dirtworks (dirtworks.net)
Pest control, fertilizers, bagged compost

DripWorks (dripworksusa.com)
Drip irrigation systems and supplies

Extremely Green (extremelygreen.com)
Pest and weed control, fertilizers

Gardens Alive (gardensalive.com)
Pest control, fertilizers

Hydrofarm (hydrofarm.com)
Lights, greenhouses, nursery containers and soil mixes

Morton's Horticultural Products (mortonproducts.com)
Nursery containers, greenhouses and accessories

Peaceful Valley Farm Supply (groworganic.com)

Soil amendments, cover crop seeds, pest and weed control, season extenders

Planet Natural (planetnatural.com)

Pest control, composters, fertilizers

Vermicomposting

For complete instructions on how to set up, maintain and extract the castings from your worm bin, go to wormwoman.com.

Pest Identification

bugguide.net

insectidentification.org

Insect Identification Laboratory at Virginia Tech, idlab. ento.vt.edu

INDEX

1,000 Weed Games, 332

alternate THC consumption methods, 377

Amsterdam, 463

anatomy of cannabis, 476

Anslinger, Harry, 51

Aryans, 19

brain chemistry, 502

Bush, George W., 86

cannabinoids, 497

Cannabis Cup, 336

Carter, Jimmy, 85

Chocolate Chip Cookies with Walnuts… and Weed!, 412

Clinton, Bill, 85

curing cannabis, 577

D.A.R.E., 338

Dogon, 15

drug testing, 343, 428, 524, 529

Enlightenment, 26

etiquette, 372

Forchion, Edward, 90

Ford, Henry, 64

Frankfurt Resolution, 462

glaucoma, 88

glossary, 350

Gore, Al, 85

Grand Theft Auto, 340

Grass card game, 331

green butter, 398

green oil, 401

Grinspoon, Lester, M.D., 519
Hash Bash, 79
hash, 382
Hazelnut Rum Chocolates, 406
Hearst, William Randolph, 46
Hemp for Victory, 62
hemp products, 494
hemp, 431, 492
hemps, false, 496
hermaphrodite, 478
hiding pot smoke, 380
High Times magazine, 340
hydroponic, 587
indica, 472
Jamestown, Virginia, 29
Jefferson, Thomas, 30
Johnson, Gary, 87
joints, 379
Kerry, John, 86
Kesey, Ken, 74
koalas, 341
LaGuardia Report, 57
Law Enforcement Against Prohibition (LEAP), 427
Le Club des Hachichins, 34
Leary, Timothy, 72
legal timeline, 439
Lice Klispie Tleats, 410
Linguini with Garlic Weed Butter Wine Sauce, 414
Ludlow, Henry, 42
Marihuana Tax Act, 55
McGurk effect, 342

medical reports, 512

Medieval period, 24

munchies explained, 511

Napoleon, 32

National Organization for the Reform of Marijuana Laws (NORML), 77

O'Shaughnessy, William Brooke, 36

Obama, Barack, 86

Office of Strategic Services, 65

Kennedy, John F., 69

paraquat, 84

patent medicines, 41

Peanut Butter Cups, 408

Perlowin, Bruce, 432

photoperiod, 560

Polo, Marco, 22

price of pot, 346

Prohibition Era, 48, 422

Rastafari, 82

sativa, 472

smoking methods, 273

smoking methods, alternate, 376

soil, 539

stealth pipes, 378

Stoner Games, 332

Stoner Trivia, 333

Stony Awards, 347

tie-dye, 348

Towelie, 302

Wo/Men's Alliance for Medical Marijuana, 349

Yang-shao, 17

BOOKS

Alice's Adventures in Wonderland, 306
Ask Ed: Marijuana Gold, 307
Aunt Sandy's Medical Marijuana Cookbook, 307
Baked!: Marijuana Munchies to Make and Bake, 308
Bong Bible, The, 308
Bongwater, 309
Botany of Desire, 310
Cannabible, The, 311
Cannabis Breeder's Bible, The, 311
Cannbis Companion, The, 312
Dr. Kindbud's Weed-O-Pedia, 313
Emperor Wears No Clothes, The, 313
Eye Voltage: A Stoner's Book of 40 Mind-Blowing Optical Illusions, 315
Fear & Loathing in Las Vegas, 315
Green Weed: The Organic Guide to Growing High-Quality Cannabis, 316
Grow Your Own Organic Weed: Everything You Need … Except the Seeds, 317
Little Green Book, The, 317
Handbook of Medicinal Herbs, 318
Marijuana Chef Cookbook, The, 318
Official High Times Pot Smoker's Handbook, The, 319
On the Road, 61
Pot Book, The, 319
Pot Culture: The A-Z Guide to Stoner Language & Life, 320
Pot Stickers, 321
Quotable Stoner, The, 321
Reefer Movie Madness: The Ultimate Stoner Film Guide, 322
The Savage Detectives: A Novel, 322
Spliffigami: Roll the 35 Greatest Joints of All Time, 323

Stoner Coffee Table Book, 323
Wonder Boys: A Novel, 324

FAMOUS FOLKS
Angelou, Maya, 325
Apatow, Judd, 283
Benson, Doug, 284
Bruce, Lenny, 285
Carlin, George, 286
Carroll, Jim, 326
Chappelle, David, 287
Clarke, Robert, 289
Cyrus, Miley, 290
Diaz, Cameron, 290
Etheridge, Melissa, 291
Galifianakis, Zack, 291
Ginsberg, Allen, 326
Harrelson, Woody, 292
Hedberg, Mitch, 292
Herer, Jack, 293
Kerouac, Jack, 327
Lawrence, Martin, 294
Martin, Steve, 295
Morrison, Jim, 295
Murray, Bill, 296
Nelson, Willie, 297
Phelps, Michael, 297
Pryor, Richard, 298
Scott-Heron, Gil, 293
Silverman, Sarah, 299
Silverstein, Shel, 329

Sinclair, John, 328
Stern, Howard, 300
Timberlake, Justin, 301
Wavy Gravy (Hugh Nanton Romney), 302
White, Shaun, 303
Williams, Montel, 304
Williams, Ricky, 304
Williams, Robin, 305

MOVIES

Alice in Wonderland, 93
Animal House, 94
Bad Teacher, 96
The Big Lebowski, 97
Bongwater, 98
The Breakfast Club, 99
Caddyshack, 100
Cheech and Chong… Up in Smoke, 102
Clerks, 103
Club Paradise, 104
Dazed and Confused, 105
Dogma, 106
Dude, Where's My Car?, 108
Easy Rider, 110
Emperor of Hemp, 111
Eyes Wide Shut, 112
Fast Times at Ridgemont High, 113
Fear & Loathing in Las Vegas, 115
The 40 Year Old Virgin, 116
Friday, 117
Get Him to the Greek, 118

Grandma's Boy, 120
Good Morning, Vietnam, 121
Half Baked, 122
Harold & Kumar Go to White Castle, 124
Homegrown, 125
Hot Tub Time Machine, 126
How High?, 128
Humboldt County, 129
It's Complicated, 130
Jay & Silent Bob Strike Back, 131
Knocked Up, 132
Leaves of Grass, 134
Magic Trip, 135
Mallrats, 136
Naked Lunch, 138
National Lampoon's Vacation, 139
Old School, 140
Outside Providence, 141
Pineapple Express, 143
The Wizard of Oz, 144
Private Parts, 145
Pulp Fiction, 146
Reefer Madness, 148
Revenge of the Nerds, 149
Road Trip, 151
Rolling Kansas, 152
Scary Movie, 153
Sex Pot, 154
Smiley Face, 156
The Stoned Age, 157
Super High Me, 158

Super Troopers, 160
Tenacious D in the Pick of Destiny, 161
Waking Life, 162
Walk Hard: The Dewey Cox Story, 164
Your Highness, 166

MUSICIANS
311, 234
Adrian Rollini & His Tap Room Gang, 235
Afroman, 236
Andy Kirk and His Twelve Clouds of Joy, 236
Arlo Guthrie, 237
Barney Bigard Sextet, 238
Bea Foote, 238
Beatles, The, 239, 334
Ben Harper, 240
Benny Goodman & His Orchestra, 240
Black Sabbath, 241
Blue Steele & His Orchestra, 242
Bob Dylan, 243, 334
Bob Marley, 243
Bone Thugs-N-Harmony, 245
Boston, 245
Brewer & Shipley, 246
Brian Robbins, 247
Buck Washington, 248
The Buster Bailey Rhythm Busters, 248
Cab Calloway, 249
Cats and the Fiddle, The, 250
Cee Pee Johnson and Band, 250
Country Joe & The Fish, 251

Corrado, 252
Cyprus Hill, 252
Dave Matthews Band, 253
David Peel & The Lower East Side, 254
DOA, 254
The Doors, 255
Dr. Dre, 256
Ella Fitzgerald & Chick Webb, 256
Eminem, 257
Flaming Lips, 258
Georgia White, 259
Grateful Dead, The, 259
Green Day, 260
Hazel Meyers, 261
Ice Cube, 261
The Harlem Hamfats, 262
Jazz Gillum & His Jazz Boys, 263
Jefferson Airplane, 263
Jimi Hendrix, 264
Julia Lee & Her Boy Friends, 265
Kid Cudi, 266
Larry Adler, 266
Lil Green, 267
Louis Armstrong, 268
Musical Youth, 268
Neil Young, 269
Noble Sissle's Swingsters featuring Sidney Bechet, 270
NOFX, 270
Nuggets Compilation, The, 271
OutKast, 271
Pink Floyd, 272

Peter, Paul and Mary, 273
Peter Tosh, 273
Phish, 274
Queens of the Stone Age, 275
Reefer Blues: Vintage Songs About Marijuana, 275
Radiohead, 276
Rick James, 276
Roots, The, 277
Rosetta Howard & The Harlem Hamfats, 278
Snoop Dogg, 278
Steve Miller Band, 279
Stuff Smith & His Onyx Club Boys, 280
Sublime, 280
Tom Petty, 281
Weezer, 282

TELEVISION
21 Jump Street, 214
7th Heaven, 214
Aqua Teen Hunger Force, 169
Arrested Development, 167
Barney Miller, 214
Beavis & Butthead, 170
Blossom, 215
Bored to Death, 173
Cannabis Planet, 174
Chappelle's Show, 177
Cops, 176
Curb Your Enthusiasm, 215
Da Ali G Show, 178
Dragnet, 180

Entourage, 181
Family Guy, 182
Frasier, 216
Freaks & Geeks, 216
Glee, 217
Home Improvement, 217
Hooked: Illegal Drugs and How They Got that Way, 217
How I Met Your Mother, 218
How to Make It in America, 183
It's Always Sunny in Philadelphia, 184
Jay Leno, The Tonight Show, 212
Jimmy Kimmel Live, 212
Kenny vs. Spenny, 185
King of the Hill, 218
Late Night with Conan O'Brien, 211
Late Show with David Letterman, 213
Looney Tunes, 186
Madmen, 187
Maude, 218
Mr. Show with Bob and David, 189
Murphy Brown, 219
Parks and Recreation, 219
Party Down, 191
Penn & Teller: Bullshit!, 219
Pot TV, 193
Real Time with Bill Maher, 195
Ren & Stimpy, 194
Rosanne, 220
Saved By the Bell, 220
Scooby-Doo, 196
Sex and the City, 221

Skins, 198
South Park, 199
Step by Step, 221
Strangers With Candy, 221
Teletubbies, 200
Tenacious D, 200
That '70s Show, 201
The Andy Griffith Show, 214
The Boondocks, 171
The Colbert Report, 175
The Cosby Show, 215
The Daily Show with Jon Stewart, 179
The Dukes of Hazzard, 216
The Facts of Life, 216
The Kids in the Hall, 218
The Man Show, 188
The Muppet Show, 190
The Sarah Silverman Program, 220
The Simpsons, 197
The Whitest Kids U' Know, 206
The Wonder Years, 222
Three's Company, 222
Tonight Show with Johnny Carson, 210
Trailer Park Boys, 203
Two and a Half Men, 222
Weeds, 207
Wilfred, 208
Yo Gabba Gabba!, 205

ABOUT CIDER MILL PRESS BOOK PUBLISHERS

Good ideas ripen with time. From seed to harvest,
Cider Mill Press brings fine reading, information, and
entertainment together between the covers of its creatively
crafted books. Our Cider Mill bears fruit twice a year,
publishing a new crop of titles each spring and fall.

Visit us on the Web at
www.cidermillpress.com
or write to us at
12 Port Farm Road
Kennebunkport, Maine 04046